# Designing Interdisciplinary Curriculum
# in Middle, Junior High, and High Schools

# Designing Interdisciplinary Curriculum in Middle, Junior High, and High Schools

**RICHARD E. MAURER**
*Anne M. Dorner Middle School, Ossining, New York*

**Allyn and Bacon**
Boston London Toronto Sydney Tokyo Singapore

Copyright © 1994 by Allyn and Bacon
A Division of Simon & Schuster, Inc.
160 Gould Street
Needham Heights, Massachusetts 02194

**Library of Congress Cataloging-in-Publication Data**

Maurer, Richard E.
    Designing interdisciplinary curriculum in middle, junior
high, and high schools / Richard E. Maurer.
        p.    cm.
    Includes bibliographical references (p.    ) and index.
    ISBN 0-205-14117-X
    1. Interdisciplinary approach in education—United States.
2. Education, Secondary—United States—Curricula.  3. Curriculum planning—United States.  I. Title.
LB1628.5.M38    1994
373.19—dc20                                                          93-723
                                                                     CIP

Printed in the United States of America
10  9  8  7  6  5  4  3        97  96

*For my parents, and Jeannette and Regina*
*who assisted in the correspondence,*
*and especially Elizabeth.*

# About the Author

**Richard E. Maurer,** Ph.D. (Fordham University) is the principal of Anne M. Dorner Middle School in Ossining, New York. During his more than nineteen years as an educator, he has been a teacher, school psychologist, and administrator. In addition, he is an adjunct professor of education at the University of the State of New York at New Paltz. Since 1990 he has been a member of the U.S. Department of Education's Blue Ribbon Schools Recognition Panel. He has written articles and conducted workshops throughout the country on effective classroom management and instruction techniques. He is the author of three other books: *Elementary Discipline Handbook: Solutions for the K–8 Teacher, Special Educators Discipline Handbook,* and *Managing Conflict: Tactics for the School Administrator.*

# Contents

## Section Three   High School Curriculum                                      129

## Section Four   Conclusion                                                    239

# Preface

*T*his book began while I was waiting to enter the White House to be greeted by the president of the United States. As a principal of a recently nationally recognized middle school I was invited, along with other principals, administrators, teachers, and students, to a reception at the White House. During the two-day recognition ceremony I had the opportunity to speak with many educators about what made their schools so special. Restructuring to meet the changing needs of the students was a common organizational strength of many of the schools. A predominant type of effort at curriculum restructuring was one that allowed for interdisciplinary or integrated curriculum projects. Overwhelmed by the discovery of such rich and varied approaches to teaching content area knowledge, I decided to collect the more promising interdisciplinary units.

Every secondary school that was awarded national recognition during the 1988–1989 and 1990–1991 school years asked to participate in a national project to disseminate knowledge about interdisciplinary curriculum. I also had the opportunity to read the applications of many of these schools while doing research at the U.S. Department of Education in Washington, D.C. In addition, I serve as a panel member to help select schools to be recommended for national recognition. Appendix C provides a description of the Blue Ribbon Schools Program.

The term *interdisciplinary* refers to the process teachers use to organize and transfer knowledge under a unified theme. Another term, *integrated*, is often used to describe this same process. Both terms refer to removing the distinguishing barriers between subjects, disciplines, or content areas. The result is that students are exposed to themes that borrow supporting knowledge from all subject areas. The product of this unification, the interdisciplinary curriculum, helps students construct their own integrated knowledge from their experiences.

The book is divided into three sections. In Section One, "Understanding Interdisciplinary Curriculum," you will be exposed to current research concerning interdisciplinary curriculum. Chapter 1 describes interdisciplinary curriculum in detail by showing various types and purposes. Integrated curriculum is advocated by educators today as one of the solutions to restructuring our schools. The concept changes the purpose of schools, the role of teachers, the role of students, the scope and sequence of what we need to teach, and student achievement. In this chapter, you will see that many professional educational organizations and much educational research support the incorporation of interdisciplinary curriculum.

Chapter 2 presents a step-by-step process for designing interdisciplinary curriculum. Topics discussed include what to integrate, how to develop objectives, themes, and time to accomplish the task. Five different sequence models are described, with actual charts developed to help you understand the design process. Finally, the development of higher order thinking skills and authentic assessment are discussed.

In Chapter 3 the role of teachers working together on teams is developed. At the secondary level, where the content of the different disciplines can be specialized and sophisticated, teachers need to work together if curriculum is to be integrated. In this chapter, you will discover ways of helping a group of teachers develop into a team, and you will see how some teams become unsuccessful. Most important, however, you will view teams and the process of teaming as today's recognized hero in our schools.

Section Two contains 23 examples of successful interdisciplinary curricula that can be used in middle schools or junior high schools. The age range of middle school students and that of junior high students can be broad. You will note, however, that these curricula can easily be adapted to fit the level appropriate for your students. Many middle schools reported the active involvement of teams as a fundamental organization of the respective schools.

Section Three presents 19 interdisciplinary curricula at a high school level. The level of sophistication varies from simple concepts and themes to sophisticated and difficult subject areas. It is somewhat surprising that so many curriculum units at the high school level were received. One usually thinks of high schools as the foundation of content subject area disciplines. Here, it is evident that schools of excellence do consciously attempt to integrate curriculum.

The curricula in Section Two and Three are varied and are presented in most cases as they were given. The idea is to show you that there is no one way, and no one perfect way, to integrate curriculum. All the curriculum units are presented in a similar format. The subject areas integrated are listed, as well as the name of the school and staff involved in development, teaching, and organization. The phone number of the school is listed so you can call to find out more about the interdisciplinary units. In all cases, it is the teachers listed who do the work of teaching these curricula. The principal's name is listed because no school can offer these curricula without administrative support—and to give you a contact person at each school.

Section Four, the Conclusion, deals with issues related to implementation, assessment, and the future of interdisciplinary curriculum.

The length of the curricula varies considerably. Some units are printed in their entirety; others are given only a short description. Do not judge these curricula on the amount of space occupied in this book. All the curricula presented here are excellent. The choice of format was the author's, and decisions on length were based on variety of units, themes, organization, and limits in space.

You are encouraged to develop one or more of these units in your own instructional program. Choose one and ask a colleague to read it. Together, talk about the possibility of implementing the unit. Talk to other teachers, support personnel, and administrators. Then modify what you need to make it happen. Call the school listed if you need more information. Most teachers like to share what works successfully. Take a risk—implement what you have developed. Share it with others, refine it, and offer the unit again to other students.

You may also want to develop your own curriculum unit or refine one that you are already using based on ideas in this book. You will find numerous ideas on how to do this throughout the book. Appendix A provides model sequences to map your own design. Since all curriculum is always developing and changing, some of the curriculum as presented in this book may have been changed by its developers as it has been used. This means that the unit has been refined, updated, and made more successful. Appendix B provides a detailed listing of the schools involved and the curriculum units in case you would like to learn of new or further developments with interdisciplinary curriculum.

Thank you to Frances Kochan of Florida State University for her thorough and expert analysis of the manuscript. I would also like to thank the staff of the Blue Ribbon Schools Program and, in particular, the acting director of the School Recognition Division at the U.S. Department of Education, Jean Narayanan, for her assistance and cooperation. Also, the cooperation of the principals and teachers of the 42 schools of excellence that are represented here is much appreciated. Finally, I would like to thank my own staff at the Anne M. Dorner Middle School in Ossining, New York, who have shown me how interdisciplinary curriculum can be used in different formats and settings.

# Section One
# Understanding
# Interdisciplinary Curriculum

# 1 Applying the Concept

The class of 24 seventh-graders descended on the middle school library with enthusiasm and determination. Each student had just been placed on a team with three other students and given the task of finding information about life in colonial America. Shepherding all this energy was the social studies teacher. Quickly and methodically the students started discovering information in the reference section, the history section, and the technology and science section. Four students even cornered the media specialist and were asking her all kinds of questions about her trip to colonial Williamsburg in Virginia. In each student's mind was the three-day time limit given to them to complete a worksheet of activities.

Waiting for them in three days was the assignment provided by the English teacher. Each team was to write and publish a newspaper based on what they knew about colonial times. Included would be features on colonial news, weather, sports, politics, and even cartoons. This newspaper was to be exhibited in the school cafeteria for all to read.

The process of getting from collecting information in the library to writing and then to printing is one that places heavy demands on the student's ability to think, discuss, make decisions, apply skills, and cooperate with others. The students know all too well that the grade for both courses, English and social studies, will not be based on collecting information or filling in a worksheet. Rather, their mastery of the colonial period in history will be judged on their final exhibition — the newspaper.

This scene, which can be envisioned at all grade levels K–12 with various degrees of sophistication, is a simple example of interdisciplinary curriculum.

## What Is Interdisciplinary Curriculum?

Interdisciplinary curriculum is the organization and transfer of knowledge under a unified or interdisciplinary theme. Most researchers (Beane, 1990; Martinello & Cook, 1992; Jacobs, 1989; Fogarty, 1991) view interdisciplinary applications on a continuum of curriculum integration. Listed here are the common types of interdisciplinary curriculum that can be viewed on this continuum, from the simplest to the most complex.

### Correlated

Here teachers in a secondary school apply the same scope and sequence to their respective courses but make minor adjustments in the time the different elements are taught. For example, in the eleventh grade students may be required to read *The Robber Barons* in English class at the same time of the school year their American History teacher is lecturing on the industrial growth of America. In addition to content area correlation, teachers may also teach skills in a correlated sequence. In one eighth-grade English class, the teacher taught students how to outline at the same time that the social studies teacher was requiring students to keep specific notes on her lecture.

### Multidisciplinary

In this type the teachers actually create a new course which weaves the content area of the different disciplines into a unified course of study. For example, one teacher in the seventh grade offered a ten-week mini-course on genealogy. In this course the teacher combined knowledge of immigration, economics, politics, geography, foods, writing, and art into a course in which students traced their cultural past. A similar course in the twelfth grade was offered by a teacher on debating. Here students picked a variety of controversial topics that interested them, took opposing views, researched the matter, practiced oratorical technique, and performed live debates on the community's cable educational television channel.

### Interdisciplinary

This approach organizes curriculum around broad themes which by their nature contain elements of most areas of knowledge. Examples of such broad themes might be *revolution, justice, conflict,* or *change.* One high school English teacher organized her curriculum around the theme of *identity.* In analyzing the required reading for the course, students were directed to look for ways the authors dealt with the development of the character's self-image. In one of the movies viewed by the class, *Ordinary People,* the theme of identity was traced in the relationships within a family.

Beane (1990) believes that the use of themes to organize curriculum (e.g., wellness) can unify the personal concerns of adolescents (e.g., fitness) with social concerns (e.g., environmental protection).

### Integrated Day

This type of integration requires an extensive reorganization of the entire school. Schools organized around a particular philosophy such as Socratic teaching may be one such example.

In planning for interdisciplinary themes, one should be aware of two extremes in what Jacobs (1989) refers to as the "potpourri problem" and the "polarity problem." In the former case, teachers just sample bits of knowledge from different subjects but never really integrate them. In the latter case teachers use so many integrated themes that the content essential to the course is lost to the students.

## Applications

To understand how the different types of interdisciplinary curriculum described on this continuum can be applied, let's look at our colonial newspaper project. This project can be developed using any of the design types of interdisciplinary curriculum described.

### Correlated

In a middle school this unit can be taught with the social studies and English teacher developing their curriculum sequence so that both are dealing with colonial issues at the same time. During the six-week period in which the social studies teacher is describing the American revolution, the English teacher, who teaches same students, requires the class to read and analyze the book *Johnny Tremain*. Teaching the same content by sequencing the time factor is a good example of correlated curriculum.

### Multidisciplinary

The colonial newspaper project is an example of a type of multidisciplinary curriculum. While the English and social studies teachers have correlated the time of their presentation, this project integrates the curriculum a step further. It requires students to step out of their content area courses and view colonial history and culture as a whole. The newspaper project is the unifying factor. Figure 1.1 illustrates how this project unifies the content of many different courses.

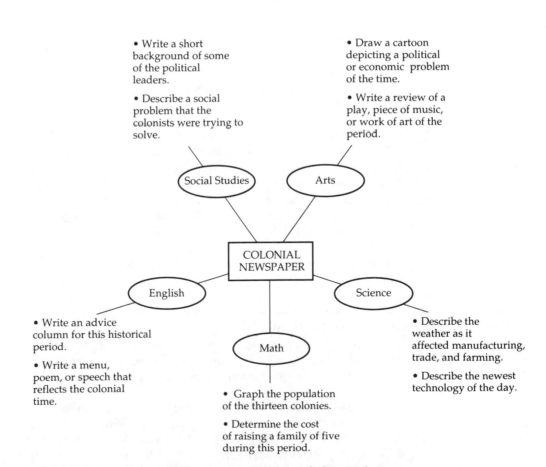

**FIGURE 1.1**  Colonial Newspaper Integrated Curriculum

### Interdisciplinary

If a teacher organizes a course around a broad theme such as *revolution* or *communication* and includes the American revolution as one of the factors covered, that would be an example of truly integrated curriculum. Using the theme of *revolution*, students would be able to understand the process of revolution in relation to their common experience of changing responsibilities at home and in the community as well as to the common social phenomena of political change. Using the theme of *communication*, a teacher could relate the media blitz aimed at today's adolescents to the power of the media to influence local, state, national, and world events.

### Integrated Day

This type of curriculum presentation involves total immersion. For example, some schools require that students actually live a full day or more in the role of a person in colonial times. Students acquire the dress, the speech, the food, and the political debates that raged during this time. One school in New York State requires as part of the unit on colonial history that its seventh-graders spend a night guarding Fort Putnam, the revolutionary fort on the grounds of the West Point Military Academy.

## The Purpose

The purposes of integrated curriculum are many and varied. It can be used for these reasons:

- It teaches students how to transfer knowledge.
- It involves the entire community as a learning environment.
- It teaches students how to analyze, explain, and apply knowledge.
- It is result oriented.
- It teaches students how to make decisions.
- It teaches students how to work cooperatively with others.
- it encourages individuality and diversity.
- It improves students' retention of knowledge.
- It provides meaning to students' experience.
- It is fun.

## Providing Opportunities to Think

Every student of education has heard of Bloom's taxonomy (Bloom, 1956). This taxonomy lists six major categories in the cognitive domain, as follows:

1. *Knowledge:* Remembering previously learned material
2. *Comprehension:* The ability to explain the meaning of things
3. *Application:* The ability to use information in a new setting
4. *Analysis:* The ability to evaluate the relevance of information
5. *Synthesis:* The ability to put parts together to form a whole
6. *Evaluation:* The ability to judge the value of material

As education students, we are taught that effective instructional objectives should include all six cognitive domains. Yet, driven by pressure to "cover" the curriculum material and by the need to teach to the test, most instructional objectives in today's schools deal only with the first domain, knowledgbe. In fact, very few of our instructional objectives reach these last domains. Taylor (1991) reports that 97.4 percent of teacher-made exams test for knowledge or information. Time, not the lack of interest or desire, has forced us to abandon reaching the higher order thinking skills.

As education students, we were taught that true critical and creative thinking take place in the last three cognitive domains: analysis, synthesis, and evaluation.

Advances in understanding how the mind works have undermined the once-sacred belief that we need to use memorization and rote work to force-feed vast quantities of information and data. Perkins (1991, pp. 4–8) refers to such instruction as the "chocolate box approach." We force students to put isolated bits of information in different "boxes" within the mind in the hope that the mind can expand to accept the increasing volume of knowledge.

It is a common belief today (Resnick & Klopfer, 1989, pp. 3–4) that knowledge is not acquired from "covering" vast amounts of memorized information. Rather, knowledge is "owned" when one can use information to make generalizations, analogies, explanations, and connections. This ability to transfer knowledge and to design new knowledge structures is what thinking is all about.

Perkins (1986) calls it design analysis, Caine and Caine (1991, p. 82) refer to it as patterns, and Spady and Marshall (Spady, 1991, pp. 67–72) promote transformational outcome-based education. They all advocate the need for instructors to help students make connections in knowledge. They postulate that the brain searches for patterns and connections, that every one of our experiences contains information from all the different disciplines, and that redundancy and immersion aid in understanding.

Interdisciplinary curriculum is a curriculum design and a method of instruction that fosters all of the above. When students are involved in the study of themes using an interdisciplinary approach, they are using such high-order thinking skills as explaining, making analogies, interpreting, applying, exhibiting, and generalizing. Students are asking themselves what parts fit to make the whole, what would be a good method to display this pattern, what is the purpose of information as related to the theme, and whether this information supports the theme. Explanatory and evaluative arguments abound both within the student and, as we will see, among students.

The colonial newspaper integrated project will assume students have applied skills in the first few cognitive domains. Moreover, the unit will require students also to engage the various higher order thinking skills. In planning and publishing the colonial newspaper, we will find students searching for connections among the various pieces of information and data found in their library research. They will be seen explaining to each other the importance of certain information for inclusion in the paper and the irrelevance of other material. They will make analogies between the proposed colonial paper and current newspapers published. The skills of organizing, writing, editing, keyboarding, and a host of others will be applied to make this paper work.

Listening to one of the groups preparing the colonial paper, we hear the following dialogue, which illustrates the higher order thinking taking place.

*Maria:* Let's decide first which of these items [facts and data the four members collected on colonial history] are the most important.

*Regina:* How do we do that?

*John:* Well, let's look at today's paper and see what items are important today.

*Maria:* Yeah! We could write our stories like today's paper. Use the same type of columns and stuff, outlining, ah, you know what I mean.

*Joe:* I was thinking. All this stuff we have on important people: John Adams, Thomas Jefferson and the others. Why not do a column called "Man-on-the-Street"?

*Marielle:* You mean "Person-on-the-Street," don't you?

*Joe:* O.K., O.K. We could interview all these folks with one question. That way they all are included.

*John:* That's good. Is there an important issue we could ask them about? I mean, which issue do you think the readers want to know about?

*Marielle:* Let's talk about that. Which issue would be the most important?

As the conversation continues, the students begin to search for connections among the varied pieces of information they have collected. They start to explain, argue, and evaluate the information for importance. Analogies with today's paper and events are discussed and debated.

## Learning Cooperatively

A vast amount of research points to the value of cooperative learning. Teachers across the nation have been exposed to this methodology and are incorporating its techniques into the classroom. Interdisciplinary curriculum is a natural place for cooperative learning. This section will describe how cooperative learning works and illustrate how it was structured into the colonial newspaper theme.

Developed and taught at John Hopkins University, by Robert Slavin (1986), student team learning has taken on many different formats. The format most widely used with interdisciplinary curriculum involves grouping students together in heterogeneous groups that work toward a common goal and common team success. The goal can be a project or exhibit. There is some debate whether grading should be based on the success of the group members as a whole or whether individual effort needs to be graded as well. Teachers tend to use both methods in grading, as well as a third method that incorporates both an individual and a group grade.

For cooperative learning to be successful as a learning technique, it must offer a reward or grade, it must hold each individual accountable, and it must offer equal opportunity for success (Salvin, 1991, p. 73). There has been much debate about the value of grades as a reward, because grades are external rewards. Grades, however, are part of education as we now know it and therefore must be considered part of the instructional assessment process. When we look at outcome-based education, you will see some alternatives to traditional grading that should be considered. Individual accountability is extremely important. Every student needs to demonstrate mastery of the material in the lesson. There must be a common core of learned knowledge or skill that is recognized as essential. Each student probably will learn other things in the lesson that are different, but it is each student's level of proficiency on the common core that must be assessed. Equal opportunity means that a few members of the group cannot do all the work with the others acting as bystanders. Depending on ability level, each member of the group must contribute something to the project. It is the task of the teacher to structure the lesson in such a way that this opportunity exists.

The value of working cooperatively is recognized as an essential skill of the U.S. workplace. Peters and Waterman (1983, p. 132) talk about project teams and project centers as the most important way in which excellent companies solve and even manage problems. Companies refer to their work force by names like "Team Xerox" and "Team Pepsi!" not only to describe themselves but also to motivate workers. Learning how to work together and to work on teams begins in school.

Students engaged in cooperative groups using integrated curriculum have established what Bennis and Naus (1985, p. 119) refer to as the collegial organization. Students determine power, status, and influence based on peer recognition. The teacher is not in the hierarchical position of making specific decisions about how to complete the project. The decision-making process is participatory. An individual's ideas are welcome, and individual commitment to the project is necessary for the whole team to be successful.

For teachers using cooperative learning, there is more work involved in organizing the project around group work and in organizing the teams so they are basically equal in ability level. There is, however, less work in the day-to-day instruction. By *work,* we are referring to the teacher-as-lecturer model, in which the teacher knows all the information and his or her task is to disseminate this body of knowledge to the students. In a cooperative work model, the best way to describe the teacher's role is that of coach. The teacher encourages, asks questions, instructs when a problem is encountered or a skill is needed to move the groups to the next step. The teacher must realize that all groups will do things differently and that all groups will not learn exactly the same things. Teachers need the ability to handle the resulting ambiguity.

One benefit of cooperative learning that is seldom mentioned is the unanticipated rise in student self-esteem. Because all students use interpersonal skills, because each student's contribution is valued and helps bring success to everyone on the team, and because each student can see the immediate effect of his or her contribution, there is a feeling among students of positive self-worth. The chance that a student will, in the future, be motivated to complete a cooperative group project increases to the extent that the student feels good about him- or herself.

If we use an integrated theme as the curriculum organizer and cooperative learning as the instructional format, our colonial newspaper learning situation would look something like this.

*Groups*   The teacher divides the class into groups of four students each. Each group has one student whom the teacher judges as having above-average ability, one student with below-average ability, and two students of average ability.

*The Assignment*   Each group is given the project of publishing a two-page newspaper based on colonial times. The group has four topics to cover: important people, technology and science, customs and culture, and government and politics. The group of four students is told that they are to decide which one of them receives which topic. Each student must have one topic, and all four topics must be covered.

*Teacher as Worker*   The teacher will spend two days lecturing, demonstrating, and holding a large-group discussion on the major aspects of the colonial period and on the four assigned topics.

*Students as Workers*   Students meet in their respective groups and divide the topics among themselves. Each student then goes to the library to research and gather information related to his or her topic. The group then comes together to determine what will be included in the paper, how it will be done, and who will be responsible for different tasks in the writing and publishing.

*Teacher as Coach*   The teacher needs to monitor and guide the individual students as they search for information. During the group discussions the teacher is needed to offer suggestions and examples, and to act as a resource for the students who are putting together the paper.

*Assessment*   Each group will receive one grade for the completed group project. Each student in the group will get two grades, one that is given to every member of the team for group effort, and the other a grade based on the student's individual effort.

## Outcome-Based Performance

Outcome-based performance is not a program in itself. The term refers to a belief among teachers that if one designs the direction and structure of learning, all students, given enough time, can learn. It implies that what is taught, how it is taught, and how it is assessed are consistent with the direction one wants to go. Students are encouraged to discover relationships between and among knowledge bases and then to apply these newfound concepts and skills in solving problems.

Interdisciplinary curriculum units usually are part of a more general curriculum plan. These plans have exit outcomes that are readily observable and are known to all participants before the unit begins. The way to do this is to organize the curriculum backwards. That is, first decide on the general exit outcome: what you want the students to learn as a result of participating in this curriculum unit. An example would be "to have all students become critical decision makers who are capable of using information to solve problems." Next, determine the program outcomes for the different subject areas involved. In our case they would be "to discover history information from different sources, analyze the information, and decide which is important to put in the newspaper." The same program outcomes would need to be determined for the other subjects involved. The next step is to plan course, then unit, and then specific lesson outcomes for the curriculum unit. To ensure congruence, all of the units are organized backwards, starting from the general exit outcomes. An outline of this plan would be as follows:

Curriculum is
designed
down.                    Exit outcomes
                         Program outcomes
          ↓              Course outcomes
                         Unit outcomes        Instruction is
                         Lesson outcomes         taught up.   ↑

The instruction for this unit proceeds from the bottom up. That is, the teacher first teaches the lesson, which then builds the unit objectives, which build the course objectives, which build the program objectives, which ultimately produce the desired exit outcome.

The instruction plan for our colonial newspaper unit would look like this:

*Instruction Outcome:*   Students will research five pieces of information related to colonial history.

*Unit Outcome:*   Students will research, design, and publish a colonial newspaper.

*Course Outcome:*   This seventh-grade curriculum will cover American history from the Pilgrims to 1848.

*Program Outcome:*   Students will connect and evaluate the information, ideas, and issues reflected in written materials about this period of our nation's history.

*Exit Outcome:*   All students will become critical decision makers who are capable of using information to solve problems.

## The Advocates

Many current educational reform movements advocate the incorporation of integrated curriculum and instruction. Specific sources can be located in the reference section of this chapter. Some examples follow.

• The America 2000 Schools initiative calls for a new partnership between schools, businesses, parents, and educators. It asks our nation to focus on specific goals and to provide the necessary research and funding to reach these goals. One of the major approaches supported by America 2000 is the need to teach students how to see patterns and connections among the different facts they learn.

• The New America School Development Corporation is helping school improvement design teams restructure how schools teach curriculum. Interdisciplinary curriculum is one of the major priorities of these new designs.

• Many states are planning for integrated curriculum. In New York State a Compact for Learning has been designed that brings together schools, communities, and businesses to reform local education. The Curriculum and Assessment Councils formed under this compact are developing outcomes in each major curriculum areas. These outcomes will encourage teachers to look for ways to integrate the curriculum. In California an educational reform task force for young adolescents has published major recommendations advocating interdisciplinary studies.

• The National Middle School Association has published a handbook and numerous books designed to help practitioners organize curriculum across subject areas.

• The Association for Supervision and Curriculum Development (ASCD) has published many resource materials explaining the need, the purpose, and the how-to of integrating curriculum. One of the ASCD's subdivisions is the Interdisciplinary Curriculum Network.

• The professional educational association of Phi Delta Kappa has published material on integrated curriculum.

• National curriculum associations have been writing new curricula that emphasize curriculum integration. For example, the American Association for the Advancement of Science (AAS) in its Project 2061 has attempted to reform science, technology, and mathematics education in the United States. The National Council of Teachers of Mathematics (NCTM) advocates the application of mathematical principles and concepts as essential to the long-term study of math. Language Arts has introduced an integrated whole language study approach that incorporates reading, thinking, and writing. The National Commission on Social Studies in the Schools has said that the term *social studies* itself emphasizes multidisciplinary study. The National Commission on Music Education has supported the connection between the arts in general and broader themes of culture, civilization, and history.

• The National Association of Secondary School Principals (NASSP) has published numerous materials and has offered staff development workshops on integrated curriculum.

• Three major reform efforts in the nation are strong supporters of integrated curriculum. The Coalition of Essential Schools has as one of its nine major principles the belief that "less is more." This means that coverage of curriculum material is less important than fostering the ability to use knowledge. Another principle calls for student exhibitions of knowledge that require students to integrate what they have learned and show how it can be applied.

• Another reform movement, the National Network on Outcome Based Education, focuses on student outcomes rather than coverage of the curriculum. This movement calls for schools to rethink what they want students to know and to work backward from these exit outcomes in organizing instruction and curriculum.

• A third reform movement comes from the Effective Schools Research Association, which publishes periodic research notes that have advocated interdisciplinary curriculum.

• In a major Carnegie Foundation research study on preparing our nation's youth for the next century, the value of interdisciplinary curriculum was strongly emphasized.

## Summary

Interdisciplinary curriculum refers to the organization and transfer of knowledge under a unified or interdisciplinary theme. Applications of interdisciplinary curriculum range from very simple to complex. Four types of interdisciplinary curriculum are described here: correlated, multidisciplinary, interdisciplinary, and integrated day. In addition to broad, abstract themes, you can use topics, concepts, problems, projects, and even skills as a basis for curriculum unification. Most problems associated with designing integrated curriculum occur either because the material is poorly integrated or because the activities become too important in themselves and the content that is being learned is lost.

Interdisciplinary curriculum is positively correlated with increases in students' higher order thinking skills, cooperative learning, and outcome-based performance. At its best, integrated curriculum encourages students to discover relationships and to apply this newly acquired knowledge to solving real problems. The America 2000 schools, various professional education associations, curriculum associations, businesses, and some of the new design teams under the New America School Development Corporation strongly advocate the use of interdisciplinary curriculum in our nation's schools.

In the next chapter, you will learn the specific steps to take to design a successful interdisciplinary curriculum.

## References and Resources

### References

Arnold, J. (1990). *Visions of teaching and learning: Eighty exemplary middle level projects.* Columbus, OH: National Middle School Association.

Association for Supervision and Curriculum Development. (1991, October). Integrating the curriculum. *Educational Leadership, 49*(2).

Beane, J. A. (1975, Summer). The case for core in the middle school. *The Middle School Journal, 6,* 33–34.

Beane, J. A. (1990). *A middle school curriculum: From rhetoric to reality.* Columbus, OH: National Middle School Association.

Bennis, W., & Naus, B. (1985). *Leaders: The strategies for taking charge.* New York: Harper & Row.

Bloom, B. (1956). *Taxonomy of education objectives. Handbook I: Cognitive domain.* New York: David McKay.

Caine, R. N., & Caine, G. (1991). *Making connections.* Alexandria, VA: Association for Supervision and Curriculum Development.

California State Department of Education. (1987). *Caught in the middle: Educational reform for young adolescents in California public schools.* Sacramento: Author.

Carnegie Council on Adolescent Development. (1989). *Turning points: Preparing American youth for the 21st century.* Washington, DC: Author.

Commission on Standards for School Mathematics Curriculum. (1989). *Curriculum and evaluation standards for school mathematics.* Reston, VA: National Council of Teachers of Mathematics.

Fogarty, R. (1991, October). Ten ways to integrate curriculum. *Educational Leadership.*

Gray, L. I., & Hymel, G. M. (1992). *Successful schooling for all: A primer on outcome-based education and mastery learning.* Roseville, MN: Network for Outcome Based Schools.

Jacobs, H. H. (Ed.). (1989). *Interdisciplinary curriculum: Design and implementation.* Alexandria, VA: Association for Supervision and Curriculum Development.

Liberman, A., & Miller, L. (1990, June). Restructuring schools; What matters and what works. *Phi Delta Kappan,* pp. 759–764.

Lloyd-Jones, R., & Lunsford, A. (Eds.). (1989, March). *English Coalition report: Democracy through language.* Lubora, IL: National Council of Teachers of English.

Mancall, J., Lodish, E., & Springer, J. (1992, March). Searching across the curriculum. *Phi Delta Kappan,* pp. 526–528.

Martinello, M. L., & Cook, G. E. (1992, February). *Interweaving the threads of learning: Interdisciplinary curriculum and teaching*. Curriculum Report. Reston, VA: National Association of Secondary School Principals.

National Commission on Music Education. (1991, March). *Growing up complete: The imperative for music education*. Reston, VA: Author.

National Commission on Social Studies in the Schools. (1989). *Charting a course: Social studies for the 21st century*. Washington, DC: Author.

New York State Education Department. (1990). *The compact for learning*. Albany: Author.

Perkins, D. (1986). *Knowledge as design*. Hillsdale, NJ: Lawrence Erlbaum Associates.

Perkins, D. (1991, October). Educating for insight. *Educational Leadership, 49*, 4–8.

Peters, T., & Waterman, R. (1983). *In search of excellence*. New York: Harper & Row.

Project 2061. Council on Science and Technology Education. (1989). *Science for all Americans*. Washington, DC: American Association for the Advancement of Science.

Resnick, L., & Klopfer, L. (1989). *Toward the thinking curriculum: Current cognitive research*. Reston, VA: Association for Supervision and Curriculum Development.

Slavin, R. (1986). *Using student team learning*, 3rd ed. Baltimore, MD: Center for Research for Elementary and Middle Schools, Johns Hopkins University.

Slavin, R. (1991, February). Synthesis of research on cooperative learning. *Educational Leadership, 45*, 73.

Spady, W., & Marshall, K. (1991, October). Beyond traditional outcome-based education. *Educational Leadership, 49*, 67–72.

Taylor, R. (1991). *Using integrated, thematic teaching strategies to increase student achievement and motivation*. Oak Brook, IL: Curriculum Design for Excellence.

Varble, M. E., & Stephan, V. (1991, December). Integrating a whole language approach in secondary school. *Curriculum report*. Reston, VA: Association of Secondary School Principals.

Vars, G. (1987). *Interdisciplinary teaching in the middle grades*. Columbus, OH: National Middle School Association.

## Resources

*America 2000 newsletter*, U.S. Department of Education, Office of Public Affairs, S.W., Washington, DC 20202-0131.

Coalition of Essential Schools, Brown University, Providence, RI.

Ebersole, B. Interdisciplinary Curriculum Network, Association for Supervision and Curriculum Development, Department of Education, University of Maryland, Baltimore, MD 21228.

National Network of Outcome Based Education, Johnson City Central Schools, 666 Reynolds Road, Johnson City, NY 13790.

New American School Development Corporation, 1000 Wilson Boulevard, Suite 2710, Arlington, VA 22209.

# 2 Designing Interdisciplinary Curriculum

## Elements of Interdisciplinary Curriculum

True interdisciplinary curriculum includes several basic elements:

- Common objectives
- Common theme
- Common time frame
- Diverse sequencing patterns
- Applied learning strategies
- Varied assessment

### Common Objectives

The best way to start is to organize backwards. First decide what you want students to learn. Ask yourself, "What is the exit outcome?"

Next, map the content. If you are working with another teacher or teachers, sit down and share curriculum topics and objectives for the next month or, in a secondary school, the next quarter. An example of an eighth-grade content mapping for the third quarter of a school year is illustrated here.

*Social studies:* Origins and period of the American Civil War

*English:* Major book report, including references and footnotes

*Science:* In earth science, study of topography

*Math:* Statistics and use, construction, and interpretation of various types of graphs

From this map, teachers may be able to develop a correlated interdisciplinary unit built around the Civil War. In social studies students will be exposed to historical facts about time. In English they can read a novel or nonfiction book about the Civil War. In science students can learn how geography influenced political and military decisions before and during the Civil War. In mathematics, students can use statistics to construct graphs of population, industry, culture, per capita income, and other information.

Once all the curriculum instruction the students will engage in over a given period of time can be seen, it is time to pick a topic that can be shared. Brainstorm with other teachers, or alone if you teach a self-contained classroom. Analyze the content map for common topics or categories. Once these have been identified, view them from an abstract position. Can a generalization be made that combines two or more of these topics or categories? If a concept can be developed, write it down. Finally, look at the topics and categories from the students' viewpoint. What are the "hot" topics of discussion among your students? Can any of these topics or categories be included within the area of concern? If so, then write them down. Once you have viewed the different topics, categories, concepts, and/or student concerns from your content map, you will need to decide which theme you want to integrate.

For example, a high school global history teacher may view the curriculum in terms of such broad themes as war, the economy, manufacturing, and human rights. It may be possible to teach this global history course around these unifying themes rather than disjointed events that span both space and time. Next, the teacher should determine the common interests of adolescents. General concerns include the need for money, independence, friends, and school. There may be needs specific to the community, such as a local political race or environmental concern. The next step is to combine the students' concerns with the focus of the course curriculum around the broad themes discussed. For example, the student's need for money can be related to the growing global economy and interdependence of the world's population.

### Common Theme

There are many ways to develop a common theme. Four of these will be briefly described here.

*Topics*   These are headings or outlines about a particular subject matter. Examples of topics would be *immigration, war, flight, oil,* or *environment.* Other topics could be current events or particular issues such as *homelessness* or *AIDS.*

*Categories*   These are a group or classification to which particular facts and experiences belong. Examples would be *islands, animals, countries,* or *dance.*

*Concepts*   These are more abstract ideas or thoughts around which discussion can take place. Concepts are more general than topics or categories. Examples would be *democracy, love, death,* or *law.*

*Student Concerns*   Although these could be any of the three types of themes just described, they are listed separately because they reflect a different view of knowledge. The first three theme structures are teacher-driven or curriculum-chosen. Student concerns view experience through the child's eyes. Around these concerns a teacher organizes knowledge and exploration to unify the curriculum. Such concerns would be how to handle the earth's endangered species, how to deal with ocean pollution, whether students should have freedom of speech and dress or a say in the school's sports eligibility policy.

Here are some questions you might ask yourself after you have chosen a theme. The answers will help you determine whether the theme you have chosen is appropriate.

- Does the common theme create a coherent view of the topic?
- Is the common theme important to each of the different subject disciplines?

It does not have to be equal in importance among the disciplines, but the theme should not be peripheral to any discipline.

- Will the students learn the theme better with the subject disciplines combined or separate?
- Does the common theme help the students overcome the fragmentation of knowledge?

### Common Time Frame

One factor that may influence your decision is time. In planning for integration, you may need to reorganize how you present the curriculum so that the common theme is presented within the same time period. For example, if sixth-grade science students are learning about animal habits along a particular river, it is important that the reading material and vocabulary words presented in language arts class correlate with the focus in science. In high school, *A Tale of Two Cities* should be assigned to English students at the same time they study the French Revolution in history class.

Whether you are planning an interdisciplinary lesson within your own class or with a group of other teachers, it is helpful to block out periods of time in the schedule. This decision can take many forms and probably should be varied during the school year to meet the time constraints of the theme chosen and the demands of the entire school schedule.

Some examples of flexible scheduling follow.

*Parallel Time*  Students are grouped with a team of teachers, and the teaching times are common. For example, in an eight-period day the four teachers on a team (English, social studies, math, and science) would teach the same periods, periods 1, 3, 5, 6, and 7 (assuming the teachers teach a five-period day). The interdisciplinary unit would be taught by all four teachers as the students moved from class to class. The teachers would not necessarily see each other during the day, so they would have to rely on careful planning to provide an interdisciplinary unit.

*Block Time*  Students are grouped with a team of teachers. Rather than changing class every period, however, they remain with the same teacher for a longer block of time, usually two periods, during which the teacher presents the interdisciplinary unit. The teacher may use the block time to teach in his or her discipline or may use the time to expand the teaching to other content areas in the unit. For some of the activities the students are completing, additional time is often needed and a block period is helpful. Often a number of teachers on the team can use the block period simultaneously.

*Block Time with Couple*  Again, the students are grouped and have a block period of time. In addition, a special class is added, which can be scheduled in the period immediately following the block time. Scheduling special classes as part of an interdisciplinary unit is often a secondary school administrator's nightmare. The students going to the special class may not all be the same ones who were in the block periods. Coupling the period on, however, allows the special teacher to continue the interdisciplinary unit into an additional period. For example, after a two-period back-to-back interdisciplinary class instruction, the students might move to a Spanish class. This works if all the students who go to Spanish have participated in the block period.

*Alternating Block Time* This block period is similar to the one described here, but it meets on rotating or alternating days during the week. For example, the schedule can be designed so that students are blocked together for two periods on Monday and then, on Tuesday, spend two periods in the class they missed on Monday.

*Grouping and Regrouping* This involves much planning among a team of teachers. However, if the team teaches the same students during the same time periods, then it is possible to regroup the students for special projects, enrichment, or remediation. This grouping would be temporary, with the students later assigned back to their regular class periods. For example, if a teacher wanted to teach a special advanced unit on math problem solving to some advanced students, classes can be regrouped for the short period in which this instruction takes place. Meanwhile, another teacher on the team might take those students not in advanced math and offer them a special skills class on giving a short oral presentation. At the end of a designated period of time, say five days, students are reassigned to their regular classes. In another version of this scheduling format, one of the teachers on the team would not teach one period for two days so that he or she could work on curriculum, plan a trip, or visit another class. The other teach teachers would regroup the students, increasing the size of each class by just a few additional students.

### Diverse Sequencing Patterns

Sequencing is the information design of your integrated curriculum. You need to present an image structure of what you are attempting to do with the curriculum. This will not only help you in planning and execution but also assist the students in grasping the big picture of the interdisciplinary curriculum. Often, a linear model of course sequence fails to capture the special relationships that exist among the various elements of an integrated curriculum. The nonlinear spatial dimension can provide a holistic understanding of the relationships among the elements. There are five sequences that are commonly used in designing interdisciplinary curriculum. Each will be briefly described and illustrated by example. Appendix A includes blank copies of the five curriculum sequences that you can copy for your own use.

   **1.** *The correlated event sequence model:* This is one of the most commonly used models in integrating curriculum. It is designed to describe the stages of events over a period of time between or among different curriculum areas. For example, in the study of the American Revolution, students in social studies may study the causes and events of the war, while in English class they read the book *My Brother Sam Is Dead* by James Lincoln Collier. Using this model, teachers in different curriculum content areas can sequence the subject matter of their lessons to coincide with each other's lessons. The courses can remain separate, but the subject matter runs parallel. Figure 2.1 illustrates how this model can be used to integrate math and social studies lessons around the theme of the U.S. census at either the middle or high school level.

| Mathematics | Social Studies |
| --- | --- |
| Data collection | History and purpose of the census |
| Statistical methods | Method of taking the census |
| Means and averages | Classification of U.S. population |
| Probability | Population forecasting |
| Graphing | Policy decision making based on census data |

**FIGURE 2.1**   The Correlated Event Sequence Model

**2.** *The webbing sequence model:* This design provides a definite space for each unit or theme in the curriculum. In addition, it allows you to show the relationships among the different units or themes. In the center of the network is placed the central theme. The example in Chapter 1 in Figure 1.1 illustrates this webbing model. In Figure 2.2, "Immigrants" is placed as the central topic. Radiating from this center are the various traditional curriculum areas such as mathematics, language arts, social studies, and the arts. As one proceeds further out from the center to the third level of organization, one finds specific learning activities. The lines among the various units indicate direct connections.

**3.** *The causal sequence model:* This model can be used to illustrate the causal relationships among curriculum elements. It is sometimes referred to as a fishbone. The beginning of the "fishbone" usually lists a complex idea, experience, or event. Branching off from the center bone are a number of effects directly related to this event or experience. Further attached to each of these effects are more distant but still positively related effects of the main event or experience.

Figure 2.3 illustrates the causal relationship of suburban expansion in the Northeast. As the ring of housing development moved farther from urban centers because of the demand for more affordable and safe housing, there were immediate and then gradual effects on a number of other factors. Figure 2.3 shows that the deer population increased in some areas closer to the urban center because of the loss of habitat further out. Also, traffic increased in some areas as people transported themselves to and from work at greater distances. One problem associated with increased contact between deer and people was the rise of Lyme disease. The traffic flow into and out of the urban centers at certain times of the day placed enormous strains on the highway network. Demands for increased road construction and improvement were felt in the state legislatures. The more gradual effect of the housing expansion was the direct conflict between the buyers of new homes and the local citizens. At village meetings one often hears heated debate over zoning laws. A second gradual effect was the increased pollution of local streams and rivers feeding the watersheds and reservoirs owned by the large urban center located 50 to 100 miles away.

**4.** *The integrated sequence model:* This model is a sophisticated pattern for interdisciplinary curriculum. Using this design approach, a teacher searches for an

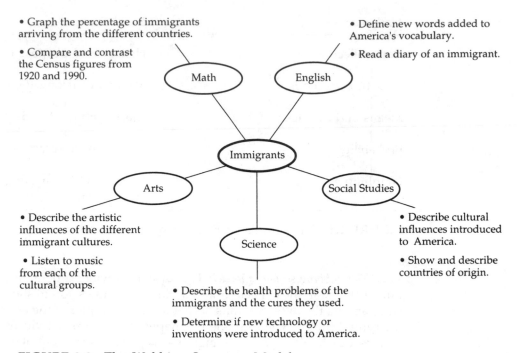

FIGURE 2.2  The Webbing Sequence Model

overall theme or pattern that can bridge a number of curriculum areas. The curriculum content is studied by looking through this overall pattern or patterns. For example, a teacher may chose "Cycle" as a theme that is present in each subject area. Drawing from the English content, the teacher discusses the role of cycles in myth and ritual, not only in ancient literature and fairy tales but also in modern

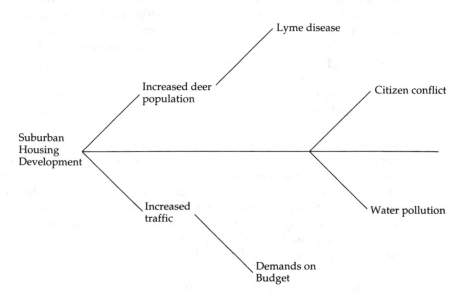

FIGURE 2.3  The Causal Sequence Model

fiction and poetry. From the history curriculum, the teacher relates the broad conceptual view that civilizations rise and fall in response to challenges as illustrated in Arnold Toynbee's cyclical view of history. In science the teacher can relate the water cycle of evaporation, condensation, and precipitation to the cycle theme. In mathematics, geometry lends itself well to the study of cycles. Psychology deals with an anxiety disorder that has cyclic qualities—manic-depressive. In technology, the study of gears in a twelve-speed bike can show how six cogs are related to two chain wheels. Planetary orbits, the circulatory system, orbitals in chemistry, religious concepts of incarnation and resurrection—all can be used to study the theme of cycle. Figure 2.4 illustrates how some of these curriculum areas can be displayed in the integrated sequence.

**5.** *The spider sequence model:* This model shows the organization of events more than it does the relationship among events as do the correlated, webbing, causal, or integrated sequencing patterns. It is a map or graphic representation of interdisciplinary curriculum by event rather than by subject area. The student often views it as an outline. In the center of this model is the main topic, and radiating from this are primary factors, events, or functions. From these primary arteries come secondary factors, events, or functions.

Figure 2.5 shows the spider model as it illustrates the organization of curriculum about the history of the Persian Gulf War in 1991. In the center is the main topic. Radiating from this core are four main ideas: (1) the history and role of oil in international economy; (2) the leaders of the Western, Middle Eastern, and Eastern nations as well as the leadership in the United Nations; (3) the military strategy of the belligerent nations; and (4) the political consequences of the war. From each of these main ideas one can see some of the secondary details to the sequence building.

### Applied Learning Strategies

Ultimately, learning requires that a student be able to perform. Learning, as discussed in Chapter 1, is not the coverage of content or the ability to memorize information. A student who has learned is one who can manipulate knowledge, create new information, ask and answer questions about reality, and be self-regulated.

Thinking should be understood as a process, not a static event. Three assumptions about thinking have become distorted. (1) the locus of thinking is often assumed to be in the person's mind rather than in the interaction between the person and the social situation. (2) the process of thinking and learning is not uniform across persons and situations. (3) resources for thinking such as knowledge and skills are often assumed to be built up over time through schooling but are, in fact, general conceptual capabilities that children have as a result of their everyday experiences or endownment (Greene, 1989).

Designing for interdisciplinary curriculum should allow for a student to learn through interaction with others and the social situation, should allow for students to express their knowledge differently, should allow the knowledge and skills to be built on the experiences and abilities of individual students and should include tasks that require students to move beyond the mastery of content to the restructuring of existing knowledge.

To accomplish this the curriculum designer needs to approach the content through multiple entry points not the single point we usually see in lesson

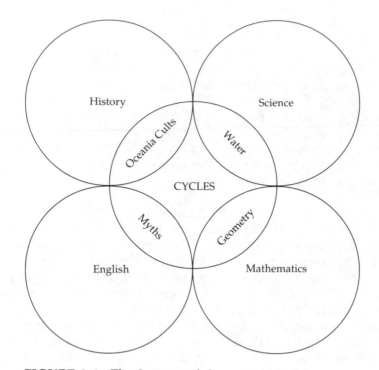

**FIGURE 2.4**   The Integrated Sequence Model

planning. Gardner (1991), pp. 245–246) talks of five entry points that correspond to his theory of multiple intelligences, which are as follows:

1. *The narrational:* Relates a story or narrative about the concept in question.
2. *The logical-quantitative:* Invokes numerical considerations or deductive reasoning.

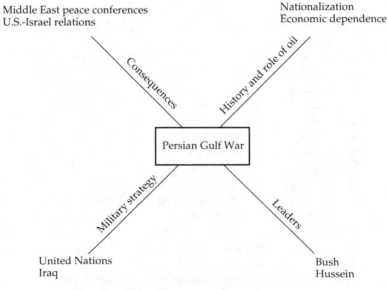

**FIGURE 2.5**   The Spider Sequence Model

3. *The foundation:* Examines the philosophical and terminological facets of a concept.
4. *The aesthetic:* Examines sensory or surface features as related to the artistic experience of living.
5. *The experiential:* Takes a hands-on approach to learning.

To ensure that knowledge is understood, students should process the knowledge and skills of the integrated curriculum using the cognitive activities associated with analysis, synthesis, and evaluation. These are the higher level thinking activities of Bloom's taxonomy, described in Chapter 1. Activities for each are as follows:

*Analysis: Separating the whole into parts*
Classify.
Outline.
Compare and contrast.
Show evidence.
Recognize patterns, assumptions.
Clarify the issues, statements, experiences.
Explain how.

*Synthesis: Combining ideas to form a new whole*
Predict.
Add to.
Create or design a plan or model.
Organize solutions, concepts, diagrams.
Develop abstractions, a scenario for the future, a process.
Generalize.
Form hypotheses based on information and/or data.
Brainstorm solutions to problems.
Propose and argue a viewpoint different than your own.

*Evaluation: Developing opinions, judgments, or decisions*
State your opinion.
Prioritize.
How would you decide?
What criteria would you use?
Judge and assess.
Select from equally appealing alternatives.
Critique an article, speech, or position.
Develop assessment strategies.
Conduct an evaluation.

A method of designing interdisciplinary curriculum to ensure that understanding takes place is to have students complete different projects. To complete a project, a student must use not only the cognitive skills of knowledge, comprehension, and application, but also analysis, synthesis, and evaluation. These projects can vary in orientation based on the multiple entry points described above. In the various interdisciplinary curricula collected for this book, many different projects are created that meet this purpose. Some examples are:

- Reports, books, newspapers, articles, pamphlets
- Mock trials, video show, school/community searches
- Puppet shows, skits, television shows, radio broadcasts
- Games, graphs, pictures, photographs, displays, cartoons
- Debates, press conferences, interviews
- Painting, sculpture, costume, artifact, murals
- Class lesson, report, acting, role playing
- Experiment, demonstration, computer display or program
- Questionnaires, poll taking

### Varied Assessment

Interdisciplinary curriculum outcomes must be evaluated if they are to have any validity with the community, parents, other teachers, and, most important, the students. Innovative curriculum ideas require that new methods of assessment be developed and implemented. There has been significant discussion of authentic and performance-based assessment, alternative forms of assessment that hold much promise for evaluating integrated curriculum outcomes. Traditional standardized tests test primarily for coverage of material, including such cognitive skills as knowledge, comprehension, and perhaps some application. But to evaluate how students are performing using higher order thinking skills like analysis, synthesis, and evaluation, we need to use other methods of assessment. We need to remind ourselves, however, that these alternative forms are still new and need much development. Research in the field is exploring the variables involved in alternative assessment forms. Some of the references at the end of this chapter may help to clarify the issues involved in this area.

Following are some steps you can take in developing performance-based assessment for your interdisciplinary curriculum unit.

**1.** *Define the outcomes of the integrated unit.* What does a good integrated curriculum project look like? What evidence will you have to show that higher order thinking skills are being used? It is important to design the curriculum backwards. First ask yourself what exit outcomes you want to accomplish. Once these are determined, finding the right assessment form will be easier.

**2.** *Define the contents of the assessment form.* It is important that the actual outcome, whether it be a written piece, a model, or a play, be a realistic task for both the teacher and the student. Decide if you plan to measure skills in a formative manner, a summative manner, or both. Determine whether you will use one outcome or will give the student a "best product" outcome to assess. Your choice will reflect your philosophical belief about the nature of learning.

**3.** *Determine the scoring criteria to be used.* Emphasize quality of work, not quantity. The scoring should be objective and manageable for the teacher to use on all students. There are two forms you can use:

*Holistic:* The raters assess their impression of the overall project. Specific criteria must be developed for the different levels of ability.

*Analytical:* The raters look for one or two specific traits in the project. Again, criteria for good and poor project presentation need to be developed.

**4.** *Establish standards.* The first time you complete an integrated curriculum unit, you probably will not have a sense of what is excellent student work and what is poor work. Look over the project outcomes and choose one or two projects that reflect excellent work. These projects then become your benchmark for measuring all others. In the next school year, you will have a benchmark established. If possible, have a team of teachers develop the scoring standards, both to give you other viewpoints and also to help them discover the validity of your nontraditional scoring process.

Part of this process requires that you establish the meaning of score. If a student obtains a "4" on a scale of scores from 0 to 4, what does this mean? Develop a written statement explaining the score so that everyone—teacher, student, and parent—understand the level of skill acquisition the score represents.

**5.** *Select the scorers.* If possible, include other teachers as scorers for the project outcomes. You should train them on the standards and organize the event. You may want to include community business people, parents, and student peer evaluators as well. Using teachers at grade levels above your own grade is another good idea. This experience will give them a good look at the learning outcomes you are trying to establish. They can then adjust their own curriculum and perhaps their assessment to reflect the skills of their incoming students.

**6.** *Feed back the results.* After the scoring has been completed, analyze the information and use it to alter your classroom instruction as needed. What trait should you focus on more, which one less, which should be dropped from the curriculum? Do the exit outcomes suggest that the skills are firmly in place? What could be done differently? Finally, the assessment information needs to be fed back to the students so they know the measurement standards before they start the final assessment process. Students should be involved at all stages of assessment—helping to determine objectives, criteria for evaluation, and evaluating their own and others work.

## Summary

Designing interdisciplinary curriculum includes the development of several elements: a common objective, a common theme, a common time frame, diverse sequencing patterns, applied learning strategies, and varied modes of assessment. Suggestions were made for selecting an appropriate theme. Scheduling sufficient time for teachers and students to develop the curriculum unit is crucial. Five different types of sequencing were described, with appropriate examples from secondary level curriculum. The models are correlated event, webbing, causal, integrated, and spider sequence. Appendix A provides blank copies of these sequences for a teacher to use in designing interdisciplinary curriculum. An important feature of integrating the curriculum is to help students understand what they are learning. Appropriately designed tasks access higher level thinking skills so students can begin to reflect constructively on the content of knowledge. Performance-based assessment will be needed to measure student outcomes on the curriculum unit. Specific suggestions for developing this type of assessment tool were described. In the next chapter you will gain an understanding of how teaming can help you design and implement interdisciplinary curriculum.

## References and Bibliography

Beane, J. (1990, May). Rethinking the middle school curriculum. *Middle School Journal, 21,* 1–5.

Beane, J. (1992, November). Creating an integrative curriculum: Making the connections. *NASSP Bulletin,* 47–54.

Brady, M. (1989). *What's worth teaching? Selecting, organizing, and integrating knowledge.* Albany: State University of New York Press.

Caine, R. N., & Caine, G. (1991). *Making connections.* Alexandria, VA: Association for Supervision and Curriculum Development.

Costa, A. L. (Ed.). (1985). *Developing minds: A resource book for teaching thinking.* Alexandria, VA: Association for Supervision and Curriculum Development.

Fagan, E. R. (1987, September). Interdisciplinary English, science, technology. *English Journal,* pp. 81–83.

Fogarty, R. (1991). *The mindful school: How to integrate the curricula.* Palatine, IL: Skylight Publishing.

Gardner, H. (1991). *The unschooled mind.* New York: Basic Books.

Gould, J. (1987). *Time's arrow, time's cycle.* Cambridge, MA: Harvard University Press.

Greeno, J. G. (1989, February). A perspective on thinking. *American Psychologist, 44,* 134–141.

Jones, B. F., Pierce, J., & Hunter, B. (1989, December–1990, January). Teaching students to construct graphic representations. *Educational Leadership, 46,* 20–25.

Lounsbury, J. H. (1992). *Connecting the curriculum through interdisciplinary instruction.* Columbus: National Middle School Association.

Marzano, R. (1991, April). Fostering thinking across the curriculum through knowledge restructuring. *Journal of Reading, 34,* 519–525.

National Association for Core Curriculum. *Bibliography of research on the effectiveness of block-time, core, and interdisciplinary team teaching programs.* Kent, OH: Author.

Presseisen, B. Z. (1991, November). *Implementing thinking in the school's curriculum.* Paper presented at the First International Congress on Psychology and Education, Madrid, Spain.

Shiever, S. (1992). *The comprehensive guide to teaching thinking.* Boston: Allyn and Bacon.

Shlain, L. (1992). *Art and physics: Parallel visions in space.* New York: William Morrow.

Spear, R. (1992). Middle level team scheduling: Appropriate grouping for adolescents. *Schools in the middle: Theory into practice, 2,* 30–43.

Van Patten, J. V., Chao, C., & Reigeluth, C. (1986, Winter). A review of strategies for sequencing and synthesizing instruction. *Review of Educational Research, 56,* 437–471.

Vars, G. (1991). Integrated curriculum in historical perspective. *Educational Leadership, 49,* 14–15.

Willis, S. (1992, November). *Interdisciplinary learning.* ASCD Curriculum Update. Alexandria, VA: Association for Supervision and Curriculum Development.

# 3 The Team as Hero

The concept of "team as hero" (Reich, 1987, pp. 77–83) means that rather than glorifying the accomplishments of the individual in an organization, or those of the maverick geniuses operating on the fringe of the organization, we should recognize the power of the team. In both business and education, teamwork has been recognized as a crucial factor in improving productivity, quality, and motivation. Kanter (1983) calls for self-regulating business work teams to perform tasks in new, more meaningful contexts. Peters (1988) believes that all business functions should be done by small multifunctional teams. In education, cooperative learning has long been recognized as a powerful instructional method to improve achievement. Chapter 1 dealt at length with the application of this method to integrated curriculum.

For integrated curriculum to work successfully, teacher teamwork is essential. At the secondary school level it is very difficult for an individual teacher to develop integrated curriculum. The curriculum is much more specialized and differentiated at this level. No one teacher can really be knowledgeable about curriculum content and subject matter. Although teachers do develop integrated curricula within their own classes, this type of integration tends to be relatively shallow and of limited duration. Teamwork then becomes the hero, as the whole—the integrated unit project—becomes better than the sum of the individual teachers' efforts.

## Team Organization

Even before the planning and development of integrated curricula occur, some factors should first be in place. The first one is shared time. Teachers who want to work together must have a time period during the day when they can meet to plan. It is not sufficient for a team of teachers to meet over lunch or after school to try to accomplish the sophisticated planning necessary for integrated curriculum. The school administration can be supportive by scheduling a planning period that is shared by teachers on the same team.

The second important factor in making integrated curriculum work is that the teachers on the team must have the same students. It makes no sense for the social studies teacher and the English teacher on a team to teach different students. Again, the administrator's creativity in scheduling can be very supportive.

A third factor is that the teachers on the team must get along. Teams put together by administrators simply for the sake of having teams, without considering personalities, will meet disaster. In developing teams, it is not uncommon to ask teachers whom they would like to work with. The teachers will select among themselves work styles or personalities adopted to their own views of teaching.

There are two schools of thought with regard to the placement of the better teachers. If these teachers are placed on the same team, they could be true risk takers. The integrated curriculum they develop and implement could serve as a model for other faculty members. Those teachers less oriented to risk could adopt the pioneering efforts of the more adventuresome. There are two problems with this type of thinking. First, the risk-taking team could get so far ahead of the other teachers that the team might be resented and misunderstood. Second, if many of the better teachers are on one team, parents will seek placement of their child on the "good" team. This type of selection breeds anger and frustration throughout the school and the community. A compromise to solve these dilemmas is to place two of the better teachers on a four-person team and then complete the team with one average teacher and one less than average teacher. In this structure, the better teachers can model for and energize the others on the team.

Team members must realize that not every part of their respective curriculum needs to be integrated. In fact, in many courses this would be impossible given that state exams are required at advanced course levels. Unless the states redefine the purpose of testing from measuring recall of curriculum content to authentically assessing students' ability to use the knowledge, the use of integrated curriculum will be limited. This is not to say, however, that integration is not the way to proceed. Teachers should start small and achieve success in their first attempt to plan and implement. After this venture, more elaborate and creative projects may ensue.

## Successful Working Teams

All teams, whether in business or in education, have two functions. The first is to perform a task. What must the team accomplish? The second function involves process: dealing with social and emotional issues that arise among team members. A team moves back and forth between these two functions, fulfilling certain needs in the course of its entire life history. Teacher teams that work successfully at planning and implementing integrated curricula can be observed fulfilling these two types of functions.

### Task Functions

The team has two primary functions: (1) to plan and develop the integrated curriculum, and (2) actually to implement the curriculum project. Each of these tasks will be described here.

The development of team activities over a period of time can be seen in the model of group performance advocated by Tuckman (1965, pp. 384–389). This model calls for four stages of group development: forming, storming, norming, and performing.

- In the *forming* stage, the members begin to meet, establish rules and roles, and seek information about each other's courses. They discuss the feasibility of coordinating curriculum.
- In the *storming* stage, the members become defensive and start thinking of reasons that their respective curricula cannot be integrated. They distance themselves from the group and solidify their own goals.
- In the *norming* stage, the members overcome their defensiveness and begin to plan the actual coordination. They orient their curriculum to each other's time schedule and, through the discussions, begin to discover that, indeed,

their own respective curricula can be enhanced through integration—and that student achievement might also improve.

- In the *performing* stage, the team actually plans and writes a coordinated curriculum. This stage is marked by a mobilization of resources and ideas to create a new curriculum presentation or project.

*Development*   As the team develops, coordination between its members will increase. At first, coordination merely consists of scheduling parent conferences together or planning joint field trips or exam or homework schedules. As development continues, teachers will begin to talk about their respective course objectives. Discovery of mutually supportive goals and objectives should lead to the beginning of coordination in timing the delivery of these objectives. Some give and take will be required here if the objectives are to be aligned. This is probably the first true test of the team's commitment to its task because it requires that some teachers change their own lessons to meet a common goal. For example, when a social studies teacher is teaching about the civil rights movement of the 1960s, an English teacher would require the students to read a novel written about that period. The ultimate coordination of planning comes when teachers actually move their curriculum objectives to a new topic that neither of them had planned to accomplish beforehand. The colonial newspaper project discussed in Chapters 1 and 2 is an example of this kind of commitment to task. At the ultimate level of coordination, teachers reach beyond their course objectives to identify an abstract idea or concept that is part of everything they teach. An example would be the adoption of a main theme like *freedom* or *justice*.

For any number of reasons, a team may get stuck at one of these stages of development. For example, a team may meet to agree on coordinating curriculum (forming) but fail to overcome the need of the different members to adhere rigidly to their own course scope and sequence (storming). In one case, a team actually planned and wrote an innovative curriculum integration project (norming) but failed to implement the project (performing) because members could not find time or room to "fit" it into the curriculum. When team development on task fails to move along, the school administrator or a consultant may need to get involved to help team members overcome obstacles to progress.

*Implementation*   This is the most exciting part, as you see the ideas and hopes of your team planning come alive in the minds of the students. There are a number of suggestions to follow as you begin.

1. Introduce the integrated unit together as a team. Show the students from the start that, as teachers, you are working together to fashion a new learning experience. If there is a project involved in the unit, explain to the students that the normal way of learning may need to be suspended for a while during this unit. Inject high expectations, enthusiasm, and fun into the upcoming lesson.

2. Inform the parents of what you are doing. A letter home or an attractive flyer announcing the unit would also alert them that some new activity is about to start. It is hoped that the child's enthusiasm will also reinforce your message. If there is a culminating activity at the end of the unit, such as a presentation, skit, or simulation, invite the parents.

**3.** Start small. If this is your first venture with integrated curriculum, be careful to take on the unit in small chunks. Many teams of teachers rush with great fanfare into integrated units so elaborate that the planning time duration alone kills any enthusiasm. On your first try, think small in the implementation. You might pilot a few mini-lessons at first to test the feasibility of a full integrated unit. The math and science teacher on a four-person team may, for example, pilot a three-day mini–integrated unit using just two of the four disciplines.

**4.** Support risk takers on your team. If a teacher or group of teachers on your team want to get started, let them proceed even if they have to plan on the run. Some teachers would like to experiment with a unit even before the rest of the team has formally planned the lessons. Encourage this innovation because such teachers will bring to the planning a wealth of experience. Modeling the integrated unit can be a valuable exercise for the team, the students, the administration, and other teachers in the building.

**5.** Look for integrated units that already work. Many companies espouse a belief called "best practices" (Stewart, 1991, pp. 41–49), which states that there are great ideas already out there that can greatly enhance the operations of one's own business. This does not mean stealing product patents or ideas, but it does mean incorporating business practices that help a company manage its operations more efficiently. There are many integrated curriculum ideas in this book that can be used or adapted to help a team of teachers get started.

**6.** The best integrated curriculum units are nurtured in school environments where change is promoted and where teams have freedom of self-management. There is no way a school administrator can make integrated curriculum just happen. The effort requires the creativity, sponsorship, and flexibility of the teachers involved. This means reducing bureaucracy so teams can get on with the implementation.

### The Process

This level of team functions fulfills the many social and emotional needs of humans working together on a task. Most of these needs can be centered around the issues of roles, norms or rules, conflict, and boundary maintenance.

**1.** *Roles* are those behavior expectations that group or team members give each other (Hare, 1976, p. 131). In teacher teams, which can best be likened to informal group structures, a number of apparent roles are played out.

- The first is the *idea* person, or the teacher who tries to keep the team on task. This role is not to be confused with the leadership role. Rather, this is the person who is more cognitively oriented and who tries to keep the group moving along in its task of developing interdisciplinary curriculum.
- The second is the *"best liked"* person, who responds to the emotional needs of the group and plays a more passive role.
- The third role that has been known to appear is that of the *deviant* person. This role is occupied by someone who talks a lot but is generally viewed with suspicion and even dislike. In group dynamics this person may express the team's anxiety about discussing an issue or even of planning together.

- The fourth role that may be present is that of *joker*. A person in this position is only marginally involved with the group discussion but uses humor to cover the rough spots of discussion and even to introduce new ideas.
- A fifth role played is that of the *silent* person. The teacher in this role says very little in discussion but responds in a positive nonverbal manner. The other group members will tolerate this role as long as the member agrees to the plans of the others. If, however, at the end of a meeting the silent member comes out against the plans of the group, a great deal of anger usually is expressed at this person.
- *Leadership* in teacher teams is a role that can best be described as informal. In most cases leadership is assumed by the person who talks the most because he or she wins the most decisions. Some teams have apointed leaders who may or may not be paid a stipend. Even on these teams, however, the real leadership may lie elsewhere.

**2.** *Norms* or *rules* are those group sanctions that are known by all members. The permanence of these norms over time may be questioned. Certainly today's teachers need to be actively involved in the change process and be able to change their instructional methods and curriculum lessons constantly to meet the needs of their students. This ability to handle uncertainty and the culture of permanent change will determine how successfully the team can fulfill its members' social and emotional needs. Some norms that need to be addressed continually are as follows:

- The objective of the team planning needs to be clear. Teachers need to know and express verbally the purpose of the curriculum integration. There does not need to be one "right" reason to integrate curriculum. In fact, teachers often have different reasons. One teacher may want to implement a unit so that cooperative learning can take place. Another may want to infuse critical thinking skills. A third member may want to see if the students can understand the curriculum better by adopting other perspectives. Whatever the purpose, each member should be clear about the needs of each other.
- Decision making needs to be based on consensus, not majority vote. No teacher should feel that he or she has been forced to be part of the integrated curriculum unit. It is better to have those teachers on the team who wish to integrate the curriculum pilot a small unit first. This can then be shared with reluctant members for evaluation.
- Communication should encourage active listening and a free flow of information. Teachers should try to understand each other's viewpoints by paraphrasing what the other is saying. A simple technique, such as, "By that, do you mean . . ." often is enough to show others that you are trying to understand their viewpoint. Teachers will feel more open to sharing if they believe they have a chance of being understood. Sharing guides, textbooks, and lesson plans is an excellent way to start breaking down curriculum barriers.
- Support for the integrated unit needs to be sought from the administration. Enlightened administrators will have established a school culture that supports innovation and risk taking. As you plan your curriculum, seek the participation of the administrator. He or she need not be part of the team meetings but should receive progress reports on the planning. His or her ideas for support or reallocation of resources can enhance implementation.

If you feel the administrator will not support the integrated unit outright, discuss among yourselves ways of introducing him or her to your more general goals and beliefs. Copying an article on integrated curriculum to share with the administrator may start the support process. Another method is to find a colleague in another school that is active in implementing integrated curricula. Ask if that school's administrator can call your own administrator to discuss the advantages of the integrated approach.

- Results are the best indicator of success. Once the integrated unit has been completed, the team should get feedback on the process. Student evaluation as well as parent, teacher, and administrator feedback will be helpful in the team's assessment of what worked and what did not. Because the school year is cyclical, the team can use this information to redesign or expand the unit for the next year.

**3.** Managing conflict is another key process function of the team. Because change is occurring and involves a number of teachers, it is safe to assume that conflict will exist in both the planning and the implementation stages. How the team members deal with the conflict will determine whether or not the integrated unit gets off the ground and whether the team stays together as a functioning unit. Some general guidelines for dealing with conflict are listed here. For further information, see Maurer (1991).

- Maintain a positive climate by avoiding power struggles for leadership and recognizing the fears of reluctant members. Go slowly and build steadily by explaining, modeling, or piloting parts of the unit. There is no need to do it all immediately. Nor does the leader need to remain the leader throughout the unit's implementation. If a number of teachers want to be leaders, plan a unit in which teachers can rotate the leadership role.
- Keep the focus of planning on the unit, not on the person. If a teacher on the team becomes uncomfortable to work with over a long period for any reason, do not focus on the personality or the person's behavior. Instead, maintain the focus of your discussions on planning of the unit.
- Recognize anger and frustration among the team members when it appears. These emotions are natural phenomena in groups. When they surface, recognize them and move on. Teacher teams are not therapy groups; most members do not want to lavish time on talking about intragroup anger. If anger becomes an obstacle to group functioning, seek the advice of an outside person, perhaps an administrator, to help the group deal with the anger.
- Focus on the mutual interest among the team members to build an integrated unit, not on the demands of individuals. If one teacher demands that something be included in the unit but other members truly believe it would not work, try to discover what interest the teacher may have in including this particular item. Perhaps the interest can be met in some other matter.
- Reach for consensus among the members. There are no right or wrong absolutes in planning an integrated curriculum. There should be room for everyone's ideas and interests. Let creativity abound so that all team members are stakeholders in the unit's implementation.

**4.** Boundary maintenance may be one of the more vital process functions of the team. All schools have multiple layers of organization and leadership. One reason school culture is so complex is that overlapping interests are permanently present. Members of a school team are usually members of a school curriculum department and probably also members of the faculty bargaining unit. In schools where shared decision making is operative, there are usually many school improvement or shared governance committees. At any one time, a teacher can be a member and/or leader of any one of a dozen different school organizations. Yet despite this abundance of membership, the traditional school culture in place even today supports and reinforces the single teacher in the classroom more than any other function.

The true task of a team member is to build and maintain boundaries between the varying overlapping memberships while at the same time attempting to penetrate the classroom boundary walls to integrate curriculum.

To accomplish this, the teacher and the team as a whole needs to display skills in synchronization with other functions and organizations at the school and district as well as skills of developing cohesiveness. Maintaining team boundaries involves constant work by the members to ensure that the team is not engulfed by larger, noisier, or more hierarchical groups. On the other hand, the team should avoid becoming so rigid that it becomes isolated.

## Unsuccessful Working Teams

There are many reasons that teamwork fails. As we have shown, schools have sufficient organizational structure to impede team growth. Parents may not support teamwork because it locks their child with certain teachers on the team. Special subject teachers may not support teamwork because they are not involved and teams restrict their own course scheduling options. In addition, personality factors among the different members, though invisible to all but the members themselves, can slowly eat away at the heart of working together.

Teams that do fail to build integrated curriculum often fail on task functions for three reasons:

**1.** The project is too large and takes too long, or there are too many resources to plan, organize, and implement. Here, the scope of the change in curriculum is so vast that when a small problem arises it is almost impossible to stop and repair it. The students get lost early on because what they are doing is so new and so all-encompassing that they cannot make the adjustment.

**2.** The project involves too many people. It is important to confine implementation of the new project to those who were part of the planning, those teachers who have a stake in the process and will make it work. Involving other teachers, parents, or administrators who have not been part of the planning can add confusion to the process. First get started, then add others as time goes on.

**3.** There is no culture in the school to support integrated curriculum. If the school administration does not believe in the concept, teachers involved in the process may have difficulty early on when they need to seek extra resources. Other teachers may not support the project and may even blame it for causing too much disruption, for having too many field trips, or for causing students to miss their class. In some cases teachers not involved in the project even blame lower standardized test scores in reading on the time the students "wasted" on the curriculum project. For the teachers involved, it is wise to take time in the planning process to help others in your building understand what you are doing.

Teams that fail to develop integrated curriculum often fail on process functions in three areas.

**1.** Communication is guarded or nonexistent, or, at the other extreme, communication is confrontational. In the former case members do not share what they are thinking or feeling for fear of rejection or ridicule. As a result, other members may believe they have such a person's support. When the project begins to be developed, the other members are surprised and then angry that this person is so strongly against its implementation. At the other extreme, when members are always confronting each other and not listening, everyone will feel misunderstood. Discussions of planning will soon bog down over minor details so that nothing is accomplished.

**2.** Team meetings are poorly organized, or, at the other extreme, meetings are too rigid. Lack of enthusiasm for the project among one or more members, long meetings without agendas, failure to reach decisions in adequate time, feeling that one is forced to participate—all contribute to meetings that will eventually kill a project. On the other hand, meetings that are driven by task completion assignments and do not allow for spontaneous interplay among team members will also destroy any creativity and fun in the project.

**3.** Team members feel they are required to work more or harder, or, at the other end of the spectrum, team members view others as doing the whole thing. If teachers feel they now have to do more in addition to what they already are doing, the project could be designed in such a fashion that it minimizes any potential creativity. Team members need to think that the project will help them deliver the curriculum in a smarter, more efficient manner. They need to see that working together collectively is smarter than closing the door and being alone with the students. The other extreme is the view that one or another of the team members is going to do the whole thing. In such cases, other team members are available but only as support. If the project is a success, the other team members may resent the one person's fame. If the project is a failure, the other team members may say, "I told you so."

These three reasons for failure exist on a continuum. If a situation arises where team members are at one of the two extremes on a factor, there is a good chance of failure. Figure 3.1 illustrates this continuum.

---

Poor communication . . . . . . . . . . . . . . . . . . . . Confrontational communication

Loose meeting organization . . . . . . . . . . . . . . . . . . Rigid meeting organization

One member decisions . . . . . . . . . . . . . . . . . . . . . . Multimember decisions

---

**FIGURE 3.1**  Continuum of Project Failure

## Summary

The concept of team as hero was discussed as the necessary structure to implement integrated curricula at the secondary level. The need to involve content specialists from differing areas will add richness and meaning to the project unit. Team organization that considers shared meeting time, the same students, mutually agreeable members, and an understanding of what parts of the curriculum can best be integrated will have the best chance of success. Teams that work successfully together manage to accomplish both task and social/emotional functions to the satisfaction of all members. Task function can be divided between planning the unit and eventually implementing it. Social and emotional functions refer to process issues like roles, norms, conflict, and boundary maintenance that are part of every group structure. Unsuccessful teams either get bogged down in planning or execution of the project or fail to fulfill the members' basic needs with regard to social and emotional issues. In the next two sections of this book, you will see examples of working interdisciplinary curriculums. Many of these units are the result of successful efforts of teachers to work together as a team.

## References and Bibliography

Bales, R. (1970). *Personality and interpersonal behavior.* New York: Holt, Rinehart and Winston.

Block, P. (1987). *The empowered manager.* San Francisco: Jossey-Bass.

Bolman, L., & Deal, T. (1991). *Reframing organizations.* San Francisco: Jossey-Bass.

Dyer, W. (1987). *Team building: Issues and alternatives.* Reading, MA: Addison-Wesley.

Fisher, R., & Brown, S. (1988). *Getting together: Building a relationship that gets to yes.* Boston: Houghton Mifflin.

Fox, W. (1987). *Effective group problem solving.* San Francisco: Jossey-Bass.

George, P. (1982, April). Interdisciplinary team organization: Four operational phases. *Middle School Journal, 13*(3), 10–13.

Gersick, C. J. G. (1988). Time and transition in work teams: Toward a new model of group development. *Academy of Management Journal, 31,* 9–14.

Hare, A. P. (1976). *Handbook of small group research.* New York: Free Press.

Kanter, R. M. (1983). *The change masters.* New York: Simon and Schuster.

Merenbloom, E. Y. (1991). *The team process: A handbook for teachers.* Columbus: National Middle School Association.

Maurer, R. (1991). *Managing conflict: Tactics for school administrators.* Boston: Allyn and Bacon.

Peters, T. J. (1988). *Thriving on chaos.* New York: Knopf.

Reich, R. B. (1987). Entrepreneurship reconsidered: The team as hero. *Harvard Business Review, 65*(3), 77–83.

Schein, E. H. (1985). *Organizational culture and leadership: A dynamic view.* San Francisco: Jossey-Bass.

Sundstrom, E., DeMeuse, K. P., & Futrell, D. (1990, February). Work teams: Applications and effectiveness. *American Psychologist, 45,* 120–133.

Tuckman, B. W. (1965). Developmental sequence in small groups. *Psychological Bulletin, 63,* 384–389.

Ury, W. (1991). *Getting past no: Negotiating with difficult people.* New York: Bantam Books.

Varney, G. H. (1989). *Building productive teams.* San Francisco: Jossey-Bass.

# Section Two
# Middle School/Junior High
# School Curriculum

*The grade levels for schools in this section vary considerably. Most middle schools include grades 6 through 8, although some middle schools that incorporate grade 5 and some have grades 7 and 8 only. Many junior high schools have grade levels 7 through 9, although circumstances vary and there are junior high schools with different grade configurations. There is a major philosophical difference between schools that are organized as middle schools and those that are organized as junior high schools. For the purposes of the integrated curricula in this section, however, this difference is not important. Any of these units can be applied to either a middle school or a junior high school. The teacher can make some modifications to take age differences into account.*

*In these units you will note some common trends. One is the introduction of the abstract idea of* concepts. *Students, as young adolescents, are being asked to move beyond merely experiencing events to assume the task of organizing them intellectually. Conceptual ideas such as culture, affective needs, self-esteem, sequence, mythology, power, and forecasting are some of the ideas presented in these units.*

*Another trend is that of understanding oneself through understanding others. Four of these units look at "culture" in different ways. All, however, ask students to begin the process of self-discovery by looking first at how others have organized their lives. The current interest in immigration and the opening of a museum at Ellis Island in New York Harbor are natural places to begin organizing such a study.*

*A third trend is that of hands-on learning. In many of these units, students are busing doing things. Whether it is actually digging up artifacts, walking across a city, constructing flags or models, or dressing up for a play, the units have incorporated the belief that one of the most powerful ways to learn is by actually becoming involved in an activity.*

*These activities include a wide variety of curricula, covering almost every content area known at the middle/junior high school level. They range from one as simple as uniting five different subjects around the theme of a single book ("Slake's Limbo") to a sophisticated unit that integrates ten content areas and replaces the typical school day ("Kaleidoscope"). You will find a unit that integrates study units into every major content area ("Study Wydown Style"), units that involve field trips ("Walk Across Orlando" and "Kentucky–Tennessee Experience"), and units which have a ten-month sequence ("Humanities Program" and "History through Literature"). For those schools that organize events for Black History Month in February, the unit "A Minority Study: The African-American" is rich with ideas. Finding units that incorporate music is often difficult. This section includes two units that have music as a major content area ("Suite for the Endangered" and "Story Telling through Dance").*

*1* *Curriculum Unit*  Historic Dig

*Subject Area*  English, social studies, math

*Recommended Grade Level*  Middle school

*Summary*  Participation in this unit enables students to gain an understanding of the concepts of *culture* and *a culture*. With teacher assistance, students work in cooperative groups to gain an appreciation of the values and differences among people.

*Objectives*

- Students will learn productive work habits.
- Students will work cooperatively in groups.
- Students will learn the nature of culture.
- Students will gain an in-depth understanding of one specific ten-year period of U.S. history.

*School and Contact Persons*

Cross Keys Middle School
14205 Cougar Drive
Florissant, MO 63033
(314) 831-2700

M. Delores Graham, Principal
Mary Louise Hawkins
Judy Bick

*Procedures*  In this unit students create group identities related to the time period/culture they are studying. The students complete a series of activities over a six-day span of time. The amount of time required for each day's activities will vary depending on how involved and detailed the teacher would like the students to become. As many classes as possible can be involved. For each class involved, there will be a specific ten-year time period assigned.

### Day 1—The Hook: "Do you dig culture?"

1. In a planning session, each teacher involved should select a ten-year time period. Teachers then present to their respective classes an overview of the unit. The overview should begin with the teacher explaining that the class has been given a ten-year period (e.g., 1900–1910) for which it must create a culture. The tasks involved in this unit are as follows:

- Develop a definition of culture.
- Complete a background and theme sheets.
- Create representative artifacts from the group's time period and bury them to be excavated by other groups.

- Complete artifact record sheets.
- Complete museum cards.
- Create a group badge.
- Compile a scrapbook.
- Write and learn lyrics to a song.
- Create a personal timeline.
- Complete selected readings.

**2.** All students then should complete a Student Survey Sheet located at the end of this unit. The teacher will tabulate a summary for each class involved and one for the entire group. Students should write a definition of the word *culture* as they perceive its meaning. The class should brainstorm their definitions and then agree on a common definition of the term.

**3.** The teacher should ask the class what a timeline is and what kind of data are recorded on one. The teacher shares a timeline that the teachers participating in the unit have already developed. It starts from 1930 and includes two important events from each of the teachers' lives.

**4.** Once the students understand a timeline, they can begin to construct their own individual ones. Many computer programs will generate timelines, and a teacher may want to ask the computer coordinator for assistance in this area. The student's timeline should contain eight to ten personal events, and these events should be imposed on a preprinted historical event template that shows events from 1975 on.

**5.** The teacher should distribute the reading list found at the end of this unit. Students need to pick reading material that will tell them about events and life during the ten-year time period assigned to them. A collection of short stories, bibliographies, novels, and newspaper clippings can be made available.

**6.** The teacher should invite the students to listen to tape recordings of a song that reflects culture. The teacher should ask the students what the lyrics of the song are saying and what they mean. An excellent song to use is Billy Joel's "We Didn't Start the Fire." Students should be reminded that eventually they will have to write their own lyrics to reflect their group culture.

**7.** Teachers should prepare videotape clips from various "family" programs from the 1950s to the present. (e.g., "Life of Riley," "Ozzie and Harriet," "The Donna Reed Show," "The Cosby Show," "Growing Pains"). After viewing these clips, the students share their perceptions of how families have changed over the years.

**8.** Each group should create a group name tag, badge, or button. The purpose of creating and wearing this is to foster group identity and a sense of *esprit de corps.*

**9.** Each group should now begin its scrapbook. Scrapbook materials for each student should include manila folders, paper fasteners (brads), six sheets of paper per student to go inside the scrapbook, markers, colored pencils, paste, scissors, and rulers. The following materials can be placed inside: timeline, survey form, summary of independent readings. As the unit progresses, more and more material can be placed in the scrapbook.

### Day 2: The Secret Society

**1.** Students should continue to work on the badges or buttons that help establish the group identity.

**2.** The teacher should distribute a copy of the "Culture Analysis Outline." This provides a list of elements of culture that the students will use while viewing films about specific cultural periods.

**3.** The students should view the video clips of the family programs that have been prepared. Students should be told they are looking beyond the plot to issues like values, problems, events of the period, geographic location, and physical characteristics of the people.

**4.** The teacher should distribute the "Background and Themes" sheet to each student in the group. After viewing each videotape, the students should complete the sheet.

**5.** After discussing the films, each teacher and group should continue working on personal timelines, readings, scrapbook covers, and research of the culture for their time period.

### Day 3: I've Got a Secret

**1.** Each group should have a discussion about their cultural period. At the end of the discussion, as students share ideas and stories, they should begin to brainstorm what items or artifacts could best represent the time period they are studying. The teacher will need to explain that each group is going to bury artifacts of their period for the other groups to dig up or discover. The archaeological term for this burying location is a *mound* or a *layer*. Distribution of the "Culture Analysis" sheet should be completed. This will help students plan and record the artifacts to be buried.

**2.** Each group needs to begin to prepare two plastic trays for the burial of artifacts. Someone on the team needs to line grid each tray into eight blocks. Popsicle sticks or string may be used to mark off the boxes. One side of the tray should be marked as the top and each square should be numbered. The sequence should look like this.

| *TOP* | | 3 | 4 | | *TOP* | | | |
|-------|---|---|---|---|-------|----|----|----|
| 1 | 2 | 3 | 7 | | 9 | 10 | 11 | 12 |
| 5 | 6 | 7 | 8 | | 13 | 14 | 15 | 16 |

**3.** Students should now begin to design artifacts to place in the grid. A copy of the "Artifact Idea Sheet" should be distributed to help the students in deciding which artifacts to design. Particular grid areas should then be assigned to each student in which he or she will place an artifact.

**4.** As the artifacts are completed, they should be stored carefully away from the view of other groups who may be using the classroom at other times during the day. An "Artifact Record" slip should be completed for each artifact made.

**5.** The teacher should allow time so that students work on the lyrics to their culture's song.

### Day 4: I've Got a Secret

**1.** Students should complete a "Before" museum card.

**2.** All artifacts should now be placed in the appropriate grid in the tray.

**3.** The work on the individual scrapbooks needs to be completed at this point. All necessary materials should be present: timelines, artifact idea sheets, "Before" museum sheets, culture analysis sheets, song lyrics, etc. Each scrapbook should have its own cover design.

**4.** A rehearsal needs to be completed for the student-created lyrics. At one point during the culminating activity for this unit, each group will present one verse of the song with lyrics reflecting their culture period.

**5.** Students should make a mural depicting the culture or civilization that the group has created.

### Day 5: The Dig (Dig it?)

**1.** Each group of students now assumes responsibility for the next historical time period to begin the dig (e.g., 1900–1911, 1940–1950).

**2.** In the classroom, students excavate the grid area for which they are responsible. Once the artifact is excavated, the student labels it and completes a museum "After" card. When all sixteen grid areas have been excavated, the group completes a culture analysis sheet for the society excavated.

**3.** After students have finished, all the artifacts should be returned to the zip-lock bags and then simply replaced on the top of the grid from which they were excavated. They will be ready for the next group. If there is enough time, allow the students to rebury the artifacts so that each group physically digs up all six layers instead of just one.

### Day 6: Show and Tell, or The Secrets Are Out

**1.** The groups should be brought together in a culminating activity where everyone can see what was discovered. Each "Secret Society" should bring their trays, "Before" museum cards, song lyrics, and murals with them to the large room. In addition, each student needs to bring all "After" museum cards.

**2.** Starting with the earliest time period, ask each group to make a presentation to the rest of the team about their society and the artifacts that were buried.

Students listening to each artifact maker will refer to their "After" museum cards to verify the accuracy of their records.

3. When all the grid areas have been described, the presenting group displays its mural and presents the verses of the song that was written to reflect the culture of the time period.

4. Teachers should now be prepared to evaluate the unit. Student scrapbooks should be collected. Students may complete a short summary evaluation of the unit.

## STUDENT SURVEY

Group Name _____

**Demographics**

1. Age _____ 2. Sex: M _____ F _____

3. Family at home:   Mother _____   Father _____   Number of brothers _____

   Number of sisters _____   Stepmother _____   Stepfather _____

   Number of stepbrothers _____   Number of stepsisters _____

   Others (list) _____

4. My family's history in the United States began with my parents _____

   grandparents _____

   great-grandparents _____   earlier _____   don't know _____

5. My ancestors originally came to the United States from

   Europe _____   Asia _____

   Africa _____   South America _____   North America _____

   Australia _____

6. How many regions of the United States have you lived in (not counting the St. Louis area)?   0 _____   1 _____   2 _____   3 _____   more than 3 _____

7. How many school systems have you attended?   1 (current one) _____

   2 _____   3 _____   4 _____   more than 4 _____

8. Which of the following is most important in helping you to make decisions? family _____ friends _____ church _____ school _____

9. Which of the following is most influential in helping you to form your opinions? family _____ friends _____ church _____ school _____

## CULTURAL CONSIDERATIONS

Do you consider the following to be marks of culture?

a. religion            yes _____ no _____ don't know _____

b. sports              yes _____ no _____ don't know _____

c. buildings           yes _____ no _____ don't know _____

d. books, plays        yes _____ no _____ don't know _____

e. music               yes _____ no _____ don't know _____

f. education           yes _____ no _____ don't know _____

g. clothing styles     yes _____ no _____ don't know _____

h. government          yes _____ no _____ don't know _____

i. hairstyles          yes _____ no _____ don't know _____

j. morals              yes _____ no _____ don't know _____

k. transportation      yes _____ no _____ don't know _____

l. economics           yes _____ no _____ don't know _____

m. legal system        yes _____ no _____ don't know _____

n. family structure    yes _____ no _____ don't know _____

o. recreation          yes _____ no _____ don't know _____

p. radio, television   yes _____ no _____ don't know _____

q. communication       yes _____ no _____ don't know _____

r. inventions          yes _____ no _____ don't know _____

s. wealth              yes _____ no _____ don't know _____

t. rites of passage    yes _____ no _____ don't know _____

u. burials             yes _____ no _____ don't know _____

v. types of food       yes _____ no _____ don't know _____

w. treatment of
   the children        yes _____ no _____ don't know _____

x. treatment of
   adolescents         yes _____ no _____ don't know _____

y. treatment of
   senior citizens     yes _____ no _____ don't know _____

z. other marks of culture (list) _____

_____

_____

# INDEPENDENT READING: BACKGROUND AND THEMES

Name _____     Group _____

*Directions:* Using the reading assignments, complete each of the following items.

Title: _____

Author: _____

## I. Background of Culture

   **A.** Time: _____

   **B.** Geographic settings: _____

   **C.** Physical description of people: _____

      _____

      _____

## II. Themes

   **A.** Values (what is important to the people): _____

      _____

      _____

      _____

      _____

   **B.** Issues (important questions of the time): _____

      _____

      _____

      _____

      _____

   **C.** Events (happenings of importance): _____

      _____

      _____

      _____

      _____

# READING LISTS

## Teacher 1: 1600—Colonial

### Poetry

"Indians" by John Fandel from *Reflections on a Gift of Watermelon Pickle . . . and Other Modern Verse.*

### Novels

*The Witch of Blackbird Pond* by Elizabeth G. Speare.
*Sword of the Wilderness* by Elizabeth Coatsworth.

### Literary Selections

From *They Led the Way* by Johanna Johanston:

   "On Trial for Thinking for Herself" (Anne Hutchinson), p. 10.
   "First Poet in Colonial America" (Anne Bradstreet), p. 18.
   "Mayor of Her Own Town" (Lady Deborah Moody), p. 23.

From *The Witchcraft of Salem Village* by Shirley Jackson. Chapter 1 is especially good.

### Play

From *Adventures for You:* "They Call Me a Witch" by Esther C. Averill.

## Teacher 2: 1700—Revolution

### Poetry

*"Paul Revere's Ride"* by Henry Wadsworth Longfellow, Introduction to Literature, p. 197.

### Novels

*Light in the Forest* by Conrad Richter.
*My Brother Sam Is Dead* by James L. Collier and Christopher Collier.
*Johnny Tremain* by Esther Forbes.

### Literary Selections

"Salt-Water Tea" from *Johnny Tremain—Adventures for Readers,* Book 2, p. 176.
"The Legend of Sleepy Hollow" by Washington Irving, *Adventures for Readers,* Book 2, p. 375.
"The Three-Cornered Hat" by Russell Gordon Carter, *Adventures for You,* p. 2.
"An April Ride—1777" by Erick Berry, *Adventures for You,* p. 73.
"That Lively Man, Ben Franklin" by Jeannette Eaton, *Introduction to Literature,* p. 187.
"Patrol at Valley Forge" by Russell Gordon Carter, *Introduction to Literature,* p. 202.

### Play

"The Mystery of Patriot Inn" by Jessie Nicholson, *Adventures for You*, p. 150.

## Teacher 3: 1800—Westward Expansion—Civil War—Immigration

### Novels

*Old Yeller* by Fred Gipson.
*Across Five Aprils* by Irene Hunt.

### Library Selections

"Old Yeller and the Bear" from *Old Yeller* by Fred Gipson, *Adventures for Readers*, Book 2, p. 2.
"Lewis and Clark" by Bernard de Voto, *Adventures for Readers*, Book 2, p. 205.
"The Kiskis" by May Vontver, *Adventures for Readers*, Book 2, p. 226.
"The Man without a Country" by Edward Everett Hale, *Adventures for Readers*, Book 2, p. 358.
"Father Lets in the Telephone" by Clarence Day, *Adventures for Readers*, Book 2, p. 238.
"The Pacing Goose" from *The Friendly Persuasion* by Jessamyn West, *Introduction to Literature*, p. 117.
"A Wild Strain" by Paul Horgan, *Introduction to Literature*, p. 214.
"A Gray Sleeve" by Stephen Crane, *Introduction to Literature*, p. 226.
Selections from *They Led the Way: Fourteen American Women* by Johanna Johnston:
　　"Into Med School by Student Vote" (Elizabeth Blackwell), p. 64.
　　"She Helped Abolish Slavery" (Harriet Beecher Stowe), p. 80.

## Teacher: 1900–1975—Global War

### Poetry

From *Reflections on a Gift of Watermelon Pickle:*
　　"Sonic Boom" by John Updike, p. 79.
　　"Hey Diddle Diddle" by Paul Dehn, p. 80.
　　"Little Miss Muffet" by Paul Dehn, p. 80.
"I, Too, Sing America" by Langston Hughes, *Introduction to Literature*, p. 489.

### Novels

*I Am Rosemarie* by Marietta D. Moskin.
*The Forgotten Door* by Alexander Key.

### Literary Selections

From *They Led the Way: Fourteen American Women* by Johanna Johnston:
　　"One Woman Race against Time" (Nellie Bly), p. 105.
　　"Women Win the Right to Vote" (Carrie Chapman Catt), p. 125.
"I Have a Dream" by Martin Luther King as reported by James Reston, *Introduction to Literature*, p. 240.
From *Black Boy* by Richard Wright, *Introduction to Literature*, p. 46.
"Hunger" by Richard Wright, *Projection in Literature*, p. 275.
"June 6, 1944" by Cornelius Ryan, *Adventures for Readers*, Book 2, p. 268.
"The Homecoming" by Frank Yerby, *Understanding Literature*, p. 115.

"The Biscuit Eater" by James Street, *Currents in Fiction*, p. 245.
"The Test" by Angelica Gibbs, *Currents in Fiction*, p. 276.

### Play

"The Diary of Anne Frank" by Frances Goodrich and Albert Hackett, *Counterpoint in Literature*, p. 466.

## Teacher 6: 1990–2050—Future

### Poetry

From *Reflections on a Gift of Watermelon Pickle:*
"Earth" by Oliver Herford, p. 81.
"Earth" by John Hall Wheelock, p. 81.
"Southbound on the Freeway" by May Swenson, p. 82.

### Novel

*Anthem* by Ayn Rand.

### Novella

"I Sing the Body Electric" from *I Sing the Body Electric—Stories by Ray Bradbury*, by Ray Bradbury, p. 150.

### Literary Selections

"The Pedestrian" by Ray Bradbury, *Explorations in Literature*, p. 368.
"Sinister Journey" by Conrad Richter, *Explorations in Literature*, p. 380.
"Examination Day" by Henry Slesar, *Explorations in Literature*, p. 398.
"Someday" by Isaac Asimov, *Explorations in Literature*, p. 408.

# BACKGROUND AND THEMES

Dig Group _____

*Directions:* Using your imagination and research, determine the background and themes of your culture.

### I. Background of Culture

    **A.** Time: _____

    **B.** Geographic settings: _____

    **C.** Physical description of people: _____

_____

_____

### II. Themes

    **A.** Values (what is important to the people): _____

_____

_____

_____

_____

    **B.** Issues (important questions of the time): _____

_____

_____

_____

_____

    **C.** Events (happenings of importance): _____

_____

_____

_____

_____

# CULTURE ANALYSIS OUTLINE

Name of Culture: _____

## I. Background of Culture

    **A.** Time
    **B.** Geographic setting
    **C.** Events (happenings of importance)

## II. Themes

    **A.** Values (what is important to people)
    **B.** Issues (important questions of the time)
    **C.** Events (happenings of importance)

## III. Economics

    **A.** Technology
    **B.** Trade/money
    **C.** Transportation

## IV. Food, Clothing, Shelter

    **A.** Food (methods of production and domesticated animals)
    **B.** Clothing/adornment
    **C.** Shelter/dwellings

## V. Political Organization

    **A.** Government/war/peace

## VI. Family and Kin

    **A.** Marriage/type of family groupings

## VII. Attitude toward the Unknown

    **A.** Religious practices/burials

## VIII. Communications

    **A.** Literacy/ability to read
    **B.** Measurement/math tools

### IX. Arts and Esthetic Values

    **A.** Art
    **B.** Music
    **C.** Dance/Drama/literature

### X. Recreation

    **A.** Games/sports
    **B.** Use of leisure time

# CULTURE ANALYSIS SHEET—2

Name of Culture _____

## I. Background of Culture

**A.** Time: _____

**B.** Geographic settings: _____

**C.** Physical description of people: _____

_____

_____

## II. Themes

**A.** Values (what is important to people): _____

_____

_____

_____

_____

**B.** Issues (important questions of the time): _____

_____

_____

_____

_____

**C.** Events (happenings of importance): _____

_____

_____

_____

_____

## III. Economics

**A.** Technology: _____

_____

_____

_____

_____

**B.** Trade/money: _____

_____

_____

_____

C. Transportation: _____

_____

_____

_____

_____

## IV. Food, Clothing, Shelter

A. Food (methods of production and domesticated animals: _____

_____

_____

_____

_____

B. Clothing/adornment: _____

_____

_____

_____

_____

C. Shelter/dwellings: _____

_____

_____

_____

_____

## V. Political Organization

A. Government/war/peace: _____

_____

_____

_____

_____

## VI. Family and Kin

A. Marriage/type of family groupings: _____

_____

_____

_____

_____

## VII.　Attitude toward the Unknown

**A.** Religious practices/burials: _____

_____

_____

_____

_____

## VIII.　Communications

**A.** Literacy/ability to read: _____

_____

_____

_____

_____

**B.** Measurement/math tools: _____

_____

_____

_____

_____

## IX.　Arts and Esthetic Values

**A.** Art: _____

_____

_____

_____

_____

**B.** Music: _____

_____

_____

_____

_____

**C.** Dance/drama/literature: _____

_____

_____

_____

_____

### X. Recreation

**A.** Games/sports: _____

_____

_____

_____

_____

**B.** Use of leisure time: _____

_____

_____

_____

_____

## Grid Areas

1. Technology
2. Trade and money
3. Transportation
4. Food
5. Clothing
6. Shelter
7. War/peace or government
8. Marriage and type of family grouping
9. Religious practices/burials
10. Literacy/ability to read
11. Measurement/mathematics tools
12. Art
13. Music
14. Dance, drama, literature
15. Games and sports
16. Use of leisure time

## ARTIFACT IDEA SHEET

Name _____

Date _____

Team _____

*Directions:* You are responsible for this grid area in your team's culture.

_____

Review the background and themes of your culture. Use your imagination to come up with an idea or ideas for the grid area you have been assigned.

Ideas for my grid area: _____

_____

_____

_____

_____

_____

_____

_____

_____

Why my ideas fit the time, setting, and themes of our culture: _____

_____

_____

_____

_____

_____

_____

_____

_____

_____

## ARTIFACT RECORD SHEETS

### ARTIFACT RECORD SHEET

Description including composition:

_____

_____

_____

_____

_____

Scale: _____

Made by: _____

### ARTIFACT RECORD SHEET

Description including composition:

_____

_____

_____

_____

_____

Scale: _____

Made by: _____

### ARTIFACT RECORD SHEET

Description including composition:

_____

_____

_____

_____

_____

Scale: _____

Made by: _____

### ARTIFACT RECORD SHEET

Description including composition:

_____

_____

_____

_____

_____

Scale: _____

Made by: _____

### ARTIFACT RECORD SHEET

Description including composition:

_____

_____

_____

_____

_____

Scale: _____

Made by: _____

### ARTIFACT RECORD SHEET

Description including composition:

_____

_____

_____

_____

_____

Scale: _____

Made by: _____

## BEFORE MUSEUM CARD

Culture:

Date of culture:

Grid area:

Function of artifact: _____

_____

_____

_____

_____

Any written message: _____

_____

_____

_____

_____

What this artifact tells about the culture: _____

_____

_____

_____

_____

Creator of artifact: _____

_____

_____

_____

_____

## AFTER MUSEUM CARD

Culture:

Date of culture:

Grid area:

Function of artifact: _____

_____

_____

_____

_____

Any written message: _____

_____

_____

_____

_____

What this artifact tells about the culture: _____

_____

_____

_____

_____

Interpreter of artifact: _____

_____

_____

_____

_____

## TIMELINE

| Date | Event |
| --- | --- |

*Date*    *Event*

**1925–1930**  Lindbergh flies the Atlantic.
Stock market crashes.

**1930–1935**  FDR elected president.

**1935–1940**  Social Security Act passed.
Berlin Olympics.
Mr. Richman born.
Mrs. Sieger born.

**1940–1945**  Pearl Harbor attacked: World War II begins.
Mr. Siebert born.

**1945–1949**  Atomic bombs dropped on Japan.
Mrs. Garrett born.
Mr. Leo born.
Truman wins the presidency.

**1950–1955**  Korean War begins.
Mrs. Martinez born.
Mr. Richman graduates from eighth grade.
Eisenhower elected president.
Korean War ends.
*Brown* v. *Board of Topeka* case decided.

**1955–1959**  Martinez has open-heart surgery.
Big Red move to St. Louis.

**1960–1964**  JFK elected president.
JFK assassinated.
LBJ elected president.
Leo goes to USAF.
Gulf of Tonkin Resolution passed.

**1965–1970**  Siebert gets married.
Siebert graduates from M.U.
MLK and RFK assassinated.

**1965–1970**  Nixon elected president.
Cross Keys opens.
Sieger witnesses lift-off.
Americans land on the moon.
Garrett starts at Cross Keys.

**1970–1975**  Leo gets married.
Leo begins at Cross Keys.
U.S. troops leave Vietnam.
Watergate scandal: Nixon resigns.
Ford becomes president.

1975–1980     U.S. celebrates bicentennial.
              BG Garrett born.
              Siebert comes to Cross Keys.
              Jimmy Carter elected president.
              Martinez goes to Peru.
              Martinez goes to Mexico.
              Americans taken hostage in Iran.

1980–1985     Ronald Reagan becomes president.
              Sieger comes to Cross Keys.
              Hostages freed from Iran.
              Richman comes to Cross Keys.
              Garrett goes to Paris.

1985–1990     Sieger's European vacation.
              Challenger disaster.
              George Bush elected president.
              Martinez comes to Cross Keys.
              Big Red move out of St. Louis.
              Cross Keys wins excellence award.
              Twin grandchildren for Sieger.
              Leo gets married for keeps.

**2** *Curriculum Unit*  Kaleidoscope

*Subject Areas*  Foreign language, music, home economics, physical education, computer, technology, English, math, social studies, science

*Recommended Grade Level  Middle/junior high school*

*Summary*  Kaleidoscope is a mixture of special area teachers, imaginative activities, and a group of enthusiastic students, coming together in a formal design to create harmonic divergence. All students in a particular grade rotate through a kaleidoscope of experiences in the practical and fine arts areas, accomplished in traditional and nontraditional classroom settings.

*Objectives*

- To provide middle school students with an integrated, hands-on, process-oriented learning experience in exploratory classes.
- To provide a structure in which elective teachers are able to work in a team teaching environment, to address perceptions of fragmentation, and to foster feelings of belonging and ownership by middle school staff.
- To provide a greater student awareness and understanding of important and relevant themes each year.
- To provide integrated instruction and learning between elective and academic subjects.

*School and Contact Persons*

Bloomfield Hills Middle School
4200 West Quarton Road
Bloomfield Hills, MI 48302
(313) 626-2517

Gary Grossnickle, Principal
Nancy Koski
Gary Ellis

*Procedures*  A three-member teaching team of the special area teachers are formed somewhat randomly each year, based on interests and expertise of the teachers. Each team works with approximately 30 students who are also given choices as to the group or groups in which they wish to become involved.

Kaleidoscope is not an addition to the usual school day's instruction, but in lieu of it. The book or core subject classes (English, math, social studies, science) continue to meet as usual, but those teachers cooperate fully in complementing the current theme and, if necessary, relinquishing time for field trips and assemblies. All elective classes meet as kaleidoscope groups.

The groups may meet in various locations depending on their needs—in the gym for dance, in home economics classrooms for cooking, in art classrooms for paper making or design, in the industrial arts area for set building, in the media center for research, in the computer lab for simulations, and in the music classrooms for anything from singing to filming environmental commercials. All aspects of the instructional theme are connected. This program is time intensive, so other priorities of the instructional schedule are put on hold during the one- or two-week period of the kaleidoscope.

The key factor in this program is not the theme, which changes every year, but the kaleidoscope program concept. The program can adapt to any theme and this makes it viable, rather than repetitive, year after year.

The areas of interest are specifically designed to integrate with the central theme. The themes for the past three years have been:

Celebration of Freedom
Touch the Earth
Cultural Diversity through Entertainment

### Touch the Earth

This unit involved students in three major areas. Detailed descriptions of the events as well as a timetable can be obtained from the school.

*Made from the Earth*   An investigation into natural foods, additives, gardening, and food processing gave the students valuable information on nutrition and its relation to physical fitness. Using natural materials, the students crated pottery, dyes, and paper.

*Save the Earth*   The problem of endangered species provided the students with motivation to raise funds for the preservation of these animals and to employ a variety of methods to raise the awareness of their fellow students. Solutions to pollution of land, air, and water were explored both theoretically and in actuality.

*Sounds from the Earth*   A celebration of the earth and its people through music involved the study of music in nature and included the creation of natural musical instruments. These instruments were then used to provide the background for original videos that students wrote and produced. These videos, one of which was awarded a medal by the Detroit Association of Film and Television, stressed the importance of saving the earth.

### Cultural Diversity through Entertainment

Seven activities make up this unit. A brief description of each follows. Detailed descriptions and a chronology of the activities are available from the school.

*Kick Off*   Students will gather in front of a giant screen to view news items showing Germany during the collapse of the Berlin Wall along with interviews with people. A speaker who has experienced a loss of freedom will address the students. Following this assembly, the students will participate in a rally complete with banners, cheers, and a march through the halls.

*Interest Areas* Students will work in one of the following areas: creating skits, designing costumes, writing and studying poetry, writing a narration, designing scenery, building sets, and composing music.

*Past* "Freedom Fighters of the Past" will be emphasized. Frederick Douglass, Underground Railroad heroes, fighters in the French and American Revolutions, and others will come alive in a series of mini-skits.

*Present* "The Walls Come Tumbling Down" is the theme. Using El Salvador, Germany, and other locales as settings, the students will act out ongoing revolutions.

*Future* "Reaching for Freedom" is the theme. Students will predict revolutionary outcomes in South Africa and China.

*America* "Let Freedom Ring" is the theme. The inherent freedom of Americans will be celebrated through dialogue with guest speakers who have recently gained their personal independence.

*Grand Finale* All the groups will combine their talents in a grand finale performance for the entire student body. One student from each group will act as a link to pass the "Torch of Freedom" between "Past," "Present," "Future," and finally to "America." To conclude the performance, everyone will join in songs about America.

*3* *Curriculum Unit*   Slake's Limbo

*Subject Areas*   English, math, geography, social studies, health

*Recommended Grade Levels*   Middle/junior high school

*Summary*   Using the book *Slake's Limbo,* students complete a series of activities that provide them with an integrated, comprehensive study of the elements of a novel.

*Objectives*   This unit is divided into four primary areas—English, social studies, math, and geography—each with its own objectives. The objectives for each will be listed separately, followed by the unit's activities.

*School and Contact Persons*

St. Louis Park Junior High School
2025 Texas Avenue South
St. Louis Park, MN 55426
(612) 541-1884

Les Bork, Principal
Karen Boisselle
L. Brubaker

*Procedures*   *Slake's Limbo* by Felice Holman, 1974. Aladdin Books, Macmillan Publishing Company, 866 Third Avenue, New York, NY 10022

### 1. "Going Underground": Geography Unit

The students will do the following:

- Locate New York City and surrounding cities and important features.
- Describe and map Slake's "place" (physical and human characteristics).
- Evaluate their sense of place and the role their own experiences play in drawing perceptions of specific places.
- Analyze how people have interacted with their environment in New York City.
- Explore and describe lives of the homeless.

Using maps of the Twin Cities, New York City, and the East Coast and the May and September 1990 issues of *National Geographic,* the students should be able to locate the key cities in the respective regions.

Using the book as a guide, the students will work cooperatively to create a map or model of Slake's world, including a written description of the map or model.

The teacher should give instructional lessons on perception, including such terms as blind rooms, hearsay details versus personal observation, long interaction versus short interaction, and personal perception maps.

In cooperative learning groups the students will brainstorm and report on the Twin Cities' human and environmental characteristics.

In small and large group discussions the students will outline the Twin City and New York City connections.

Using maps, geographic knowledge, and historical descriptions, students will explain the growth of New York City and the Twin Cities.

In cooperative groups the students will create a written plan and map of the mass transit improvements in the Twin Cities.

### 2. "Earning Money": Mathematics Unit

The students will do the following:

- Be aware of and familiar with commonly used ways of earning money.
- Consider some of the motivating reasons for desiring a steady source of income.
- Become familiar with the fringe benefits that enhance the choice of a vocation.
- Consider reasons that deductions are a factor to consider when establishing a level of income.

### 3. Journal Writing: English Unit

The students will do the following:

- Understand essential literary strategies in the novel such as plot, foreshadowing, and the like.
- Write an essay of at least one paragraph demonstrating their ability to develop individual journal themes based on topics from the novel.
- Discuss assorted topics from the novel in a small group or as a class.
- Engage in an enrichment activity that fosters a personal interpretation of the novel and an understanding of its context (e.g., mass transit, child homelessness, New York City).

*Chapter 1*  Have the students discuss the symbolic meaning of Slake having no eyeglasses and poor eyesight. Who or what is the bird? Have the students write in their journal what they feel is the meaning of this statement: "This year the leaves would stay on the trees." Have students discuss their entry in small group discussions.

*Chapter 2*  A workman's mistake decades before results in Slake's cave. Describe a situation or story where something that happened in the past unintentionally affects the present. In the journals have the students describe the new character in "On Another Track."

*Chapter 3*  In a large group discussion, ask the students what is the difference between consciousness and unconsciousness. Have the students reread this section in the chapter.

*Chapter 4*  What does the saying "the great crocodile of the third rail" mean. Slake says that he feels invisible. What does this mean? Are there any street vendors in our town? Describe in your journal how Slake "goes into business."

*Chapter 5*   In your journal, write the answer to this question: "Why didn't Slake complete his exploration and go back above ground?" In this chapter five new characters are introduced. Who are they? In small group discussions, talk about which one seems most interesting. Also talk about whether there are any grafitti in town. What does it say? Discuss which message Slake liked and why.

*Chapter 6*   Discuss how Slake feels about the man with the turban, and why? How did Willis Joe's "star fall"?

*Chapter 7*   Discuss Slake's improving material world. Describe in your journal whether there is a threat to Slake's security in his hole. What does the author mean when it is written that Slake finds a pair of eyeglasses?

*Chapter 8*   Discuss Slake's improving world.

*Chapter 9*   Speculate in your journal who the "doctor" is. What is Slake's flashback? How do you think memory works?

*Chapter 10*   The rat reminds Slake of something, but he is not sure what it is. Discuss what you think it reminds him of? Slake makes peace with it. Discuss what that says about Slake.

*Chapter 11*   Why is Slake the stronger one when the lights go out? What does it say about Slake when he holds the cleaning woman's hand? Explain the turbaned man's devolution joke. Reread and evaluate Slake's two dreams. Write in your journal what you think they mean.

*Chapter 12*   Why does Slake take the emergency seriously? What is the status of his health.

*Chapter 13*   Slake has a series of fever dreams in this chapter. In your journal write what you think they mean. Have you ever dreamed in this manner? Discuss it in a small group. What do you suppose goes through Willie Joe's mind—pros and cons—when he weighs stopping or not?

*Chapter 14*   After Joe rescues Slake, what effect does this have on him? Describe it. Have you ever had this type of experience? Describe it.

*Chapter 15*   Slake dreams that he vomits the bird. How do you interpret this? Slake receives new glasses, the effect of which is described in this chapter. What do you think the author is saying by giving Slake new glasses?

*General Discussion or Essay Topics*

1. The author uses the image of a bird stuck inside Slake. Discuss what the image means.
2. Discuss Slake's personal background (before going underground). How did this make him become a shy runaway?
3. Describe Slake's friendships. Did they change? Did they grow?
4. Discuss Slake's friendships with rat. What is the author up to?
5. Is the novel optimistic or pessimistic? Choose one and describe why in detail.

*Enrichment*

1. You are Slake. Prepare a solioquy that tells us about your world before you went underground.
2. Prepare a dialogue between Slake and his aunt that occurs when or if he returns home.
3. Prepare a dialogue between two students—Willis Joe and Slake—that occurs in Slake's hospital room.
4. Prepare a monologue of the cleaning woman describing Slake.
5. Instead of the cleaning woman, prepare a monologue of the turbaned man describing Slake.
6. Prepare a dialogue between the waitress and the restaurant owner about a new, mysterious kid, Aremis Slake.

## 4. Social Skills: Health Unit

The students will:

- Recognize putdowns.
- Recognize affirmative statements.
- Change putdowns to affirmatives.
- Identify self-esteem (good and bad) and practice good self-esteem actions.
- Be aware of and understand opinions about the homeless.

**1.** *Self-esteem:* Have the students hold small group discussions on what is self-esteem, what is good, what is bad?

Have the students complete "Slake Worksheet 1" on self-esteem. Students do their own and then go around the class and share the items they have circled. Students have the option to pass on sharing what they have circled.

**2.** *Putdowns:* Make a list of three times that Slake was put down or put someone else down. After the students have completed their lists, they are to take one of the putdowns and change it to an affirmative. Ask the students to speculate on what might have happened if this had occurred in the story.

**3.** *Homeless:* Have the class visit an organization that works with the homeless or with the poor. Ask if there is a service project dealing with the organization that might interest you. Ask the class to organize and implement the project.

Arrange for a speaker to come to the school to talk about the homeless.

Discuss with the class what may have made Slake homeless. Does the book provide an answer?

Discuss the homeless situation in your town or state.

**4.** *Choices and consequences:* On a sheet of paper list the choices Slake had in Chapters One through Three down on the left side of the sheet. List all the choices, not just the ones he made.

Divide into small groups. Have the students discuss the choices each had listed. Within the group, list the consequences for every choice written down.

Find articles in the paper dealing with the homeless, and write or report orally to the class what the article was about and/or how you felt about the opinion if one was stated.

## SLAKE WORKSHEET 1

Choose from the words below those that you feel best describe you.

| Understanding | Helpful | Smart |
| Kind | Cute | Bold |
| Tough | Dumb | Artful |
| Flirt | Fast | Loving |
| Honest | Poor | Fair |
| Hopeful | Rich | O.K. |
| Confused | Friendly | Slow |
| Good | Popular | Unpopular |
| Good-looking | Ordinary | Supportive |
| _____ | _____ | _____ |

**4** *Curriculum Unit* Vacation USA

*Subject Areas* Math, language arts, social studies

*Recommended Grade Levels* Middle school/junior high

*Summary* As the theme of this unit, students plan a two-week vacation, by road, to an area of the United States.

*Objectives*

- The students will gain an understanding of how the disciplines relate to and depend on one another.
- The students will increase their knowledge of different areas of the United States.
- The students will learn to work together in teams.

*School and Contact Person*

Wassom Middle School
Forest and Gorgas Avenue
Fort Campbell, KY 42223
(502) 439-1832

Carolyn Dove, Principal
Dennis McGee
J. C. Kellar
Nancy Coleman
Kim Butts

*Procedures* The class should be divided into teams of four students each. The goal of the unit is for each team to plan a visit to specific points of interest, including historical, entertainment, and recreational stops. Each of the four content areas has specific requirements that are collected to form a complete description of the student's imaginary journey.

**Social Studies**

The students must trace their route onto road maps starting and ending at Fort Campbell, Kentucky. Smaller, secondary roads are encouraged for much of the trip to take advantage of increased map-reading skills and to provide a closer look at the region that would be offered by using only the Interstate highway system. In order to emphasize the history of the region, at least three stops must be made at sites of historical significance; for example, Vicksburg Battlesite or San Jose Mission National Site. Two stops for pure amusement, such as Graceland or Six Flags over Texas are required. Five scenic stops, to better observe the geographic attributes of the region, are also included. This requirement accents the close relationship between the economic and the ecological characteristic of the region traditionally studied independently in science.

### Science

The students must list all the biomes through which their trip will take them. The students will be expected to mape these and include information on the temperature and rainfall expected and on seasonal changes for each biome. A description of the plants and animals that are found along the way, as well as how they have adapted to the different climates, is included. Finally, a continuing description of the geographical attributes of the regions is used to tie together the ecological picture of the region.

### Math

Students must keep track of all money spent for travel, food, lodging, entertainment, and miscellaneous expenses. Using mileage charts, the students calculate distance driven and time spent on the road. The students are required to construct a pie graph showing the percentage of money spent in each category. Finally, they construct line graphs showing the distance driven and money spent each day.

### Language Arts

Students are required to write a narrative of what they "see" on their imaginary trip. Complete descriptions of places visited as well as an imaginary daily journal of the trip will be required. Extra credit is given for the inclusion of postcards, maps, and the like of the actual places.

### Library/Media

The librarian will be used as a resource person to the teams as they gather information about the specific trips. The computer can be used in depicting the various biomes encountered and daily weather information available through the National Geographic's Weather Machine Network. State road maps and booklets describing points of interest are available from a variety of sources. A local travel agent can provide a short discussion with the entire class about how to plan a trip. *National Geographic* magazine has videotapes on the physical geography of North America.

The following pages include worksheets that students can use to help complete the unit.

# VACATION USA

In this unit you will take a two-week vacation to some regions of the United States. When you complete your vcacation, your group will be turning in a journal. The requirements for your vacation are as follows.

## Social Studies

_____    Road map of each state you traveled through (starting with Fort Campbell, KY).

_____    You must make at least *three* historical stops—for example: (1) Mud Island, (2) Trail of Tears, (3) Vicksburg Battlesite, (4) Natchez Trace Indian Trail, (5) San Jose Mission National Site; *two* amusement stops, such as (1) Graceland and (2) Six Flags over Texas; and *five* scenic stops: (1) Boatride on the Mississippi River, (2) Big Bend National Park, (3) Lake of the Ozarks, (4) Bull Shoals Lake, (5) canoe ride down the White River.

## Science

_____    List all biomes you will be traveling through. Include specific states. Include a map of your vacation route. Show all biomes.

_____    Describe the climate of each biome. You must include temperature and rainfall. Also describe seasonal changes.

_____    Give examples of animals found in each biome. Describe ways in which animals have adapted to their environment.

_____    Give examples of vegetation found in each biome. Describe ways in which the plants or trees have adapted to the environment.

_____    Conclude your report by describing the land features. Was the area flat or hilly? Did you drive by the ocean, lakes, or rivers? Were there any unusual land features?

## Math

_____    Keep track of money spent for travel, food, lodging, entertainment, and miscellaneous items.

_____    Use a mileage chart to calculate distance driven.

_____    Estimate driving time.

_____    Construct a pie graph showing percentage of money spent for each area.

_____    Construct a line graph showing relationship between distance driven and money spent for each day.

**Language Arts**

Each group of *four* students will hand in a completed journal containing the following:

_____    All math, social studies, and science requirements.

_____    A journal entry for each day of the trip (at least *14* entries). The entries must include descriptions of how you would imagine things to be — for example;

> Today we made it to San Antonio and visited the Alamo. It was really neat. It was very interesting to learn that Davy Crockett fought and was a well-known defender of the Alamo. The fort itself was fresh. The way the wall was built around the fort makes it hard to believe that anyone was able to defeat the people inside this Mexican military headquarters.
>
> The drive to San Antonio was really kinda boring. This land is very flat and it was very hot. Of all days the air conditioning went out on the car today. It must have been over 100° inside the car because it was 99° outside. 99° is very normal for Texas this time of year.
>
> We passed an oil rig on the way. Also we stopped and bought some miniature souvenir cotton balls. Cotton is one of Texas's major agricultural crops.
>
> We saw a lot of wild turkeys and quail. This made Mark hungry for Thanksgiving dinner, but everything makes Mark hungry. He wanted to stop and try to catch a turkey. We wanted to know if he wanted us to leave him on the side of the road so the next people passing by could pick up a real "turkey."

_____    Any extra pictures, postcards, and the like included in your journal will be considered as *extra credit*.

## VACATION USA

Name _____

Due—will be informed at a later date.
Order of Vacation Notebook:

1. 14 pages of language arts journal
2. Science biome map
3. Science temperature/rainfall map
4. Science report:
   A. List of biomes
   B. Temperature/rainfall
   C. Animals
   D. Plants
   E. Land formations
5. 4 individual money charts (math)
6. 1 bar graph of money spent
7. 1 bar graph of miles driven
8. 1 pie graph
9. 1 outline map of all the United States (social studies)
10. Individual state maps (with route marked)
11. 10 pages of research (of the 3 historic, 5 scenic, and 2 amusement stops)
12. Any extra credit
13. Everything should be housed in an attractive and creative cover.

## VACATION USA

Names: _____

_____

Name of place visited _____

Type of stop _____ historical _____ amusement _____ scenic

Number of stops in this category _____

Where is this stop located? (state, city, interstate exit)

_____

_____

_____

On which day of this trip will this stop be made? _____

_____

About how much money will be spent here? _____

What did you see and do at this stop? (Use your research to answer this question. This information should be used when you write your journal for language arts.

_____

_____

_____

_____

_____

_____

_____

_____

_____

_____

_____

_____

_____

_____

Vacation USA Expense Worksheet

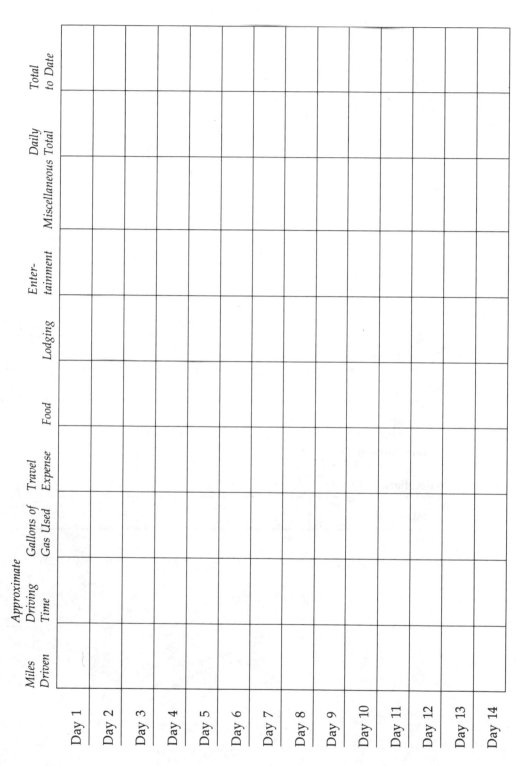

| | Miles Driven | Approximate Driving Time | Gallons of Gas Used | Travel Expense | Food | Lodging | Enter-tainment | Miscellaneous | Daily Total | Total to Date |
|---|---|---|---|---|---|---|---|---|---|---|
| Day 1 | | | | | | | | | | |
| Day 2 | | | | | | | | | | |
| Day 3 | | | | | | | | | | |
| Day 4 | | | | | | | | | | |
| Day 5 | | | | | | | | | | |
| Day 6 | | | | | | | | | | |
| Day 7 | | | | | | | | | | |
| Day 8 | | | | | | | | | | |
| Day 9 | | | | | | | | | | |
| Day 10 | | | | | | | | | | |
| Day 11 | | | | | | | | | | |
| Day 12 | | | | | | | | | | |
| Day 13 | | | | | | | | | | |
| Day 14 | | | | | | | | | | |

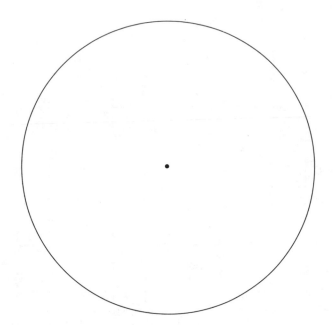

|  | Amount Spent | Percent |
|---|---|---|
| Travel Expenses |  |  |
| Food |  |  |
| Lodging |  |  |
| Entertainment |  |  |
| Miscellaneous |  |  |
| Total |  |  |

**5**  *Curriculum Unit*  History through Literature

*Subject Areas*  English, history

*Recommended Grade Levels*  Eighth grade (middle school)

*Summary*  The project seeks to integrate the English and history courses by presenting thirteen literature selections in the context of U.S. history and by reinforcing the English writing process within the history classes.

*Objective*

- To demonstrate to the students that knowledge is integrated.
- To enhance the understanding of literature selections by coordinating their study with the appropriate historical period.
- To coordinate the teaching of writing between English and history classes.
- To support the humanities through joint English/history projects.

*School and Contact Person*

Fugett Middle School
500 Ellis Lane
West Chester, PA 19380
(215) 436-7242

Robert Shapley, Ph.D., Principal
Susan Blevins, English teacher
Brooks Morris, history teacher
Karen Satz, English teacher
Larry Woodruff, history teacher

*Procedures*  All eighth-grade students participate in writing a joint English/history research paper. The topic is based on the history curriculum and is assigned by the history teachers. Standard research procedures are taught by the English teachers, including proper bibliography and note-taking methods. Adjustments are made according to various ability levels. In addition to this research paper, the history teachers follow the writing process for a variety of other writing assignments within their classes.

The English and history teachers agreed to implement a common writing process. The English teachers emphasize the five-step model according to the West Chester Area School District policy for the writing process, with particular emphasis on brainstorming as a prewriting activity, preparing a rough draft, revising, and proofreading. The history teachers support the writing process by requiring rough draft copies to be submitted along with final copies of all formal written assignments and by the use of proofreading checklists.

Attached is a schedule of the eighth-grade English/history coordinated instruction for a school year, September through June. All of the literature selections can be found in *Prentice Hall Literature, Silver Edition*, which is the required anthology for all eighth-graders at Fugett Middle School.

**J.R. Fugett Middle School: The Coordination of Eighth-Grade English and History Instruction**

| Month | U.S. History Unit | Literature Selection | Enrichment |
|---|---|---|---|
| September | Unit I: Native Americans and Exploration | "The Origin of Fire" "Medicine Bag" | Native American program |
| October | Unit II: Colonial America | | |
| November | Unit III: The American Revolution | | Library report (work to be supervised and graded by both English and history teachers) |
| December | | | |
| January | Unit IV: The Constitution | *Johnny Tremain* "Raymond's Run" "A Retrieved Reformation" "Thank You, Ma'am" "Roberto Clemente: A Bittersweet Memoir" | African-American history program |
| March | Unit V: A Growing America | | Women's history program |
| April | Unit VI: The Age of Jackson and Westward Expansion | "Grass Fire" "The Day the Sun Came Out" *Roll of Thunder, Hear My Cry* | |
| May | Unit VII: The Civil War | "Harriet Tubman: Guide to Freedom" "The Man without a Country" "The Drummer Boy of Shiloh" | Slide presentation and field trip to Gettysburg (historic orienta- tion to be super- vised by history teachers; "Gettysburg Address" analysis to be supervised by English teachers) |
| June | | | |

**6** *Curriculum Unit* Study Wydown Style

*Recommended Grade Level* Middle school/junior high school

*Subject Area* All subjects taught in the sixth through ninth grades.

*Summary* The staff of this school is committed to the development of study skills for all students across the different subject areas. Attention is given to the student's learning styles as the students become actively involved in setting goals and action plans for their achievement. The organization of this study skill plan is extensive. There is a project director and an after school program, parents are informed and offered workshops on the plan, and there exists a mini–lesson plan file in each core and special subject area.

*Objectives*

- At the beginning of the year, a time management and organization system is put into place.
- During the course of the year, staff members emphasize one efficient study skill per week.

*School and Contact Person*

Wydown Middle School
6500 Wydown Boulevard
Clayton, MO 63105
(314) 726-5222

Jere Hochman, Principal
A. J. Walker, teacher in charge of study skill program

*Procedure* The following material is from a much more comprehensive manual called *Study Wydown Style*.

**Introduction**

Study Wydown Style is the result of a State of Missouri Grant. Components of the program include: this parent and teacher study guide, mini-lesson packets, a parent home-study workshop, and an after school program to individualize help for students.

The purpose of Study Wydown Style is to help students incorporate efficient study skills into their personal study habits. At the beginning of the year, a time management and organization system is put into place. With the system in operation, staff members emphasize one efficient skill per week. Team planning sessions for staff and a one page addition to the *Wydown Newsletter* allow everyone to reinforce the importance of knowing the identified skill.

Choosing to not include a skill in one's own study habits is quite different from never knowing the skill. In this program, a student can discuss how a single skill fits into personal study habits. An individual's learning styles strengths can be emphasized as a parent and/or teacher helps the student to value skills necessary for academic achievement. The After School Program will assist in this effort. Strong study skills are valuable wherever they are used, but for work completed outside the classroom, they are essential.

## Learning Style

Style is a mode of expression or performance peculiar to an individual, group, or time period. It is a positive word which allows for the individual differences among people. A body of current information now exists regarding the learning styles strengths and preferences among students involved in the pursuit of learning. Ken and Rita Dunn have authored an excellent overview of learning styles and have made specific suggestions regarding curriculum, as well as the study skills and habits which aid in the retention of curricular content. The Dunns' overview will be used in both teacher and parent workshops to explain the goals/styles/skills matches involved in Study Wydown Style. In addition, the program will make use of Myers-Briggs and Swassing-Barbe materials.

As a result of Study Wydown Style, each student in school will assess his/her learning style preference via surveys. Results will be available to students, parents, and teachers. The program provides a system for helping students match their learning styles to curriculum challenges. Styles information only adds an "extra dimension" to the content message. It does not detract from a traditional lesson.

Classrooms should be viewed as places where all types of learning and teaching styles can be practiced with confidence. Time constraints often require that teachers teach only one skill method to an entire class as compared to teaching each student a personal method. This makes it possible to hold students accountable. Once students have mastered the study method taught in class, they can adapt it to fit their preferred learning styles. The After School Program is a unique component added to our present program. It is important in helping students make adaptations. Students, parents, and teachers have opportunity to make referral for the program and then to evaluate the after school component.

## The Human Triangle: Parents–Students–Teachers

In any successful school program, parents, teachers, and students have important roles to play. During the school year, no person's role changes as the result of Study Wydown Style, but each person's role can be more clearly defined. The tasks to be accomplished by any person can be described, discussed, and negotiated.

One of these tasks is homework. Homework is a task in which communications can often become confused. It is important to know what is expected of each person. Students will have an hour or more of homework each evening. Parents need to maintain a positive emotional distance where homework content is concerned. The completion of homework is the student's job. Students will remember and learn from mistakes. The manner in which those mistakes are highlighted is crucial to the student's desire to continue open communication with others. A positive attitude is always beneficial to any endeavor. It is hoped that Study Wydown Style will provide the system to communicate effectively about necessary school roles.

During each trimester, teachers and students will take time to assess strengths and weaknesses of individual styles and study habits. The purpose of these assessments is to keep communications objective and positive. Students can get and give information regarding achievable goals for their personal growth. In addition, the parents receive for signature a study skills evaluation sheet. This sheet also serves as a springboard for positive communication at home and school. Understanding each role in the homework process makes it possible for teachers, parents, and students to make mutual decisions regarding a study plan for academic success.

In Study Wydown Style, teacher(s) will be responsible for the following:

1. Teach required skill lessons.
2. Monitor homework folders.
3. Reinforce the notebook system.
4. Use Wydown heading format.
5. Use long-range planning calendar.
6. Use Wydown assignment sheet where appropriate.
7. Initial study skills evaluation forms.
8. Refer students to after school program if advisable.
9. Give assessments and surveys.
10. Use survey results to help with student needs.
11. Conference with students and parents of students experiencing difficulty.
12. Keep a positive attitude, keep communications open, and compliment effort.

Student(s) will be responsible for the following:

1. Keep an organized and up-to-date homework folder.
2. Use a notebook system.
3. Complete assignments in an appropriate and timely way.
4. Use formal heading on all work submitted.
5. Use appropriate listening skills.
6. Use appropriate reading skills.
7. Use appropriate writing skills.
8. Use appropriate test-taking skills.
9. Take responsibility to get necessary help.
10. Use after school program when necessary.
11. Fill out assessments and surveys.
12. Keep a positive attitude, keep communications open, and recognize personal growth and achievement.

Parent(s) will be responsible for the following:

1. Consider education a valued investment.
2. Provide a place in the home for study.
3. Expect approximately one or more hours of homework per night.
4. Help students budget time necessary for homework.
5. Be consistent about time and place to study.
6. Limit radio or TV time when necessary.

7. Give help when requested.
8. Help students maintain necessary materials.
9. Sign the study skills evaluation form upon request.
10. Watch the *Wydown Newsletter* for up coming skills topics.
11. Attend the parent workshop, if possible.
12. Keep a positive attitude, keep communications open, and compliment effort.

### Goal Setting and Motivation

External and internal motivators are important as students set goals for their academic achievement. Personal goal setting is a positive aspect of Study Wydown Style. **A GOAL + visualization + affirmation can equal success.** The ongoing effort by teachers and parents to help students make their own choices regarding goals and methods of achieving them can be enhanced during the school year by Study Wydown Style lessons and workshops.

Parents and teachers who are involved in helping others incorporate skills into their personal styles should remember that it is helpful to describe consequences and be consistent in their use. In selecting positive consequences, one should also remember to make the choice appropriate for the age level of students. It should be something valued by them and should be earned. "If you follow directions, something good will happen." Conversely, "If you choose not to follow directions, then you will be held accountable." Again, the accountability factor must be appropriate for the grade level and in harmony with existing family/school programs and procedures. Consequences can be given with a minimum of time, trouble, and discomfort remembering that consistency is essential to the system. The parent workshop held in September deals with consistency and the powers of persuasion available to adults as they help middle school students deal with motivators for good study habits.

Students often need help with the realities of the time framework that they set for goal achievement. At school we will use an assignment calendar and the Wydown weekly assignment sheet. Note *planned time* plus *time spent* column on the weekly sheet. Through negotiation, there can be a family plan of specific steps to follow for the achievement of a goal. For family planning purposes, there is a monthly and weekly "time budget" sheet available. Budgeting time is complex for students with many activities built into their "at home" homework schedules.

### After-School Program

The After School Program is a unique component of Study Wydown Style. Students of all ability levels can use the after school program. The program is best used a single day each week, or it may be used for three consecutive days in any given week.

Students, parents, and teachers will make use of referral and evaluation forms involving the program. The purpose of the program is to provide individualized help in achieving better performance in Wydown's curricular work. A student may have a need for help with organization and management or with daily assignment chores or with a single long-term assignment. A student may want to know more about his/her study habits. Assessment of strengths and how to use those strengths when completing homework chores can be extremely helpful during the middle school years.

The after school program will meet for one hour, 3:30–4:30, on three afternoons of certain weeks of the school year. 3:30–4:30 is the time for the program. Students referred are involved for at least three sessions. After the required sessions, additional time can be determined by the student, parents, and/or teachers. Referral should be made for any student who is not functioning at his/her perceived potential within any given class. Referral is also welcomed for any student who simply wants more structure with home work necessities. The more specific the prescription on the referral form, the more specific the activities will be after school. Specific information regarding the program will be attached to the *Wydown Newsletter* as well as the referral form.

Staff for the after school program includes a teacher, teacher aide, and Dr. Walker, the teacher in charge of Study Wydown Style. All of us at Wydown welcome the chance for students to get individualized attention with regard to goals/styles/skills matches.

## STUDY WYDOWN STYLE

Date _____ / _____ / _____

To the parents of: _____

From: _____

Skills emphasized in the Study Wydown Style program are important to academic success. Areas of concern have been discussed with your child. We would like to keep you informed of these areas so that you can help your child improve in necessary study skills.

Improvement is needed in the following areas:

_____ Homework folder

_____ Notebook system

_____ Arriving prepared for class

_____ Listening and following directions

Please sign and return this sheet before _____ / _____ / _____

Parent signature _____

Parents may wish to make comments on reverse side:

**7** *Curriculum Unit*  Humanities Program

*Recommended Grade Level*  Middle/junior high school

*Subject Areas*  English, social studies, math, foreign language, science, religious studies, visual and performing arts

*Summary*  This unit integrates the different curricula content over an entire school year around the theme of the diversity and interrelatedness of the human family.

*Objectives*

- To understand how humankind uses myth to understand the world.
- To develop plays and music to interpret the different myths.
- To learn to synthesize material from many disciplines.
- To understand how the Roman and Arabic numeral system and Greek geometric systems originated.
- To use science to study humankind's understanding of the world.
- To see how modern literature is related to myths, the Bible, history, and ancient literature.

*School and Contact Persons*

The Bishop's School
7607 La Jolla Boulevard
La Jolla, CA 92037
(619) 459-4021

Joan Breher, Principal
Brooke Suiter
Margaret Bowles

*Procedure*  The year begins with a study of mythology and its impact on civilizations from several points of view. In the Early Civilizations course the students learn about humankind's use of myth to understand the world, while in English they look at the development in literature of Greek–Roman myths. The Christian Traditions course explores the fertile relationship between myth and self-understanding in both Christianity and other religions. Foreign language students learn about the Latin origin of the romance languages as well as terms that have Greek origins.

In the arts courses students investigate, develop, and initiate creations based on topics in the curriculum. The courses Production 8 (drama and dance) and Chorus 8 involve dancers, actors, and musicians in work that includes plays (written in English class) based on various world myths. Design 8 and Studio 8 explore and create art influenced by mythological concepts of the universe and its inhabitants. Often guest artists are invited to introduce the students to medieval, Indian, Japanese, and African music.

Throughout the year students and teachers continue seeking and showing the relationships between these disciplines. In the Earth Science course students learn about tectonic plate theories that explain the formation of the continents on which the early civilizations built. They also study astronomy, where they reencounter the names of Greek and Roman mythological characters and creatures. Additionally, the course in Mathematics 8 integrates with other subject areas by using the Roman numeral system and by investigating early calculating devices. The students graph astronomical bodies to reinforce concepts studied in science.

Reading, writing, discussing, and creating—the students and teachers explore answers to such universal questions as: What is a hero/heroine? Who am I and how do I fit into the scheme of life? What does it mean to be civilized? What are the causes of conflict and how can conflict be resolved? Beginning with the study of prehistory and the ancient Near East, through exploration of Mycenaean and Minoan, Trojan, Greek, Roman, Egyptian, Byzantine, and Persian civilizations as well as Islamic and Arabic culture and the civilizations of Africa, China, Japan, and the Americas and the Middle Ages, the students are involved with the humanities and apply them to the tasks of daily living in the community.

## 1991–1992 Eighth-Grade Humanities Curricula

| | Enrichment | Early Civ. | English | Christian Trad. | Design 8 | Product 8 | Science | Math | Language | Chorus | Studio 8 |
|---|---|---|---|---|---|---|---|---|---|---|---|
| **September**<br>September 3–6 | Intro to Humanities | What is Civilization? Perspective/ bias | Wizard of Earthsea; Mandalas | Religion and myth; Judaism | Who am I? | | Origins of Earth, Universe, solar system | Graphing constellations; calendars & time | Myths of Quetzalcoatl | Early music | |
| September 9–13 "the Rescue" (9/11) | "Apollo to Paleolithic/ | Prehistory Roman neolithic | Greek to Mythology | Judaism objects | Childhood dance and | Greek music time line theatre | Geological | | | | |
| September 16–20 | | Ancient Near East | God/ goddess monologue | Judaism | Fantasy | | Fossils | | | | |
| September 23–27 | | | Write dialogue using myths | Christianity: Birth narratives | Mytholog-ical Zoo | | Constellations and star groups | | | | |
| **October**<br>September 30–October 4 | Mr. Updegraff on Greek epic poetry | Ancient Near East | Trojan War; world mythology | Birth narratives | | Silent Films | Scientists of the early age | Pythagoras Geometry | Etymology of Words; Greek and Latin origins | Early Music Myths in Music | |
| October 7–11 | | Myth vs. history; Minoan & Mycenaen Trojan War, hubris | Playwriting Using world mythology | Teachings of Jesus | Computer icons with alphabets, numerals, geometric shapes | "Shopping Bag Lady"/ Contemporary monologues | Science/ religion/ mythology | | | | |
| October 15–18 | Transparencies from Design 8 | Bulletin-board: Byz., Greece, Rome, Egypt, Persia | Playwriting: Human Comedy | "Shopping Bag Lady" | | | Reference points and measure-ment | | | | |
| October 21–25 | | Greece | Deliver myth Plays 11/1 | Teachings of Jesus | | Receive myth plays | | | | | |
| **November**<br>November 5–8 | | Rome | Human comedy | Passion narratives | Set building and other projects | Myth plays | | Roman numerals | Origins of Romance languages | Winter Sun | |
| November 11–15 | Roman art & architecture Slides; Pompeii | Rome | | Passion narratives | | | Minerals, rocks, disasters, Pompeii | | | | |

## 1991–1992 Eighth-Grade Humanities Curricula (Continued)

| | Enrichment | Early Civ. | English | Christian Trad. | Design 8 | Product 8 | Science | Math | Language | Chorus | Studio 8 |
|---|---|---|---|---|---|---|---|---|---|---|---|
| *November* | | | | | | | | | | | |
| November 18–22 | | Roman culture | Eagle of the 9th | Acts—Early Christianity | | | Plate tectonics | | | | |
| November 25–27 | | Byzantine civilization | Eagle | | | | | | | | |
| *December* | | | | | | | | | | | |
| December 2–6 | | Islam | Eagle | Islam | Painting | Myth Plays | | Arabic numerals Arabic influence on math | Moors in Spain Arabic influence on Spanish | Winter ?????? | |
| December 9–13 | | Islam | Eagle | Islam | | | | | | | |
| December 16–20 | Myth plays | India | Short story | Hinduism | | | Erosion | | | | |
| *January* | | | | | | | | | | | |
| January 6–10 | Indian musicians 1/8 | Nectar in a Sieve | Writing unit | Buddhism | Design banners | | Mapping/ topography | | | | |
| January 13–17 | | Nectar in a Sieve | | Chinese Religions | | | | | | | |
| *February* | | | | | | | | | | | |
| February 3–7 | African Musicians and Dancers 2/5 | Africa | Midsummer Night's Dream | Religion and myth; Judaism | Childhood objects Fantasy | African tales | TBA | Ratios and percents using historical information | TBA | Rhythm | Printmaking wood blocks silk screen |
| February 10–14 | | Africa | Midsummer | Judaism | | | | | | | |
| February 18–22 | African Tales 2/19, 2/20 | China | Midsummer | Judaism | Chinese dragons | | | | | | |
| February 24–28 | | China China/ Japan/ Africa boards due 2/18 tasks due 3/2 | Midsummer | Christianity: birth narratives | | | | | | | |
| *March* | | | | | | | | | | | |
| March 2–6 | African tales 3/4, 3/5 | Japan | Rebels of the Heavenly Kingdom | Birth narratives | Computer designs | Scenes from A Midsummer Night's Dream | Oceanog- raphy | Positive and negative numbers elevations | Indian influence on Spanish | Shakes- pearean music | Large painting |

## 1991–1992 Eighth-Grade Humanities Curricula (Continued)

| March | Enrichment | Early Civ. | English | Christian Trad. | Design 8 | Product 8 | Science | Math | Language | Chorus | Studio 8 |
|---|---|---|---|---|---|---|---|---|---|---|---|
| March 9–12 | Storytellers | Japan | Rebels | Teachings of Jesus | | | | | | | |
| March 16–20 | Japanese Musicians 3/18 | Japan | Storytelling | Teachings "Shopping Bag Lady" | | | | | | | |
| March 23–26 | | Messo America, N. American Indians | | Teachings | | | | | | | |
| April 3–Story Telling Contest Period I | | | | | | | | | | | |
| *April* March 30–April 3 | Storytelling contest 4/3 | Americas | Storytelling contest | Passion Narratives | | MSND | Weather | Weather & temperature conversions | "El Cid" & "Rolando" | Madrigals | Stained Glass & Enameling |
| April 6–10 | | Americas | History of English | Acts—Early Christianity | | | | | | | |
| April 20–26 | Fencing Demonstration 4/22 | Middle Ages | Canterbury Tales | Acts—Early Christianity | | | | | | | |
| April 27 / May 1 Arts Week | "Carmen" 4/23 MSND scenes 4/29 | Middle Ages | Canterbury Tales | Islam | Banners | | | | | | |
| *May* May 4–8 | Medieval musicians | Middle Ages research paper due 5/1 | Canterbury | Islam | | | | Geometry History of measurements | AP exams | Madrigals | TBA |
| May 11–15 | Bayeaux Tapestry slides 5/13 | Middle Ages | Jekyll & Hyde | Hinduism | Religious symbols Banners | Explore themes from Jekyll & Hyde | National parks paper | | | | |
| May 18–22 | Percussion 5/20 Bishopbury banquet 5/22 | Oral reports 5/18 | Jekyll & Hyde | Buddhism | Painting, color theory | | | | | | |
| May 26–29 | | | Mandalas Jekyll & Hyde essay What Is Human? | Chinese religions | | | | | | | |
| June 1–3 | | Review | Review | Review | | | | | | | |

*8* *Curriculum Unit*   Back to the Past: An Immigration Experience

*Recommended Grade Level*   Middle/junior high school

*Subject Areas*   Reading, English, social studies, math, science, foreign language, physical education, home economics, art, music, computers

*Summary*   This unit provides the student with an understanding of lives and experiences of workers of Lowell, Massachusetts, from the "mill girls" of the early 1800s to the latest immigrant groups of the 1900s. An emphasis is placed on the shared experiences that helped unite workers despite their many differences.

Through role play, students investigate why people came to Lowell, what the conditions were in their country of origin, what types of material culture (artifacts) people brought with them, and what experiences awaited the new immigrants.

*Objective*

- To make students aware of their own immigrant past
- To trace the development of the United States through the Immigration process
- To appreciate the uniqueness of what each immigrant group has brought or added to the U.S. "melting pot"
- To promote both multicultural and international awareness

*School and Contact Person*

Alcott Middle School
1490 Woodtick Road
Wolcott, CT 06716
(203) 879-2517

Robert F. Gerace, Principal
Frances Flynn
Arline Tansley
Francis Masi
Victor Delcioppo
Mary Glendening
Donna CelCioppo
Joan Vastola
Gloria Gubitosi
Vivian Rosenthal
Barbara Skrebutenas
Florence Goodman

*Procedure*

*Student Projects*   Students are grouped to draw:

**1.** Continent maps with country delineations for hall display. Each student researched and constructed a flag for individual countries to place on maps. *Theme:* We all came to America.

2. Central hall display of map of New York Harbor featuring Statue of Liberty and Ellis Island. Students supplied immigration papers and memorabilia from relatives to surround map.
3. International recipe book:
   a. Students supplied recipes for dishes representative of their heritage.
   b. Groups of students collected and typed recipes using word-processing skills learned in computer class.
   c. Committee of students created a cover design with the assistance of the art teacher.
   d. Cookbook was bound and distributed to all students and teachers at the International Festival.

### Writing

1. Students research their names through family discussions.
2. Family trees
3. *Research papers:* Cooperative effort between English and social studies departments. Students will research a particular country or U.S. state to find out the history of immigration from or to that area.
4. Students may choose to research the process by which a person can become a U.S. citizen.
5. Students use the information they have gained about various countries and cultures to write their own myths and folk tales.
6. Students who have immigrated to the United States are encouraged to to present written and oral reports on their experiences here and abroad.

### International Festival   Prior to festival days:

1. Students participated in the creation of the International Cookbook.
2. Students create life-sized flags of the countries from which a majority of their families had come.
3. A calendar of holidays around the world was created on the computer and displayed. Copies of individual months were used as placemats.
4. Students researched their heritages and created an 8½ × 11 block representing their ancestry. Blocks were laminated and tied to form a "quilt of cultures," which was displayed.
5. Physical education teacher organized groups of students to present international ethnic dances. Students were encouraged to display their singing, dancing, and instrumental music.
6. Students submit a small picture, which is placed on a simulated passport that they carry on festival day.

### Festival Day

1. Students bring in ethnic foods they have prepared, which correspond to recipes they submitted for the cookbook.
2. All students gather in the gym cafeteria to enjoy the music presentation and international buffet.
3. As students leave, they receive a bound edition of the cookbook as a memento.

*Miscellaneous Activities*

1. Diversity crossword puzzle
2. Newspaper articles on current immigration and past history of immigration
3. Students with special talents are encouraged to demonstrate them for each class (e.g., origami).
4. Students create posters and displays of languages around the world.

*9* *Curriculum Unit*  A Minority Study: The African-American

*Recommended Grade Level*  Middle/junior high school

*Subject Areas*  Science, social studies, art, math, home economics, music, language arts, reading

*Summary*  This unit is summarized with a "Peanut Day." Each student brings to school something made of peanuts, and the whole grade has a toasting party. Later a program is held viewing Dr. Martin Luther King Jr.'s speech "I Have a Dream." One student from each section shares his or her paper concerning a famous Black American he or she has researched.

### Objective

- To familiarize the students with the roots of prejudice and discrimination Blacks have suffered throughout the history of our country

### School and Contact Person

Washington Middle School
First and Vine
Maryville, MO 64468
(816) 562-3244

Glenn Jonagen, Principal

### Procedures

*Social Studies*

1. Locate on an African map the regions that produced the largest number of slaves and develop two theories on why these regions produced the largest amount of slave trade.
2. Explain the origin of the word *slave*.
3. Discuss a relevant form of discrimination in class.

*Science*

1. Give a brief history of the life of George Washington Carver and a brief summary of his development of the use of peanuts and sweet potatoes.
2. In class, make peanut butter and peanut bread.

*Math*

1. Collect, organize, and display data taken from literature about peanut production from various countries and states.
2. Write multistep story problems using a peanut theme.

*Art*

1. Students will view an exhibit of African art at a local gallery.
2. Students will discuss the cultural and social implications of the images in reproductions of contemporary art by African-American artists.

*Home Economics*

1. Share the history of the images of Mrs. Butterworth and Aunt Jemima.
2. Make pancakes as a cooking unit.

*Music*

1. Teach and give history of songs from Africa (Mangwani Mpulele, Tina, Singu)
2. Teach and give history of songs from Black Americans: ("He's Got the Whole World in his Hands," "Nine Hundred Miles," "On My Journey," "This Old Hammer," "When the Saints Come Marching In," and the like)

*Language Arts*

1. Develop a plan and final paper that includes:
   • Topic sentence stating the name of a prominent African-American and one reason that the person was chosen
   • Person's date and place of birth
   • Three facts about the person's background
   • A summary of one's overall impression of African-Americans

*Reading*

1. Identify four to five facts concerning the life of Dr. Martin Luther King Jr.
2. Participate in a panel discussion with ideas on prejudice and discrimination.
3. Develop six to eight questions and conduct an interview with Black university students concerning their experiences.

*10* *Curriculum Unit* Ancient Greece

*Recommended Grade Level* Middle/junior high school

*Subject Areas* English, social studies, math, science

*Summary* An interdisciplinary study of Greek culture, myths, legends, art, science, and math are included in this comprehensive 60+ page unit.

## Objectives

- The students will become aware of the many Greek contributions to the world.
- The students will develop an appreciation for the Greek achievements in art, science, and government.

*School and Contact Person*

Conway Middle School
4600 Anderson Road
Orlando, FL 32812
(407) 275-9263

Debora Graves, Principal
Robert Mantone
Marilyn Whitley
Mary Lynn Williams
Jerald Kelly
Holly Potter

## Procedure

*English/Language Arts* The English classroom provides a variety of materials to fit into an interdisciplinary unit on Greece. This is an opportune time to stress the development of literature for which the Greks were so largely responsible. Greeks developed the plays of comedy and tragedy as well as the fable for which Aesop is so famous.

At the end of the unit, students developed an Oprah Winfrey–style talk show. Students wrote down questions they would like to ask the mythological characters. Students volunteered to role play the many characters about whom they had read. The students brought in their own costumes (sheets for togas and other props). The classroom was decorated with plants, ivy, and borrowed columns from the social studies classrooms. Students took turns role playing and answering the many questions that the "audience" had prepared for the talk show's "guests."

*Science* The study of Greek scientists who explored the stars as well as math can be included here. Students can choose one Greek scientist to follow during the unit. The study of the constellations provides an excellent hands-on learning opportunity. Students can locate and chart various constellations and relate them to stories and mythological figures in Greek literature. Another area of interest is the study of the Hoppocratic oath. Students can discover how it is used today and compare today's doctors to those who took the oath in Greek times.

*Social Studies*   The textbook is used to cover many ancient Greek terms and words. Geography can be incorporated into this unit here by introducing map skills. Art and architecture are studied through hands-on projects. Ancient and modern-day Olympics are compared and contrasted. Students are introduced to the Greek language. Mazes and bingo games are used to reinforce the course content. Reports are also required.

1. A report on Athens or Sparta. The student should tell about the city with regard to daily life and kind of government. Pictures should be provided to describe the city. The report should have a cover and a bibliography.
2. A report on a great philosopher and scientist should be completed. The students should select one of the following men and do a complete report on his life: Pericles, Aristotle, Euclid, Hippocrates, Plato, Homer, Herodotus, Themistocles.
   • Tell when and where he was born and his early life.
   • Tell about his later life, his accomplishments, and the things he did to be remembered.
   • Tell about the last part of his life and the effect he had on our way of thinking.

*Projects*

1. Imagine spending a day in ancient Athens. Visit the marketplace, gods, the temple, the acropolis, and a typical home. Write about what you might see and do.
2. Construct a Greek marketplace from cardboard, wood, and other materials.
3. Write a Greek play about a famous person in ancient Greece.
4. Write a speech on the rights and responsibilities of being a citizen in Athens. Compare those rights to your rights and responsibilities as a citizen of the United States and as a citizen of the world.
5. Make a diorama showing the life-style in Sparta.
6. Write a letter to the Council of 500 in Athens or the kings of Sparta making suggestions for improving the quality of life in that city-state.
7. Draw a picture showing contributions of Greece to our life in the modern world today.
8. Use an atlas to find examples of U.S. cities and towns that have Greek names.
9. Find three books in the library or your classrooms that contain information about Greece. List the books in correct bibliographical form.
10. Use vocabulary words from Ancient Greece. Write up several clues for each word. Clues can be used for a Password game. The class is divided into two teams. Two people from each team begin the game. Ten points are scored if a team guesses on the first clue, nine points if a team guesses on the second clue, and so on. For the second vocabulary word, two more players are selected.

*Math*   Students are introduced to Greek number system, work Greek decoder puzzles, and learned how numerology was used to tell fortunes.

*Culminating Activities*

- *Greek Salad Day:* Through the help of the parents, a period is set up to serve the students Greek salad. This requires only lettuce, feta cheese, green or black olives, and Italian dressing. While the students eat their salads, other students can perform adaptations of Greek plays or original plays that they have written themselves in English or reading.
- *Olympics:* This can be handled as a field day. Students may compete in events similar to those of the early Greek Olympics.

## ANCIENT GREECE—BINGO

Below are 32 words associated with Ancient Greece. Below the list of words are some blank squares which, when filled, will make a bingo card. Write one word from your list in each box. Mix the words as you write them in the boxes. There will be seven words you will not use at all.

Your teacher will ask you questions about Greece. Find the answer and place a marker on it. You may get Bingo horizontally, vertically, or diagonally.

| Democracy | Solon | Assembly | Council |
| Macedonia | Odyssey | Sparta | City-State |
| Aristotle | Persia | Pericles | Acropolis |
| Archimedes | Hippocrates | Alexander | Parthenon |
| Hellenistic | Athena | Aegean | Corinth |
| Athens | Greece | Iliad | Euclid |
| Socrates | Academy | Plato | Zeus |
| Crete | Poseidon | Olympics | Marathon |

|  |  |  |  |  |
|---|---|---|---|---|
|  |  |  |  |  |
|  |  |  |  |  |
|  |  | BONUS |  |  |
|  |  |  |  |  |
|  |  |  |  |  |

*Directions:* Cut apart cards below. Use to call questions for Ancient Greece—Bingo.

| | | | |
|---|---|---|---|
| Type of government in Ancient Greece | Patron goddess of Athens | Country located between Ionian and Aegean seas | Ruler during the Golden Age of Greece |
| Homeland of Alexander | All citizens belonged to this | School founded by Plato | Conqueror of Greece and most of the known world |
| Pupil of Plato—Teacher of Alexander | Militaristic city-state | Sea to the east of Greece | Battle in which the Greeks defeated the Persians |
| Inventor of pulley-lever | High hill | Story about the Trojan War | Games played in honor of Zeus |
| Civilization based on combining cultures of Egypt, Greece, Western Asia | Building on the Acropolis | Wrote teaching of Socrates | Greek poet who wrote the *Iliad* and the *Odyssey* |
| Wrote Code of Laws | Gulf dividing mainland Greece into two parts | Inventor of Geometry | God of the Sea |
| Story of the adventures of Ulysses | Democratic city-state | King of gods | Sun god |
| Enemy of Greece | Taught by questioning | Island south of Greece | Father of medicine |

## ANCIENT GREECE–CROSSWORD PUZZLE

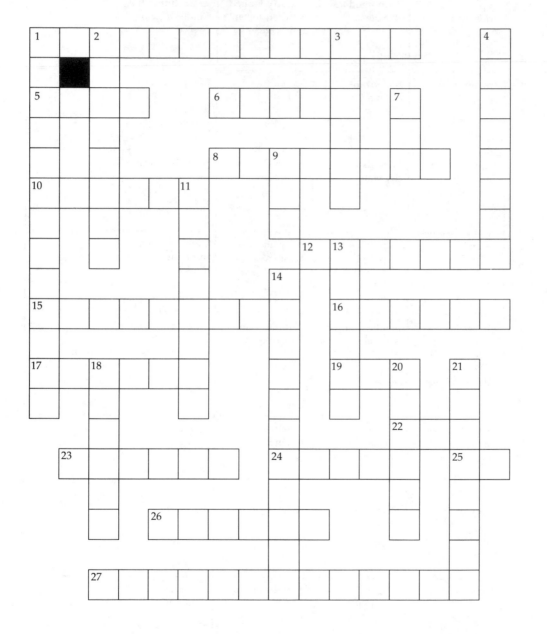

## ACROSS

1. Sea south of Greece
5. Aegean city-state destroyed by Greece
6. Clothing worn by ancient Greeks
8. God of the sea
10. University built by Alexander
12. Wrote code of laws
15. Town with its own government, laws, and army (two words)
16. Democratic city-state
17. God of the sun
19. A set of rules or customs
22. Zeus was the god of this
23. Patron goddess of Athens
24. Poem written by Homer
25. Abbreviation for southeast"
26. Military city-state
27. Played in honor of Zeus (two words)

## DOWN

1. Archimedes
2. God of the grape
3. Wrote book on geometry
4. Inventor of the pulley
7. A place in Alexandria where animals from all over the known world were kept
9. Poseidon was god of this
11. Famous battle against Persians fought here
13. Temple, priest, and priestess who gave advice from the gods
14. New civilizations formed after the conquests of Alexander
18. Public speaker
20. Athena was goddess of this
21. Poem about Ulysses written by Homer

## ANCIENT GREECE—CROSSWORD PUZZLE ANSWERS

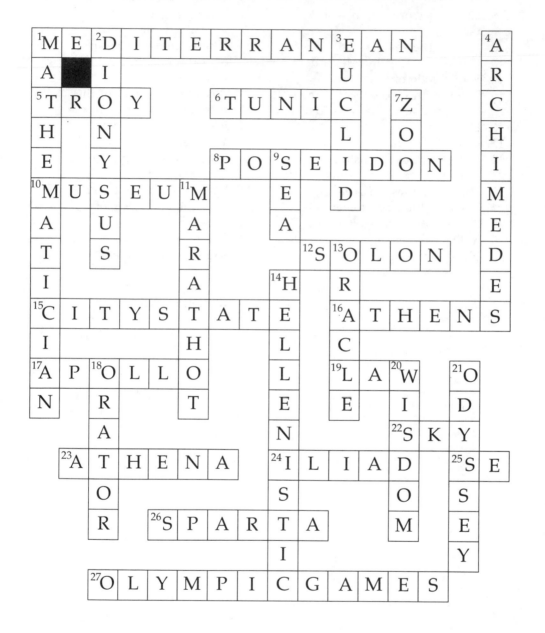

*11*  *Name of Curriculum*  The Spirit of America

*Recommended Grade Level*  Middle/junior high school

*Subject Areas*  Math, language arts, social studies, science, media, business, computer

*Summary*  Students will choose a specific era or event from 1900 to 1992 and will summarize how the spirit of patriotism was demonstrated. Students will become aware of trends in music, literature, and fine arts and how these influenced the American way of life. Activities will focus on group participation, ending in project displays and a culminating presentation for the whole school.

*Objective*

- To understand how patriotism is expressed in the United States
- To understand major trends in American culture
- To demonstrate the American spirit of patriotism

*School and Contact Person*

Brewster Middle School
Building 40 MCB
Camp Lejeune, NC 28542-5005
(919) 451-2561)

Elizabeth Thomas, Principal
Jackie Wagner
Carole Hill
Susan Wolf
Sonya Brooks
Chuck Woodul
Melinda Compton
Anna Campbell

*Procedure*  Some of the movies and videotapes mentioned in this unit can be replaced by similar material that a school may have available. These movies and videotapes are constantly being updated. If a teacher is interested in the current material being used, it is best to call the principal at the school.

**Objectives: Social Studies**

1. Students will outline the major late nineteenth-century/early twentieth-century influx of immigrants and how this influenced our social and political developments.
2. Students will demonstrate that the years 1920–1940 were a time of rapid change, economic, prosperity, and depression.

3. Students will summarize political, technological, and social changes in the United States from 1945 through the 1960s.
4. Students will outline the effects of foreign policy since 1945 and the purpose of the United Nations.
5. Students using computer and multimedia resources will apply these skills to American history.

## Activities: Social Studies

1. Movie: *Golden Door*—immigrants
2. Time line—immigrants
3. Bar graph—immigrants
4. *Scholastic News* articles and activities from the magazine on immigrants and Elis Island.
5. Written and oral reports on significant immigrants
6. Geographical maps on Pacific; World War II (students had to locate and define a legend), Pearl Harbor, Hiroshima/Nagasaki, Japanese conquests in 1942, Battle of Midway
7. Jigsaw activity between groups on European/Hitler/World War II. Questions and answers by "expert" groups.
8. "Soundies"—Video of 1940s (panagram)
9. "Cruisin the '50s"—notes on movie

## Objectives: Language Arts

1. Students will take notes on a timeline dating from 1914 to 1990. This timeline represents poetry of famous authors and historical events of these times.
2. Students will read poetry for content and connotation, and decide how the historical events influenced the writers and how they portrayed "the American spirit."

## Activities: Language Arts

1. Choose American writers. Examples of simple background readings are the poetry of Countee Cullen and Langston Hughes—for example, "As I Grew Older" by Langston Hughes, and "Any Human to Another" and "From the Dark Tower" by Countee Cullen.
2. Conduct class and group readings of the aove poetry. One poem is modeled to be read for content and connotation. As groups, choose one of the three poems to read for content and connotation.
3. Individually, read a poem from any time period. (You might make time cards and handing the students these cards to work on a specific time period of one another.) Ask the students to write the poem, giving the author the credit and writing the connotation in essay form.

## Objectives: Earth Science

1. Students will describe varied careers in science.
2. Students will demonstrate that science depends on accurate measurement.

3. Students will discuss current societal issues related to earth science.

**Activities: Earth Science**

1. Open discussion of the importance of energy:
   - What it is like with energy?
   - What it is like without energy?
   - Various types of electricity: wind power, hydro, solar, geothermal

2. Ecosystem and its components:
   - Predators and prey
   - The food chain (invite guest speakers)
   - Hands-on: snakes

3. Discussion of current events:
   - Acid rain (hands-on):
     - Experiment to test the acidity and alkalinity of rainwater, faucet water, lemon juice, tomato juice, vinegar, distilled water.
     - Students learn to follow through on an experiment, forming a hypothesis and testing it.
     - Learned how to read litmus paper and pH scale.
   - Biomes:
     - Open discussion of tropics, tundras, rainforest, oceans
     - Videos of oil spills

4. Recycling (hands-on):
   - Students made paper out of recycled material.
   - Guest speaker discussing the program in Onslow County called "Keeping America Beautiful."
   - Emphasis on *precycling* versus *recycling*.

**Objectives: Mathematics**

1. Students will add and subtract fractions.
2. Students will compare two fractions.
3. Students will determine the difference between two times.

**Activities: Mathematics**

1. The music teacher was invited to the class to demonstrate the use of math in music counting (division of beat).
2. Students created various rhythm patterns and performed them on the synthesizer or by other methods (hand clapping).
3. Students learned to discern the relative duration of note values and how various rhythms are noted.
4. Students listened to various types of music, such as jazz, rock oldies, and beach music.

### Objectives: Careers

1. Students will investigate the influence of personal interests, aptitudes, career values, and attitudes on career choices.
2. Students will explore their individual interests and abilities in fine arts occupations.
3. Students will relate the importance of technology, productivity, and citizenship to the development of independent workers.
4. Students will examine the effect of technology on workers.
5. Students will participate in job tasks related to current technology.

### Activities: Careers

1. Fine arts vocabulary
2. Overhead notes on the three major groups of fine arts occupations, requirements, example of an occupation in each.
3. Video ("Norman Rockwell: An American Dream")
4. Art director: Students design their own album cover.
5. Video ("We Are the World"): Occupations other than performer involved in making videos
6. Mini-research on favorite recording artist or group accompanied by pictures and music and presented to class.
7. Handouts:
   • Show Business Is Mostly Business"
   • "Careers in Music"
   • "Fine Arts and Humanities Careers"
8. Extra credit: Puzzles

### Goals: Computer

Students will use multimedia practices and techniques to develop presentations and reports. These practices and techniques include using an authoring program and laser disc to combine text with real photographic images. Students will select an approved topic of interest from the time period 1900–1990. This topic will be developed into a hyperpresentation.

### Objectives: Computer

1. Students will demonstrate their use of the program Tutor-Tech to form their research into a hyperpresentation that will allow them to report on their topic of interest.
2. Students will incorporate Print Shop images into the hyperpresentation.
3. Students will demonstrate proficiency using a laser disc player as part of their presentation.
4. Students will demonstrate their abilities using a Macintosh computer and the program Visual Almanac to research visual images on a laser disc player.

**Activities: Computer**

The first step for the students involved with computer presentations was to learn the basics of the program-Tech by Techware, Inc. This program allows the students to organize their research in a fashion that makes sense to them. In doing so, students created an original "authored program." An important part of these "programs" were the Print Shop graphics the students were able to incorporate into their presentations. Another feature of their presentations were the photographic images the students were able to display on the laser disc player.

The Visual Almanac played an important role for the students. It enabled them to research text and images that they wanted to incorporate into their programs. Once they had selected what they wanted their programs to show, they combined the text and visual images with Tutor-Tech.

By researching for visual images using Visual Almanac, students were able to get the frame numbers for images they felt added to their research. With the laser disc player plugged into their computers (Apple IIgs) via the modem port, students were able to write the Tutor-Tech commands (using the frame numbers they had researched) that would enable their program to command the laser disc player to display the appropriate images.

Some of the topics for which the students authored programs were doughboys, Black doughboys, sports, jazz, immigration, and Vietnam. By combining research topics like these with computer technology, students made the spirit of America come to life.

**Objectives: Physical Education**

*Recreational Dance*

1. Students will demonstrate positive self-concept and social confidence through participation in recreational dance.
2. Students will participate in square/folk/contemporary and popular dance (e.g., aerobics, electric slide, shag, twist).

**Activities: Physical Education**

1. Physical education teachers were asked if they could specifically teach the students the following dances: the Charleston, the continental, the electric slide, and the bus stop.
2. Students were asked to volunteer to perform these dances on stage.

Listed below are some ideas for topics that will allow the students to do hands-on projects. These ideas can be applied to many subject areas.

1. *Research paper:* These should be kept short.
2. *Filmstrip:* Students may create their own filmstrip and cassette in which they communicate the knowledge they have gained about a particular topic.
3. *Video:* Student-made videos with sound. Pictures from books and magazines may be used. See the librarian for the necessary materials.
4. *Charts:* Charts that inform in a variety of ways.
5. *Maps:* Student-made

6. *Games:* Students may make a game that challenges or tests other students from the material that they have studied.
7. *Book:* Students may write a book. This is really writing for meaning.
8. *Newspaper:* Students may write their own newspaper related to the topics that they are studying.
9. *Computers:* Whether using the computers in the lab or making use of those on your team.
10. *Oral presentations* by students of materials that they have studied.
11. *Brochures:* A good way for students to research and communicate their knowledge in geography.
12. *Picture scroll:* Student artists will draw pictures and write a script related to topics in class.
13. *Diary of a particular time event* (e.g., wars, awareness of environment, an author's success and failure of writings, musicians and their success and failure of job searching)
14. *Other* (approved by teacher)

*12*  *Curriculum Unit*  Cultural Fair

*Recommended Grade Level*  Middle school/junior high

*Subject Area*  English, social studies, math, science, music, physical education, home economics

*Summary*  Students will work in small groups to complete a number of required projects and a number of elective projects that illustrate the features and cultures of other countries.

*Objectives*

- To participate in cooperative learning group projects
- To complete a number of individual projects
- To prepare a demonstration booth for a specific country for a spring cultural fair

*School and Contact Person*

Edgewood Middle School
929 Edgewood Road
Highland Park, IL 60035
(312) 432-3865

Gregory Mullen, Principal
Bridget Booker
Sally Henderson

*Procedure*  The class is divided into small groups of six or seven students. Each group is assigned a specific country as its project country. Each member of the group will do a certain number of individual projects and receive individual grades. There will also be a number of group projects. These will receive one overall group grade and will be counted as a grade in math, science, language arts, and social studies for each member of the group. The work of the group projects should be evenly divided among members so that one or two people are not overloaded.

Along with the projects listed below, the students will have the opportunity to try out for some special activities that will occur on the night of the Cultural Fair. The special activities will include, among others, ethnic dancing, singing, and speech giving. The fair will be held during the first week of May.

*Individual Projects*  The following projects will be required for each individual member.

*Social studies:* Research papers, current events project
*Math:* Currency project, graphing project

*Language arts:* Speech, letter writing
*Science:* Three-dimensional biomes project

**Required Group Projects**    The following projects are required of every group:

1. *Flag of the country:* On poster board, in colors, made on both sides
2. *Banner:* Computer printout, including name of country, decorated and colored in
3. *Six-inch cube:* Decorated with scenes from your country obtained from magazines, embassies, travel agents, and other sources
4. *Three-dimensional project:* Related to some aspect of your country such as land formation, architecture, and so on
5. *Travel brochure:* A hand-made booklet approximately twenty pages long highlighting information about the country that tourists would want.
6. *Physical features map:* Salt dough relief map showing elevations and physical features of your country.
7. *Import/export trade partners map:* Use a world map and special purpose maps to show the trade partners of your country

**Elective Group Projects**    Each group is required to choose three additional projects from the following list below. Other ideas are acceptable, but they must be approved by the teacher first.

1. Made a board game involving information about the country.
2. Make an electric game about the country.
3. Make puppets wearing the native dress of the country.
4. Make a diorama of a scene from the country.
5. Make a timeline of the history of the country.
6. Make an informational chart about one aspect of the country such as language or religion.
7. Make a second three-dimensional project.
8. Make a replica of a game native to the country.

**Cultural Fair**    Each group will complete the following activities for the Cultural Fair:

1. Set up a booth attractively displaying all completed projects. The students will have a 6–8 foot table and the wall space behind it. A table cover is a good idea.
2. Students should bring food native to the country for the guests to sample. This should be home made by the students using recipes from the country.
3. Home-made costumes depicting the native dress of the people of the country should be worn, if possible.
4. Students should be knowledgeable about their country in case they are quizzed about the country by the teachers visiting the booths.
5. If possible, students should display artifacts from the country. Items might include coins, newspapers, travel posters, dolls, jewelry, crafts, and the like.

**Project: Graphing**

*Class*  Mathematics

*Purpose*  Students will learn to understand create four basic types of graphs—line, bar, circle, and picture.

*Classroom Acivities*

A. The class will discuss the kind of information that fits the various types of graphs.
B. Sample student graphs from previous years will be displayed and discussed.
C. Students will be given sample graphs done by the teacher.

*Student Directions*  The following will be done as part of the Cultural Fair project. The students will be required to make four graphs, including a bar, line, circle, and picture graph.

The grade will be 50 points based on accuracy, interesting selection of materials, neatness, proper titles, spelling, and other factors.

The teacher will provide the student with a packet of up-to-date statistics on the country. Students are welcome to use other statistics, but all data should be reviewed with the teacher before use. Students can graph the data in any order they wish, but all four graphs need to be utilized.

**Project:**

If a visitor from . . . came to Chicago

*Class*  Mathematics

*Purpose*  Students will gain an understanding of the monetary system of various countries and how these systems relate to the system used in the United States.

*Classroom Activities*

A. Collection of currency from twenty or more countries will be displayed and discussed.
B. Sales checks from various countries will be displayed and discussed, noting the way the various numbers are made differently and how the comma and decimal are often used differently than in U.S. money notation.
C. Students who have traveled to other countries may relate how they handled the use of other currencies.
D. Students are invited to bring in and share other currencies they may have.
E. Conversions will be done with the various currencies.
F. Students will complete a twelve-page booklet of money conversions for each country.

*General Directions*  Students should think about various tourist attractions in and around Chicago to which one would take a visitor from their country. Students should collect advertisements or souvenirs from these places. They should figure out the cost of going to these places in U.S. currency and then figure out the cost in the currency of their country.

Students should mount each attraction attractively and neatly on a separate page. The ten attractions shown must represent a variety of interesting sites as well as a range of prices.

Examples of attractions are museums, amusement parks, fast food restaurants, Sears Tower, theater, professional sports, art galleries, zoos, river cruise, Board of Trade, and movies.

Advertisements can be found in magazines, newspapers, pamphlets, and brochures. Students can also use ticket stubs or program covers.

If the cost is not listed in your information, students should make up a reasonable price. To vary costs, a student could take two or four people or buy the most expensive seats or the cheapest, and so on. If something is free, a student could use the cost of parking or the cost of a souvenir.

**13** *Curriculum Unit*  Suite for the Endangered

*Recommended Grade Level*  Middle school/junior high

*Subject Areas*  Music, science, English, journalism, drama

*Summary*  By integrating the theme of the endangered species across a number of curriculum areas, students can become more aware of the fragile balance of nature that exists for so many species.

*Objectives*  To help student and audience participants become more aware of the endangered species in our animal kingdom

*School and Contact Person*

Blair Junior/Senior High School
440 North Tenth Street
Blair, NE 68008
(402) 426-4941

Steve Shanahan, Principal
Lloyd Kilmer, Assistant Principal
Linda M. Donohue, Instrumental Music and Coordinator
Terri Weeces, Science
Rebecca Wuilf, English
Robert Bair, Journalism
Joseph Anderson, Drama

*Procedure*

*School Band*

A. To develop the musical, technical, and ensemble skills necessary to perform "Suite for the Endangered"
B. To become aware of the tonal colors, dynamics, rhythmic effects, and stylistic changes in the music that depict the endangered species associated with each movement
C. To develop an awareness and appreciation for performing contemporary compositions
D. To develop an understanding of a musical suite as a collection of different musical compositions written in various styles but having a common theme
E. To coordinate performance of the music with a visual slide presentation on endangered species

*Science*

A. To develop an awareness of the endangered species in our animal kingdom by studying and researching this area

   **B.** To determine given characteristics of these species, their normal habitat and geographical locations

   **C.** To encourage the school and community to begin to become aware of the endangered species situation and to begin to take responsible action to preserve the endangered

*English, Journalism, and Drama*

   **A.** To develop the students' awareness of the endangered species by the use of research and writing skills

   **B.** To review, select, compose, and edit a series of visual slides of the endangered species to be shown during the actual performance of the music

   **C.** To plan, coordinate, and assemble the sound, lighting, and visual effects for the performance of the "Suite for the Endangered"

*References and Materials*

1. "Suite for the Endangered," a concert band musical selection composed by Paul and Teresa Jennings, published in 1989 by Musicworks, and distributed by Jenson Publications. The music is suitable for middle level/junior high school bands.

2. *Available books: Vanishing Species* by Ron Wilson, published in 1979 by Albany Books; *Whales, Dolphins and Porpoises* by Sir Richard Harrison, published in 1988 by Facts on File, Inc. (used for slide visuals). Various other media resources are available in the local library.

3. Two slide projectors with approximately fifteen slides each, projected onto a full-stage screen.

4. The stage and the auditorium were dark except for 40 music stand lights used on stage so the 90 student musicians could view the music.

*14* *Curriculum Unit*  Walk Across Orlando

*Subject Areas*  English, math, science, geography

*Recommended Grade Level*  Middle school/junior high

*Summary*  This unit is a study of Orlando, Florida, designed to help students become familiar with the geography, history, economic base, major industries, municipal structure, and natural resources of the city.

### Objectives

- To enable students to understand the complexities of the infrastructure that supports the community
- To help students understand what having roots in a community means
- To help students see themselves as one of the fastest growing cities in America

### School and Contact Persons

Conway Middle School
4600 Anderson Road
Orlando, FL 32812
(407) 275-9263

Debora Graves, Principal
Kim Davison
Marcia Carow
Sammie Nicholls

*Procedures*  This unit is divided into two components. The first is a series of classroom activities the students undertake to prepare for the walk. The second component is the walk itself. The classroom activities can be divided into four content areas, discussed next.

### Language Arts

The students are grouped onto teams for these activities. Each team must choose one of the following research projects to complete.

- A photo exhibit featuring pictures that group members take of important locations in Orlando
- An original rap about Orlando
- An original Orlando banner
- An original play or skit about some phase of Orlando life and history

Each student is also required to complete an individual research project. For resources the students must use back issues of newspapers, interviews with long-time Orlando residents, and/or other print media to describe significant events from Orlando's past. Such items might include the famous Hillcrest School fire or the crash of the McCoy Air Force jet.

Finally, each student is required to choose a topic from the following list and conduct research concerning the item. The students will need to talk informally with people in the community, schedule and follow through with appointments and interviews with key community leaders, and write letters to municipal agencies and business requesting information.

- The renewal and regentrification of downtown Orlando
- Programs for senior citizens
- The homeless problem in Orlando
- Orlando's sports opportunities
- Medical services
- Orlando's parks and recreation
- Crime in Orlando
- Orlando's lakes and waterways
- Orlando's public services (law enforcement and fire protection)
- Public transportation (county, Airport Authority, Amtrak, taxis, rapid transit)
- Education in Orlando and the central Florida area
- Information flow and communications network
- Social services and volunteer organizations in Orlando
- Tourism in Orlando
- Orlando's municipal government
- Roadways and traffic control in Orlando
- Orlando's zoning laws

These activities are conducted during school time. Parents usually accompany the students for the visits and interviews, which provides a nice way to involve parents in the school activities. As examples of such research, one student interviewed the chief of police, two students attended the Pass in Review Ceremony at the Naval Training Center, four students toured the local press facilities, one student job shadowed a surgeon at a hospital, one student spent a day at a day care facility, six students helped serve lunch to the homeless at a local community kitchen, and two students attended a rehearsal of the Florida Symphony Orchestra.

### Geography

In this content area the students concentrate on Orlando's historical landmarks, historical buildings, and a history of Orlando. The local museum provides an outreach package that helps the students make a timeline of major events in Orlando's past. The entire class takes a field trip to the Orlando Historical Museum.

### Science

In this area the students study animals and plants indigenous to the Orlando area. They also research the history of Lake Eola and conduct water analysis experiments using water samples retrieved during the Walk across Orlando.

### Math

In this area the students study lapsed time by using the dates of the historical buildings studied in geography. Also, they learn how to draw an Orlando map to scale and to calculate the distances they walk on the Walk across Orlando.

### Summary Composition

All students are required at the end of the classroom phase of the project to write a comparison/contrast composition by comparing Orlando with any other city they have lived in or visited.

### The Walk

This is undoubtedly the most popular phase of the unity. The students are divided into four groups. A city bus ride is used to get everyone to the downtown area. Prearranged tours include such places as a bank, public library, Church Street Station, several churches, WFTV Channel Nine, and Lake Eola. Part of the day is spent locating the historical buildings, and another part is enjoying lunch at a local park. The students then return to the school on a city bus.

*15* *Curriculum Unit*   Dickens' England

*Subject Areas*   English, social studies, music, art, foods, clothing

*Recommended Grade Levels*   Middle school

*Summary*   Through a series of activities, students will gain an appreciation of the writer Charles Dickens.

*Objectives*

- To enlighten students about the Victorian period in England and encourage cultural awareness of this period
- To teach students the etiquette of the period and promote good manners
- To promote an appreciation of live theater
- To prepare students to watch "A Christmas Carol" from a different frame of reference

*School and Contact Person*

East Hills Middle School
2800 Kensington Road
Bloomfield Hills, MI 48304
(313) 332-9286

Donald Hillman, Principal
Liz Golding

*Procedures*   Dickens' Day (these activities should be done two or three weeks ahead)

1. In classes various works of Charles Dickens we discussed and a study of Victorian England was undertaken through customs, traditions, and behavior.
2. Students studied the dress of the Victorian period. A costumer from professional theater presented a talka bout the clothing of the period. The students had the opportunity to model some costumes reflecting the period. The costumer also spoke to the students about proper etiquette for their trip to see "A Christmas Carol."
3. In home economics class, the students made scones and shortbread for a tea.
4. Students had the opportunity to see films of *David Copperfield* and *Oliver Twist.*
5. The day before Dickens' Day, all students made tea sandwiches using fancy cutters. They also made Devonshire cream for the scones.

**Dickens' Day**

On Dickens' Day, from 8:30 A.M. to 12:00 noon, students went to five mini-sessions entitled "Dickens' England."

1. The students made Victorian cutouts and designed a Victorian outfit on them and then colored it in. Another art activity had the students making fancy windows of the Victorian period using black paper and brightly colored paper to fit into the cutout designs, similar to stained glass.
2. The students attended a class discussing the life of Charles Dickens.
3. In another class the students heard a talk about England and viewed a slide show about the country.
4. In the fourth session the students discussed the British influence on rock music. (The students decided the Victorian period music was not as motivating for them.)
5. The last session was a class on Victorian etiquette, particularly the formal way to have tea. The students came dressed for tea.

For the tea a Victorian tea table was set with lace, silver tea service, and candles. The background was a Victorian window draped with attractive period draperies. The student's mothers served the tea and the following items.

- Scones with Devonshire cream and raspberry jam.
- Shortbread
- Tea and finger sandwiches of various kinds: cucumber, cream cheese and date nut, cream cheese and pineapple layered with egg salad, cream cheese and watercress, and cinnamon twists.

### Post-Dickens' Day

After Dickens' Day students were treated to a field trip to a professional theater to see the production of "A Christmas Carol." The following day the students were asked to do a writing assignment describing one of the activities using unusual descriptive words and details.

## 16 Kentucky-Tennessee Experience

This 47-page curriculum unit involves a three-day field trip through Kentucky and Tennessee. The trip is divided into three "experiences." The first is a visit to Chattanooga, Tennessee, where students visit the Confederama Hall of History, Ruby Falls, the Rock City Gardens, and the Chattanooga Choo-Choo. The second experience is in Nashville, Tennessee. Here the students learn about the founding of the city, the role of Native Americans, the importance of the Cumberland River to the development of the city, the Civil War battles fought in the area, a visit to the Ryman Auditorium (the Grand Ole Opry House), the Parthenon (full-size replica of the ancient Parthenon of Greece), and the Hermitage (Andrew Jackson's home). The third experience is a guided tour of the Mammoth Caves National Park in Kentucky. For each of the stops on the field trip, students are required to complete worksheets on what they have seen. The trip incorporates units of study from art, English, social studies, and science.

*Contact*

Greater Atlanta Christian School (junior high)
P.O. Box 4277
Norcross, GA 30091
(404) 923-9230

William Burton, Principal
Elaine McGuire
Brad Kinser
Pamela Cook
Michael White

## *17* We Didn't Start the Fire

Using the theme of Billy Joel's popular song of the same name (Storm Front) this unit encourages students to write their own newspaper. After watching the music video of this song, students are divided into small groups and instructed to collect topics for each year from 1975 to the present. They may choose events, people, "things" such as inventions and discoveries, literature (all kinds), concepts, and so on. Events can be political, economic, scientific, or social. Each group of students should determine which topics are most important for each year (six or seven topics). Students are encouraged to find and include topics that have been less publicized or may seem obscure but are no less important in their influence. In writing the paper, students should write in the present tense, and in organizing the articles should use the format of a real newspaper. Special features may be included, such as a comic section and advertising.

*Contact*

Canyon Vista Middle School
8455 Spicewood Springs Road
Austin, TX 78759-1049
(512) 331-1666

Don Dalton, Principal
Cathy Miller

## 18  Annual Science Olympiad

Students in this junior high school are divided into small groups for each of the five events. Each event requires teamwork, group planning, and cooperation. The five events are linked to particular courses. They are an Egg Drop (science and social studies), Bridge Building (math), Picture This (reading), Sail Car Races (English), and Pentathlon (physical education and electives).

The Egg Drop involves students designing and building a container to safely protect an egg dropped from varying heights. The Bridge Building contest involves building a bridge of certain measurements and materials that will hold the strongest weight. Picture This is much like Pictionary except that students must draw scientific terms or concepts. For the Sail Car races, students design and sail cars built to certain specifications using index cards and glue. The cars are moved across the race floor by students blowing into a straw. The Pentathlon involves each team traversing five obstacles on a course similar to the television program "Battle of the Network Stars." The team that spills the least amount of water wins.

### Contact

Helen Cannon Junior High School
5850 Euclid Avenue
Las Vegas, NV 89120
(702) 799-5610

Teri Smith, Principal
Monte Bay

## *19*  Middle East

This unit helps students understand the geography and the strategic location of the Middle East as measured by maps. It also helps the students understand the similarities and differences among the various Middle East cultures. In math the students identify the Syrian numerals 1–10 and Arabic money as measured by worksheets. In science the students note the similarities and differences in weather conditions between the Middle East and the United States as measured by daily graphing activities. In language arts the students write letters to people in Saudi Arabia. During Operation Desert Storm the students wrote to the soldiers. Other activities include guest speakers, mosque drawings with Islamic beliefs, authentic clothing from Saudi Arabia, and artifacts and slides of the Middle East.

### Contact

Caloosa Middle School
610 South Del Prado Boulevard
Cape Coral, FL 33990
(813) 574-3232

Marilynn Strong, Principal
Debra Hanson
Teri Theall
Catherine Schons
Yvonne Isaac
Debbie Schieber

## 20   Reader's Digest

The students create their own version of the *Reader's Digest*, including sections like Word Power, Life in these United States, Campus Comedy, Condensed Novels, and a Travel Diary. To complete this project, students learn how to develop skills such as locating the main idea, increasing vocabulary, reinforcing, outlining, condensing, collecting data, and presenting facts in a story form. All areas of study are incorporated in this project.

*Contact*

Timberland Regional Middle School
44 Greenough Road
Plaistow, NH 03865
(603) 382-7131

Deborah Rogers-Thorton

## 21   The Planets

This unit is presented during four class periods, two in the music class and two in the school's planetarium. In music class the students study the composer Gustav Holst and his orchestral suite *The Planets*. Discussion of mythology and the physical characteristics of the planets helps students to understand how Holst's composition incorporates certain elements of music. The third lesson in the planetarium allows students to see the planet's physical characteristics. The final day of the unit combines music and planet viewing. During each of the classes, students complete worksheets to help them understand the planetary system.

*Contact*

Arcola Intermediate School
Eagleville Road
Norristown, PA 19403
(215) 631-9404

Anrew Case, Principal
Joyce Bustard
M. Eileen Meko
Ted Williams
Gerald Mallon

## 22    Manufacturing Technology

This eighteen-week unit makes students aware of the technological problems facing the nation. It shows students how mathematics, science, and technology are used both by business and in everyday life. Students first form then buy stock in a corporation. The class then chooses, designs, and conducts market research for a product. The class analyzes costs for the product and determines its profit margin. Orders for the product are then taken and manufacturing begins. Students learn and control every phase of the corporation, including accounting and using a computer.

A second part of the class activities centers on how to learn to use a computer to control a plotter and a study of basic electronics through the design of a computer control circuit. Using a software program called SASA, Jr., the students control rocket launches and analyze flight data.

*Contact*

Wasson Middle School
Forrest and Gorgas Avenues
Fort Campbell, KY 42223-5000
(502) 439-1832

Carolyn Dove, Principal
Worth Lovett

## 23  Storytelling through Dance

The curriculum for this unit explores the aesthetics of dance and the experience of movement. Based on the belief that children need to have interactive experiences in arts education, each of the study units of this curriculum begins with the children recalling events and familiar situations shared with their classmates. New information is introduced by the teacher or discovered as a class. The different units investigate the relationship of movement and nonverbal communication with dance, the relationship of music to dance, the relationship of the choreographer to dancers, and that of the audience to the performers. Students learn how to "read" dance, to interpret movement, and to articulate wht they see.

The final unit of study reviews the information explored and challenges the students to synthesize the experiences by creating a theater/dance piece that illuminates the process of creating a ballet. This curriculum unit can integrate language arts, reading, music, art, and physical education subject matter. The curriculum units were written by the New York City Ballet Education Department. Performing artists from the New York City Ballet visit the school, an educational ballet is performed at the school, and students have the opportunity to go to Lincoln Center in New York City to view a ballet production.

*Contacts*

Anne M. Dorner Middle School
Van Cortlandt Avenue
Ossining, NY 10562
(914) 762-5740

Richard E. Maurer, Principal
Faye Dittelman
Kellie Reardon
Jane Hackenburg
Victoria Wessman

At the New York City Ballet, contact:
Michelle Audet, Director
Mararet Foley, Assistant Director
37 West 65th Street, 6th Floor
New York, NY 10023

# Section Three
# High School Curriculum

*H*igh school curricula are usually driven by state, county, school district, or even citywide testing programs. As a result, the curriculum is very rich in content. To prepare for the tests, teachers need to cover a great quantity of material in a very brief time period.

High school teachers are often under enormous pressure to cover the material. The thought of doing something new usually elicits complaints that there is no time in the curriculum. Integrating curricula can be seen as an extra time burden. However, if planning is done correctly, a teacher can integrate curriculum units with other teachers and still cover the required curriculum. In this section there are many excellent examples of how this can be accomplished.

Some themes emerge from the curricula units that have been collected. The first is a heavy emphasis on skill acquisition. Three units (History in the Making, Research Skills, Visions of the Future) that ask students to learn to use computer and research skills. These skills are fused with specific curriculum content, but the processes acquired are universal and can be applied to other disciplines. In these units students should learn how to use a computer for word processing and to access and manipulate information, as well as learn how to apply a process of issue analysis.

A second theme is technology. Four units (Rocketry, Amusement Park Science, Algebra/Chemistry, and Food Science) emphasize students' learning how to use technology to understand and to solve problems. A third theme is helping students understand their role and responsibility in today's world. Four units (Psychology in Literature, Pursuing the Dream: Puritans and

*Immigration. This Land Is Your Land, Visions of the Future)* ask students to define their personal place in their world. Identity development is a major phase of a high school student's life. These units, in unique ways, help students craft an understanding of how life fits together. A fourth theme is regional emphasis. There are three units (*The Southern Way, The Creation and Organization of the Pacific Northwest States, Study Trips*) that immerse students in the life and culture of specific regions. In the case of *Study Trips*, the region is all of Europe.

These units offer a wide variety of organizational sequences. Some are very detailed (*Pursuing the Dream: Puritans and Immigration, Algebra/Chemistry, Research Skills*), some preempt the school day (*Dickens' England, Philosopher's Party, Scholar's Academy*), and some have themes that change each year (*Journeys, Scholars' Academy*).

**24** *Curriculum Unit*  Like the Stars That Never Set: A Study of Native American Cultures of the Pacific Northwest

*Subject Areas*  English, and history

*Recommended Grade Levels*  High school

*Summary*  In understanding the history of the state of Washington as well as that of our entire nation, it is important for students to recognize that there was a group of people here before the arrival of the white settlers. This unit will help students understand the past and present cultural diversity of the nation.

*Objectives*

- To understand early Native American cultures of the Pacific Northwest
- To work cooperatively in analyzing, synthesizing, and evaluating information
- To develop creative and productive problem solvers
- To complete five higher order thinking skills (HOTS) activities
- To face and solve five moral and ethical dilemmas

*School and Contact Persons*

Anacortes High School
20th and J Avenue
Anacortes, WA 98221
(206) 293-2166

John Irion, Principal
Kevin Miller
Mark Knight

*Procedures*  This unit is organized according to the ten foundational activities of humans as developed by Dr. Roger Taylor. If you are interested in further information about this theory, consult *Using Integrated, Thematic Teaching Strategies to Increase Student Achievement and Motivation* by Roger Taylor.

With each of the ten basic human activities specific tasks are required of the students. The tasks themselves are organized according to Bloom's taxonomy: Knowledge, Comprehension, Application, and High-Order Thinking Skills (Analysis, Synthesis, and Evaluation). In this unit, High-Order Thinking Skills are called HOTS Projects. Listed below are the ten foundational activities with their corresponding tasks.

**Pacific Northwest Indians**

The following material is organized under ten foundational activities of humans.

### 1. Economics, Transportation, Tool-making

*Knowledge*

Identify means of survival.
Identify means of exchange.
Identify means of transportation.
Identify means of making tools.
Identify routes of travel.

*Comprehension*

Distinguish between eastern and western tribes.
Understand environmental connections with goods produced.

*Application*

Demonstrate means of exchange.
Draw a map of tribes and trade routes.
Demonstrate methods of production.
Make models of tools.
Demonstrate fishing methods.

*HOTS Projects*

Why did specific Indian tribes choose to live where they lived?
Where are there different Indian tribes?
Where did the Indian tribes come from?
Compare the economic system of the Northwestern tribes with tribes elsewhere.
Compare myths of economics of the Northwestern Indians with myths from other cultures.
Evaluate the effectiveness of transportation and relate it to the strength of individual tribes.
Evaluate the effect of the horse on Indian society.
Compare reservation economics with prereservation economics.

### 2. Communications

*Knowledge*

List means of communication.
List different languages.

*Comprehension*

Distinguish between eastern and western tribal languages.
Generalize similarities and differences between tribal languages.

*Application*

> Make a map of language differences.
> Draw pictographs.
> Demonstrate different means of communicating.

*HOTS Projects*

> How did communication contribute to the relative strength and weakness of tribes?
> Why didn't Indian tribes have written languages?
> How did specialized trade languages enhance economics between tribes and the general relationship between tribes?

### 3. Protecting and Conserving

*Knowledge*

> List ways of preserving traditions.
> List tribal ways of protecting culture, life, good, etc.
> List tribal ways of conserving and maintaining tribal life.

*Comprehension*

> Explain differences of preservation.
> Explain differences of conservation.

*Application*

> Demonstrate modern means of conserving.
> Demonstrate modern means of preserving family traditions.
> Survey student attitudes toward conservation.
> Chart modern military strategy and early Indian military strategy.

*HOTS Projects*

> Why didn't the tribes have a garbage problem?
> How did certain tribes dominate?
> Explain different myths of conservation found in different cultures.

### 4. Providing Education/Moral, Ethical, Religious Behavior

*Knowledge*

> List methods of tribal education.
> List methods of tribal discipline.
> List tribal religious rituals.

*Comprehension*

Explain differences in male and female upbringing.
Distinguish between tribes and methods.

*Application*

Write a story.
Tell a story that educates a young Indian tribal member.

*HOTS Projects*

How would we be different today if our educational system adopted the
North American Indian philosophy of education?

How did the educational methods ofcertain tribes contribute to their strengths
or weaknesses?

Does tribal education today work at maintaining culture?

**5. *Providing Recreation/Aesthetic Needs***

*Knowledge*

List free-time activities of tribal Indians.
List ways tribal Indians beautified their environment.
List types of Indian art.

*Comprehension*

Distinguish between eastern and western tribal art.
Distinguish between competitive and noncompetitive Indian recreation.

*Application*

Draw (model after an Indian art work).
Sculpt.
Play an Indian game.
Demonstrate a different form of Indian recreation.

*HOTS Projects*

Compare the value of recreation in Indian society and in our own society.
Compare contemporary Indian art to prereservation art.
Research the influence of Native American art on modern art.

**Moral/Ethical/Spiritual Reasoning Dilemmas**

In this section of the unit the students deal with moral, ethical, and spiritual issues
that are part of the ten foundations of human activities.

*1. Economics*   You are a Native American person on a modern reservation worried about many of your people who are unable to provide for themselves. Suggestions have been made that your tribe build a bingo parlor in order to create jobs. You disagree with this idea, saying it is degrading to your culture. Your idea is to increase hunting, fishing, and trade by traditional means. How would you convince others that this is the correct way?

*2. Communication*   You are one of the last remaining resources of the old Indian culture. You speak the tribal language and practice many of the old traditions. Your grandson and his friends have no interest in learning this language and traditions. How do you convince them that this is important?

*3. Protecting and Conserving*   You have been given the task of putting together a potlatch for your tribe. You are ready and willing to give away your most treasured possessions, with the exception of your favorite horse. This horse is known throughout the tribe for his beauty and strength. You scheme to find a way to keep the horse. What would you do? At the conclusion of the ceremony, one of the tribal elders asks about the treasured horse. How do you explain the horse's unavailability?

*4. Providing Education/Moral, Ethical, Religious Behavior*   You are the chief of an Indian tribe and the head of a reservation school. There has been a great deal of pressure put upon you to teach skills that the students can use to find jobs off the reservation. However, you believe in strict tribal traditions and the teachings associated with them. How do you convince people that your beliefs and teachings are for the betterment of the tribe?

*5. Recreation/Aesthetic Needs*   Your tribe has decided to build an eighteen-hole golf course on the reservation. The land necessary for the course will cut into much of the old timber left untouched on the reservation as a natural reserve. You have been chosen to speak for a small group of tribal people opposed to the eighteen-hole golf course and the destruction of the old growth timber. Prepare and present a five- to ten-minute speech attempting to persuade the tribe not to build the course.

**Productive Thinking Skills**

In this section the students develop divergent and creative thinking by completing the activities listed under each specific productive thinking model.

*1. Brainstorm Model*

   Indian tribes you can name
   Stereotypes you can think of
   Movies or books about Indian people
   Ways to save energy
   Counties in Washington
   Ways to improve Anacortes
   Names of cities in Washington

Fish of Washington
Mountains of Washington
Birds
Evergreen trees
Environmental improvements
Make a picture
Tell a story

Cook food
Use blackberries
Show your patriotism
Catch a butterfly
Avoid a way
Avoid a fight with an enemy
Understand honey bees

### 2. Viewpoint Model

How would _____ look to a _____?
A map of Washington/prereservation Indian
Bill of Rights/reservation Indian
Potlach/investment banker
Totem pole/African Immigrant
Hell/prereservation Indian
Credit card/prereservation Indian
Reservation/German Jew

Forest/logger
Forest/prereservation Indian
Forest/spotted owl
Forest/backpacker
River/fish
River/sportsfisherman
River/fisherman
Fence/prereservation Indian
Seasons/prereservation Indian
Fossil/scientist
Pictograph/archaeologist, Indian, tourist

Totem pole/historian, Indian tribesman

*Northwest Prereservation Indian View*

Acid rain
Barbed wire
Alzheimer's disease
Dreams
Northern Lights
Eruption of Mount St. Helens
Woodland Park Zoo

**3. *Involvement Model*** How would you feel if you were:

An Indian forced on a reservation
Army general ordered to put Indian people on a reservation
The last person on earth
Forced to give up your car and ride a bike only
Indian grandfather working in a shopping mall
Captured by an Indian tribe
Indian child reaching the age of adulthood

If you were a _____, what would you sense?

Salmon in a river
Eagle
200-year-old tree
Mole
Fly caught in a spider web
Snake in a zoo cage
Whale in the ocean

I only know about _____, explain _____ to me.

Wind/typhoon
Oysters/pearl
Sun/Northern Lights
Universe/infinity
Butterflies/metamorphosis
sunlight/photosynthesis
Life/death

You are a _____; describe how it feels.

Fish in a net
Eagle in the sky
Coyote in the woods
Mole underground
Indian chief
Indian boy on first hunt
Indian in big city for the first time

**4. *Conscious Self-Deceit Model*** Suppose you could have anything you wanted; what ideas could you produce if this were true?

Medicine
War
Education
Pollution
Poverty
Drug abuse
Extinction of animals

**5. Forced Association Model**   How is a _____ like a _____?

  Myth/cloud
  Gang/Indian tribe
  Tidepool/universe
  Bird/ballerina
  Totem pole/tree
  Rivers/blood veins
  Life/circle

Get ideas from _____ to improve your _____.

  Death/life
  Native Americans/environment
  Myth of Pandora/understanding of disease
  Babies/perception
  Pendulum/golf swing
  Garden/love life
  Music/car engine

I only know about _____; explain _____ to me.

  Wind/typhoon
  Sun/Northern Lights
  Universe/infinity
  Butterflies/metamorphosis
  Christmas/potlatch
  Sunlight/photosynthesis
  Anger/racial prejudice

**6. Reorganization Model**   What would happen if _____ were true?

  Indian Ghost Dance
  Animals could talk
  Life on Mars
  Santa Claus

Suppose _____ happened; what would be the consequences?

  Cure for aids
  Reservation warfare
  Major rivers dried up
  Mount Baker erupted
  Major earthquake hit Seattle
  Elvis was found alive and well and living in Anacortes

What would happen if there were no _____?

  Nuclear weapons
  Spiders

Care
Schools
Diseases
Radios
Borders

**I-Search Independent Research Projects**

Students seeking an "A" in this course will complete one I-search project.

**1.** *Paradox:* How in the land of the free could a reservation system of containing a conquered people be created and enforced?
Research the beginnings of the reservation system in America. Write a paper that includes charts, maps, pictures about the founding of the reservation system and its perpetuation. Include a modern-day perspective.

**2.** *Attributes:* Research tribal characteristics for tribal people of four different cultures. Prepare a report showing the similarities and differences, and attempt to explain them.

**3.** *Analogies:* Using a detailed structural analysis of tribal organization, show an analagous relationship with an organizational structure within the world of nature.

**4.** *Discrepancies:* Attempt to trace the early beginnings of tribal delineation. Focus primarily on the tribes of the Northwest. Prepare a paper and a presentation including charts and maps. Be sure to distinguish between what is known and what is merely conjecture.

**5.** *Provocative questions:* What is the future of the reservation system in America? What would happen if the reservation system were abolished? What would happen if the reservations united and formed their own nation apart from the United States?

**6.** *Examples of change:* Working with tribal leaders on the Swinomish reservation, find out as much as you can about how the reservation has changed over the years. Also speculate on the future of the tribe. What are its goals and aspirations for its people.

**7.** *Examples of habit:* How has the Bureau of Indian Affairs managed or mismanaged the reservation system from its beginning? Pay special attention to mistakes seemingly repeated by this bureaucracy. Attempt to explain the thinking process or cultural proclivities leading to repeated errors.

**8.** *Organized random search:* Assume you are the governor of the state in the late nineteenth century. You have the opportunity to establish a system of governing that incorporates the various Indian tribes into state rule. Create a detailed plan, and outline an action-education plan to sell your plan to the legislature and the public.

**9.** *Skills of search:* The salmon plays an important role in the industry of the Pacific Northwest. Historically, this fish has played an even greater role in society. The Native Americans held certain beliefs and practiced rituals directed toward the salmon. Direct a search centered on how this fish has been viewed and used throughout history. Be sure to concentrate on religious beliefs and also the reality of a declining fish population. Also look at our methods today of keeping strong salmon runs year after year.

**10.** *Tolerance of ambiguity:* It is strongly believed that the people who made up the great civilizations of the Incas, Aztecs, and Mayana are of the same origins as the North American Indian people. Why did these southern people develop differently from their northern relatives? Discuss the differences between these groups and draw some conclusions that might explain this situation.

**11.** *Intuitive expression:* Assume you are an Indian child on a journey to prove your adulthood. Keep a journal of your observations. Include sights, sounds, feelings, and other sensory observations. Include a detailed map of the journey. Make it a circular route.

**12.** *Adjustment to development:* Research the relationship between the many problems Northwestern Indians face today and the growing technology of our state and nation. Have these problems developed because of the increasing complexity of life, or are they simply due to the character of the modern Indian? What mistakes have we made today in dealing with reservation Indians that may have added to their problems? How can we learn from these mistakes in order to help solve Native American difficulties?

**13.** *Study creative people and process:* Examine the lives and thoughts of the great chiefs and thinkers of the Native Americans, past and present. How were they able to achieve greatness? What can we learn from their thoughts and actions?

**14.** *Evaluate situations:* Assume you are an Indian chief alive in the mid-eighteenth century. You have heard and seen evidence that another culture of "white" people is moving your way. You decide to meet this intruding culture with as much strength as you can muster. You set out to unite the tribes of the Northwest into one unified force. Write a historical-fiction account of your attempts to do this. Take the story in any direction you want, but fill it with real names and places. Include a detailed map.

**15.** *Creative reading skill:* Develop a bibliography of modern American Indian writers. Read at least three different works and write a paper demonstrating your insights and understanding.

**16.** *Creative listening skill:* Tape record interviews with Indian and non-Indian people regarding life on and off the reservation. Edit the recordings to produce an audio documentary at least 30 minutes and no more than 90 minutes long.

**17.** *Creative writing skill:* Write a novel set in the prereservation Indian Northwest. Try for authenticity and entertainment.

**18.** *Visualization skill:* Create a booklet of illustrations of Indian life. Include a landscape of Anacortes as seen from Cap Sante prior to the white settlers' arrival.

**25**  *Curriculum Unit*  Psychology in Literature

*Recommended Grade Level*  High school

*Subject Areas*  Social science, language arts

*Summary*  This course is designed to enable the student to understand psychological concepts and issues especially relevant to their lives, including such things as identity development, the emergence and modification of self-image, love and its various definitions, guilt and shame, suicide, grief, motivation and goals, self-discipline, and stress management. The study of these concepts and issues will be integrated with the study of selected pieces of literature in which these same concepts and issues are addressed.

*Objectives*

- To encourage students to think
- To allow students to examine issues relevant to their own lives
- To examine the biases and assumptions related to the different psychological theories.

*School and Contact Person*

Heritage High School
1401 West Gedded Avenue
Littleton, CO 80120
(303) 795-1353

James Ferguson, Principal
Tony Winger
Jill Rickard

*Procedure*  The course follows the outline provided. Evaluation is based on the student's ability to support the conclusions the student draws and on the student's ability to demonstrate application. The course involves working in groups, listening to guest speakers, creating role plays, maintaining journals, and writing essays. In addition to the books listed here, the course is supplemented with handouts and readings by the student. The course includes a packet of resource materials, ideas, and activities developed in a workshop by Dr. Roger Taylor.

**Psychology in Literature: Resources List**

The study of the material in these books will be reinforced with class discussions, with writing, and with activities that are intended to challenge students to think. Immediate application of the material in the psychology book will be provided through our study of the novels and other literature.

*I'm O.K.—You're O.K. by Thomas A. Harris, M.D.*   Harris's discussion of the "parent," "adult," and "child" as the three states of being within every individual will offer one theory on how an individual can understand himself and, with that understanding, move toward adulthood. This, then, will be a valuable resource for our units on identity development and on love.

*Ordinary People by Judith Guest*   Guest's *Ordinary People* traces Conrad Jarrett's search for identity as he struggles with the issues of his brother's death, his own suicide attempt, and his perceived failure to meet his mother's expectations. This will be the perfect companion piece for Harris's book and for our unit on identity development, particularly our study of the affects of the family.

*Way of the Peaceful Warrior by Dan Millman*   Millman's book, *Way of the Peaceful Warrior*, is a fictional account of his own growth and development through progressive stages of maturity as he faces life's trials and challenges. Millman's description of his life journey will be another means for exploring various methods for modifying self-image and reaching adulthood. In addition, this book will provide an opportunity to recognize and apply other theories studied in class.

*I Heard the Owl Call My Name by Margret Craven*   Craven's book is the story of a priest, Mark Brian, as he established a parish among the Indians of the Northwest. Moreover, it is a study of love as Mark learns it—love of self, love of others, love of community, and love of his god. This novel, along with selected poetry, will be the fictional part of our consideration of what love is and is not.

**Psychology in Literature: Tentative Course Outline**

I. Identity development
   A. Theories
      1. Learning theories
      2. Cognitive theories

Judith Guest
*Ordinary People*
      3. Psychoanalytic theories
      4. Humanistic theories
      5. Transactional analysis
   B. The effects of family
      1. As related to identity development theories
      2. Transactional analysis (Harris Chapters 2, 3, 5)
      3. Family systems (Bradshaw)
      4. Peck
   C. Determinism versus free will (Harris Chapter 4)
      1. Skinner versus Carl Rogers

Dan Millman:
*Way of the Peaceful Warrior*
      2. Harris (p. 86)
      3. Maslow—Combination of determinism and free will
      4. Thoreau and Emerson
   D. Recognizing and strengthening free will/becoming an adult (Harris Chapters 4, 6, 9, 10)

1. Discipline (Peck)
2. Putting adult in charge
   a. Emerson
   b. Emancipated adult (TA)
3. Reparenting
4. Developing life principles
   a. Purpose
   b. Making adult choices
5. Visualization techniques/affirmation
6. Goal setting and motivation
7. Bradshaw's recovery process
8. Maslow's self-actualization and growth factors

II. Love
   A. Definitions of what love is (Peck)
   B. Clarification of what love is not (Peck)
      1. Infatuation/falling in love
      2. Dependency
      3. Self-sacrifice
      4. Cathexis
   C. **TA—Games as substitutes for intimacy** (Harris Chapter 7)
   D. TA and marriage (Harris Chapter 8)
   E. Maslow
   F. Self-worth (Harris Chapter 12)
   G. Social responsibility

Selected poetry
and Margaret Craven:
*I Heard the Owl Call
My Name*

III. Healthy and dysfunctional life responses (substitutes for adulthood)
   A. Dealing with Grief
   B. Guilt and shame versus autonomy
   C. Escapes versus discipline
      1. Suicide
      2. Drugs
      3. Runaways
      4. Eating disorders
   D. Stress versus stress management
   E. Depression versus mental health (Peck, p. 291)

Independent reading
selections chosen from
bibliography

*26* *Curriculum Unit*  History in the Making

*Subject Areas*  English, history, computer

*Recommended Grade Levels*  High school

*Summary*  This course of study is intended to integrate instruction in word processing with work on English and social studies specific to eighth and ninth grades.

*Objectives*  Students will:

- Earn a "Maclicense" indicating that they have mastered the operations of a word-processing system.
- Learn how to integrate English and social studies curriculum content.
- Create a newspaper that demonstrates use of information and imagination.

*School and Contact Person*

Convent of the Sacred Heart
1 East 91st Street
New York, NY 10128
(212) 722-4745

Nancy Salisbury, RSCJ, Principal
Ian Humphreys
Elizabeth Poreba
Maura Ollo

*Procedures*

1. *"Maclicense"*: The students receive detailed instruction in the operation of Microsoft Workplus Spell. They complete the first four of fourteen lessons in the computer lab. The students then can earn their "Maclicense" by successfully demonstrating that they have certain skills. They then move on to complete a folder called "Essay Writing." This contains six pre- and postwriting exercises that integrate the content of social studies with a novel studied concurrently in English.

As part of this unit, students are introduced to a database file called "Booklist." They are asked to fill in their summer reading and to keep an ongoing record of their outside reading. Later in the year, the class will use the data from their booklists to formulate conclusions about their reading tastes. Later in the school year the students will be shown how to create their own files in conjunction with social studies projects.

Finally, the students are introduced to Hypercard. In groups, they will create stacks that tell stories illustrating various areas of social studies with buttons connecting to new vocabulary.

**2.** *Quest:* This unit is a search or pursuit made in order to find or obtain something (as defined by the *American College Dictionary*). Students are required to read *The Odyssey* in English class as they study ancient Mediterranean civilizations in social studies.

Students must create their own quest story. They may be as inventive as they like, but they must include the following:

- An invocation to the muse at the beginning
- A worthy goal, pursued by a worthy hero or heroine
- At least one danger
- At least one temptation
- Historically correct details
- Geographically correct settings
- A heartwarming reunion scene in the conclusion

The quest must also be:

- Set somewhere within the ancient Mediterranean world
- At least five typed pages
- Printed in the format you set up in the "Format" file

A map of the hero or heroine's voyage must be included.

This quest takes about three weeks or six periods in the computer lab to complete.

**3.** *Network News Article:* This unit requires that students work in cooperative groups to produce newspapers. These papers are related to the period the students are studying at the time. Some examples are:

- "Roman Times"—Dateline March 15, 44 B.C., the date of Caesar's assassination
- "Revolution Times"—Dateline 1770, the events leading up to the American Revolution

**27**  *Curriculum Unit*  Algebra/Chemistry

*Recommended Grade Levels*  High School

*Subject Areas*  Algebra (second year), chemistry

*Summary*  In algebra classes the students learn math concepts that will expand their knowledge of seven topics in chemistry.

*Objectives*

- To demonstrate to students the ability to adapt one curriculum to meet the needs of another
- To enhance math and science conceptual skills
- To improve long-term memory for concepts in math and science

*School and Contact Person*

Niles Township High Schools
7701 Lincoln Avenue
Skokie, IL 60077
(708) 673-6822

Carolyn S. Anderson, Assistant Superintendent
Donald Ring, Principal, Niles West
Thomas Giles, Principal, Niles North
Dorothy Fugie
Kathy Kelly
Jerry Oswald
Frank Sticha

*Procedure*  The committee of teachers who designed this unit found that about 45 percent of all students enrolled in Chemistry 12 were concurrently enrolled in Algebra 3–4. The unit addresses several topics designated by chemistry teachers as areas that require extensive use of math concepts and skills. Coverage of these topics in both math and science would greatly enhance conceptualization for the students and long-term retention.

*Table of Contents*

  **F.** Proportionality
  **G.** Logarithms
  **H.** Stem-leaf diagrams: boxplots

**III.** Project evaluation

### Topic A: Metric Measure

*Concerns*

1. As students are required to use units when recording answers to calculations in science classes, it is recommended that math teachers at least encourage students to record answers to application questions with *proper units.*
2. *Metric* units should be used whenever possible.
3. Some calculations are unit specific. For example, gas law problems must be handled in Kelvin, rather than Celsius or Fahrenheit temperatures.
4. The development and use of scientific constants are unit-based. Examples include Planck's constant and the gas law constant (R).
5. Occasionally the measurements in a problem are given without matching units. Students must know how to deal with conversions before tackling the calculation.

### Topic B: Unit Analysis/Factor-label Method

*Concerns*   This is the method of calculation used most commonly in chemistry. It would be helpful if algebra teachers could encourage its use at various times throughout the year. UCSMP Algebra refers to this method as the "rate model."

*Sample Problems*

1. A man raises 100 goats and then trades them for a sheep at a rate of 6 goats for 7 sheep. Next he exchanges his sheep for hogs at a rate of 4 sheep for 2 hogs weighing 250 lbs. each. He sold the hogs at a market price of \$97 per 100 lbs. How much money did he make?

$$100 \text{ goats} \times \frac{7 \text{ sheep}}{6 \text{ goats}} \times \frac{2 \text{ hogs}}{4 \text{ sheep}} \times \frac{250 \text{ lbs}}{1 \text{ hog}} \times \frac{\$97}{100 \text{ lbs}} = \$14,145.83$$

2. How many seconds are there in 2.5 years?

$$2.5 \text{ years} \times \frac{365 \text{ days}}{1 \text{ year}} \times \frac{24 \text{ hrs}}{1 \text{ day}} \times \frac{60 \text{ min}}{1 \text{ hr}} \times \frac{60 \text{ sec}}{1 \text{ min}} = 7.9 \times 10^7 \text{ sec}$$

3. It is estimated that 238 million tons of pollutants enter the air above the U.S. each year. Convert this figure to lbs per person per day. (Assume the population of the U.S. to be 250 million.)

$$\frac{2.38 \times 10^8 \text{ tons}}{1 \text{ year}} \times \frac{2 \times 10^3 \text{ lbs}}{1 \text{ ton}} \times \frac{1 \text{ year}}{365 \text{ days}}$$

$$\div \; 2.50 \times 10^8 \text{ persons} = 5.2 \text{ lbs/person/day}$$

4. If there are 4 glops in 3 lops and 7 lops in 5 swops and 6 swops on 2 frops, how many glops are in 15 frops?

$$15 \text{ frops} \quad \frac{6 \text{ swops}}{2 \text{ frops}} \times \frac{7 \text{ lops}}{5 \text{ swops}} \times \frac{4 \text{ glops}}{3 \text{ lops}} = 84 \text{ glops}$$

5. A car averages 65 km/hr while its gas consumption is 12.6 km/l. If gasoline costs $0.53/l, how much will it cost to drive for 4.75 hours?

**Topic C: Scientific Notation (Semester 1)**

*Outcomes*  Students will convert any number from decimal to scientific notation and vice versa. Students will add, subtract, multiply, or divide numbers written in scientific notation, rounding answers as to correct number of significant figures.

*Concerns*

1. Scientific notation requires that $1 \le$ coefficient $< 10$.
2. The coefficient is recorded with the appropriate number of significant figures.
3. Although algebra teachers rarely deal in actual measurement, the reinforcement of precision of instrument in terms of significant figures would be very valuable to science teachers.
4. Scientific notation should be reinforced throughout the curriculum for very large and very small numbers.
5. There are several algorithms for rounding numbers before a 5. At present in chemistry, to express the idea that 50 percent of the time the estimate is lower and 50 percent of the time the estimate is higher, odd numbers before a 5 are rounded up while even numbers before the 5 cause the 5 to be dropped.

Example:  4.315 $\longrightarrow$ 4.32
          8.465 $\longrightarrow$ 8.46
          (to the nearest hundredth)

**Topic D: Graphing**

*Chemistry Outcomes*

- Students will produce a graph based on data.
- Students will determine the effect of temperature on solubility by interpreting solubility.

**Applications of Linear Functions**

Chemistry teachers indicate that they need students to have a better understanding of and techniques for handling graphs or linear functions. Concerns would in the area of:

1. Setting up both horizontal and vertical axes by choosing appropriate units; for example, each unit mark might represent 10 different scales on each axis.

2. Looking at a graph on a grid where the domain is other than the "Dolciani Grid"; for example, the domain might be (2000, 500)
3. Plotting real data and finding line of best fit
4. Interpretation of data from a graph
5. Interpolating
6. Extrapolating beyond the domain used in the data

The following are problems the planning committee thought might address these concepts. It thought they could be used as (a) starter problems, (b) cooperative group work, or (c) general classroom discussions.

1. Given the following data, make a graph. Be sure to choose a large enough scale on each axis to handle all the data points.

| T[Temperature (Kelvins)] | 298 | 318 | 338 | 358 | 375 |
|---|---|---|---|---|---|
| V[Volume of air ($cm^3$)] | 20.0 | 21.5 | 22.7 | 23.2 | 24.5 |

   **a.** Draw a line that you think best fits the given data.
   **b.** Is it a direct proportion:

$$\left[ V = KT \text{ or } \frac{V}{T} = K \right] \quad \text{Explain}$$

   Volume [in $cm^3$] varies directly with temperature (Kelvins). Determine the constant of proportionality K (slope of the linear function)
   **c.** At a temperature of 325 Kelvins, what is the air volume?
   **d.** If the volume is 25 $cm^3$, then what is the temperature?
   **e.** At a temperature of 100 (Kelvin), what is the air volume?

*Note to teachers:*

1. Chemistry teachers would like to see math teachers pay more attention to units. In applications such as these, we should demand of students that they should include units on axes and expect proper units with answers. Quantities should always have units attached.
2. Answers should have an acceptable degree of accuracy. Significant digits are very important to scientists.

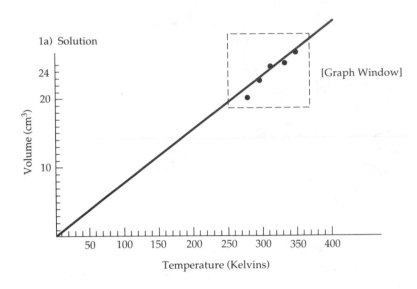

1a) Solution

[Graph Window]

Volume (cm³)

Temperature (Kelvins)

**1b.** Yes, it is a direct proportion. The line passes through the origin.

[Y = MX]   V = KT

$\dfrac{V}{T} = K$    $\dfrac{21.5}{318} = .0676$    $\dfrac{22.7}{338} = .0671$

$\dfrac{20.0}{298} = .067$    $\dfrac{23.2}{358} = .0642$    $\dfrac{24.5}{373} = .0656$

K = .067    [constant change of .067 cm³/K]

**1c.** $\dfrac{V}{325} = .067$    V = 21.8 cm³

**1d.** $\dfrac{24}{T} = .067$    T = 358 Kelvins

**1e.** $\dfrac{V}{100} = .067$    V = 6.7 cm³

### Inverse Variations

When data are graphed, data points will not always lie along a straight line. Students should be as comfortable dealing with the graphs of inverse variations [hyperbolas] as with direct variations.

The next two problems deal with graphing direct and inverse variation and distinguishing them from one another (and from other graphs). We emphasize:

### Problem 2

    **a.** Picking appropriate scales for horizontal and vertical axes
    **b.** Sketching curve of best fit and writing an equation
    **c.** Interpretation of data
    **\*d.** Interpolation between data points
    **\*e.** Extrapolation to points off the grid

*Problem 3* Given a set of data, from its graph, identify whether it is a linear function or an inverse variation, and be able to handle the appropriate mathematical model.

Although the solubilities of solids in liquids varies widely, generally increases in temperatures are associated with increased solubility. Two sets of data are given.

I.

KBr
(Potassium
bromide)

| | 60 | 70 | 80 | 90 | 100 | 110 | 120 |
|---|---|---|---|---|---|---|---|
| Solubility (g of KBr/100 g $H_2O$) | 85 | 92 | 97 | 102 | 109 | 112 | 118 |

II. $K_2Cr_2O_7$ (Potassium-dichromate)

| Temperature (°C) | 60 | 70 | 80 | 90 | 100 | 110 | 120 |
|---|---|---|---|---|---|---|---|
| Sol(g of $K_2Cr_2O_7$/100 g $H_2O$ | 48 | 58 | 70 | 90 | 110 | 140 | 190 |

For each set:

**a.** Graph the data.
**b.** Determine whether it is best described by a linear function, or an inverse variation, or neither.
**c.** If it is best described by a linear function, write the particular function equation that describes it.
**d.** If the temperature is 75 (°C), then what is the solubility?
**e.** If the solubility is 100 g/100 g $H_2O$, then what is the temperature?

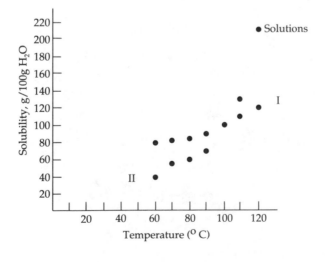

**3b.** Set I
Linear – Not a direct variation

Set                    II – Neither                    $\begin{bmatrix} \text{quadratic} \\ \text{exponential} \end{bmatrix}$  ??$\Big]$

**3c** Set I (80, 97)    (110, 112)

$$M = K = \frac{15}{30} = \frac{1}{2}$$

$$S - 112 = \frac{1}{2}(T - 110) \qquad S = \frac{1}{2}T + 57$$

**3d.** Set I
Solubility $===$
94.5g KBr/100 g $H_2O$

**3e.** Set II
(90,90)  (100,110)

$$20 \begin{bmatrix} d \begin{bmatrix} 90 & 90 \\ \times & 100 \\ 110 & 140 \end{bmatrix} 10 \\ \end{bmatrix} 50$$

d = 4
Temperature = 94 (°C)

*Problem 2*  According to Boyle's law, the volume of a gas and its pressure are inversely related; that is:

$$P(k\,Pa) = \frac{K}{V}(cm^3) \qquad \text{or} \qquad PV = K$$

**a.** Make a graph of the following data.

| Volume (cm³) | 100 | 132 | 164 | 196 | 228 | 260 |
|---|---|---|---|---|---|---|
| Pressure (kPa) | 30 | 22 | 18 | 15 | 13 | 11 |

**b.** Write the particular equation to describe the graph.
**c.** When the pressure is 160 (kPa), what is the volume?

*Problem 2*   (Solution)

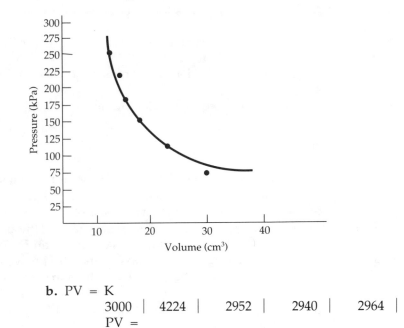

**b.** PV = K

        3000 | 4224 | 2952 | 2940 | 2964 | 2860
    PV =

**c.** (160)(V) =

*Problem 4*

*Student Problems*   A researcher measured the following frequencies and wave-lengths for visible light.

*Color*

| Red | $4.57 \times 10^{14}$ | $6.565 \times 10^{-7}$ |
|---|---|---|
| Orange | $5.25 \times 10^{14}$ | $5.714 \times 10^{-7}$ |
| Blue-green | $6.17 \times 10^{14}$ | $4.863 \times 10^{-7}$ |
| Blue | $6.91 \times 10^{14}$ | $4.343 \times 10^{-7}$ |
| Violet | $7.31 \times 10^{14}$ | $4.103 \times 10^{-7}$ |

**1.** Graph the relationship (be careful in choosing graph divisions)

**2.** Is the relationship direct: $\frac{f}{\lambda} = k$ (or inverse: $f\lambda = k$)

**3.** What is the value of k? Do you know the common name for this number?

*Instructors' Notes*

c = $f\lambda$

c = the speed of light in a vacuum = $3.0 \times 10^8$ m/sec
f = frequency of electromagnetic radiation
$\lambda$ = wavelength of electromagnetic radiation

### Topic E: Percent

*Outcomes*

- Students will calculate the percentage composition of each element in a compound when given the formula.
- Students will calculate weighted average masses of elements with multiple isotopes.
- Students will determine percentage yield in an experiment.

*Sample Problems*

1. If a sample of carbon monoxide (CO) weighs 66 g and the mass of the oxygen is 48 g, determine the percentage by mass of the carbon.
2. If the percentage by mass of carbon in a 62 g sample of sucrose ($C_{12}H_{22}O_{11}$) is 42% and the hydrogen is 6.5%, what is the mass of the oxygen?
3. Three different masses of magnesium atoms occur in nature. 78.60% of all magnesium atoms weight 24 atomic mass units, 10.11% weigh 25 amu, 11.29% weight 26 amu. What is the average weight of magnesium in nature?
4. If a student in a laboratory experiment produces 3.25 g of tin when theoretically the predicted result should have been 4.05 g, what was the student's percentage yield?

### Topic F: Proportionality

*Outcomes*

- Students will describe the effect of pressure on gas volume.
- Students will describe the effect of temperature change on gas volume.
- Students will calculate density as a function of mass and volume.

*Behavior of Gases*                                          *Density*

$P_1V_1 = P_2V_2$          P = pressure
                          V = volume

$\dfrac{V_1}{T_1} = \dfrac{V_2}{T_2}$          T = temperature (k)          $d = \dfrac{m}{V}$

                          d = density

$\dfrac{P_1V_1}{T_1} = \dfrac{P_2V_2}{T_2}$          m = mass

*Instructor's Note*   In science, units are very important because many times units vary from one set of data to the next. Unit-specific formulas may also be used (i.e., temperature in Kelvin is needed for the above relationships), and this further emphasizes the need to keep track of units. Please stress that students keep track of units at the beginning of a problem to insure cancellation and a reasonable answer. Some practice problems follow:

1. Nitrogen gas at a pressure of 2.5 atmospheres and having a volume of 22.4 liters is pumped into a new container where its volume is decreased to

18.4 liters. What is the pressure of the oxygen in the new container if the temperature is unchanging?

2. Oxygen gas at a temperature of 25°C is cooled to 273 Kelvin. Its initial volume was 5.2 liters. What is its volume after cooling (assume pressure remains constant)?

3. A helium balloon at ground level has a volume of 92 ml on a day when the pressure is 1.0 atmospheres and the temperature is 300 K. When the balloon rises to a level where the pressure is 0.65 atmospheres and the temperature is 10°C, what is its new volume?

4. The density of iron is 7.87 g/cm$^3$. What is the volume of a 0.23 k block of iron?

5. A pure copper sample has a mass of 100.0 g and a volume of 15.0 cm$^3$. What would the mass be of a copper sample with a volume of 18.5 cm$^3$?

6. Argon gas at a pressure of 2.3 atmospheres is stored in a 2.0 liter container. What would its pressure be if it were pumped into a 465 ml container?

**Topic G: Logarithms**

*Outcomes*  Students will determine the pH of solutions based on hydronium ion concentration. Students will determine the mass of radioactive material remaining after a series of decays.

*Note:* UCSMP Adv Alg  p. 495 example 2
p. 496 #5–7
p. 497 #10
p. 502 #13–15

Sample problems:

1. Determine the hydronium ion concentration if the pH is 3.7.

2. If the hydronium ion concentration is $2.5 \times 10^{-10}$, determine the pH.

3. If the half-life of radioactive oxygen is 27 sec, what mass of a 625 g sample will remain after 105 sec?

*28*  *Curriculum Unit*  Research Skills

*Subject Area*  Library media center, science, history, geography, American government

*Recommended Grade Level*  High school

*Summary*  Students will develop research strategies in the curriculum areas of science and social studies.

*Objectives*

- to discover facts concerning a specific subject area
- to be introduced to resources in the media center
- to develop research strategy skills
- to understand the importance of documentation of information

*School and Contact Person*

Thomson High School
P.O. Box 1077
Thomson, GA 30824
(404) 595-9393

Robert L. Smith, Principal
O. P. Cooper          Robert Anthony
Karen Holley          Theresa Drummer
Charlie Fowler        Barbara Dell Postor
Pam Hawkins           Larry Wiley
Brenda Van Sant       Rosa Hunt
                      Janice Williams

*Procedures*  Worksheets for four courses—Biology, American History, Geography, and American Government—are provided here. The references to specific computer commands may vary according to software & hardware needs.

# MEDIA CENTER ORIENTATION: TENTH GRADE BIOLOGY

## Objectives

1. To discover facts concerning a specific branch of science.
2. To be introduced to the resources in the media center.
3. To develop research strategy skills.
4. To understand the importance of documentation of information.

## First Day—Classroom—Date: _____

1. View and discuss the 15-minute videotape, "How to Use the Reader's Guide."
2. Introduce assignment sheets, especially new terminology.
3. Inform students of seating chart arrangement.
4. Assign each student to one of the branches of science listed below.

## Second Day—Media Center—Date: _____

1. Introduce resources to be used, including the automated card catalog.
2. Students begin working independently.

## Third Day—Media Center—Date: _____

1. Introduce the magazine index on the computer network.
2. Students continue to work independently on their assignment sheets.

## Due Date—Date: _____

1. The teacher will collect and grade the assignments for a grade in his or her class. The suggested due date is two weeks from the first class day held in the media center.
2. Students will be expected to return to the media center on an individual basis to complete the assignment.

## Branches of Science Related to Biology

1. Agronomy
2. Anatomy
3. Anthropology
4. Bacteriology
5. Biochemistry
6. Biogeography
7. Botany
8. Cytology
9. Ecology
10. Entomology
11. Embryology
12. Ethology
13. Exobiology
14. Genetics
15. Herpetology
16. Histology
17. Horticulture
18. Ichthyology
19. Mammalogy
20. Marine Biology
21. Microbiology
22. Oceanography
23. Oncology
24. Ornithology
25. Paleontology
26. Pharmacology
27. Physiology
28. Taxonomy
29. Virology
30. Zoology

Student _____     Topic _____

Teacher _____     _____     Period _____     Date _____

Lesson Components (Staple together. Blanks are for teacher use.)

_____ 4 page worksheet

_____ 1 computer encyclopedia printout (#2)

_____ 1 card catalog bibliography (#5)

_____ 1 periodical request form (#8 and #9)

_____ 1 periodical bibliography (#9)

*Note:* Every topic will not be in every reference source. You may need to use a related term, such as agronomy or agriculture. If information cannot be found in a particular source, show your teacher or one of the media personnel where you have looked, and we will indicate this on your assignment sheet.

. . . . . . . . . . . . . . . . . . . . . . . . . . . . . . . . . . . . . . . . . . . . .

### Definition

**1.** *Keywords and important people:* Using your previous knowledge and the definitions that you get for #2–3, list keywords and important people that can be used for researching more information on your topic. Add more terms as they are found.

| | |
|---|---|
| **a.** _____ | **b.** _____ |
| **c.** _____ | **d.** _____ |
| **e.** _____ | **f.** _____ |
| **g.** _____ | **h.** _____ |
| **i.** _____ | **j.** _____ |

**2.** *Information Finder* or *Software Toolworks Illustrated Encyclopedia* (*computer* versions of two encyclopedias): Browse titles, type in topic, "Alt E" to mark your text, then "Alt P," *print up to the first five frames,* and *attach printout.*

**3.** Using two of the following books and the printout for #2, read the definitions for your topic. Then write a definition in your own words.

*The American Heritage Dictionary of Science* (R 503 BAR).          Page _____

*The Cambridge Illustrated Dictionary of Natural History* (R 508.03 LIN)

                                                                                       Page _____

*McGraw-Hill Concise Encyclopedia of Science and Technology* (R 503 MCG)

                                                                                       Page _____

*The Oxford Dictionary of Natural History* (R 508.03 OXF)          Page _____

_____

_____

_____

_____

. . . . . . . . . . . . . . . . . . . . . . . . . . . . . . . . . . . .

**History**

**4.** *Chronology:* Use one of the following books:

*Asimov's Chronology of Science and Discovery* (R 509 ASI)
*Breakthroughs: A Chronology of Great Achievements in Science and Mathematics* (R 509 PAR)

*Day by Day: The Forties, . . . The Fifties, . . . The Sixties, . . . The Seventies* (R 909.82 LEO)

Find an entry on your topic in one of the chronologies, write it, and list its source.

_____

_____

_____

_____

Title of source _____ Page _____

Subject heading _____ Date _____

**5.** *Card Catalog on Computer*

- Type in "scientists" and "biography."
- Arrange books in call number order by pressing "F 9" to sort results.
- *Delete* the bibliographies.
- *Delete* the multiple copies of the same titles.
- Print the remaining nine titles by pressing "F 10" and *attach printout.*
- With one of the books listed, find a person in your field of science, answer the following questions, and list source.

Scientist _____ Birth date _____

Nationality _____ Death date _____

Major contribution _____

_____

_____

_____

Awards _____

Title of source _____

Author or
publisher _____ Page _____ Call
number _____

. . . . . . . . . . . . . . . . . . . . . . . . . . . . . . . . . . . .

**Experiments**

6. Bibliography from Card Catalog (pink paper on each table)

- Using a bibliography on "science and experiments" (several copies have already been printed to save time at the computer), find a project or experiment that is related to your topic. Briefly describe it and list its source.

Subject for project _____

Hypothesis _____

_____

_____

Materials needed _____

_____

Procedure _____

_____

_____

_____

Title of source _____

Author of
publisher _____ Page _____ Call number _____

7. Reference Books: 500s and 600s

- Using the *index volume*, which is usually the last volume in a set of books, find an article that will provide *background or supportive information* for the science project or experiment that you chose in #6.
- Write a summary of this article and list the sources.

Subject heading or title _____

_____

_____

_____

_____

_____

_____

_____

Title of source _____
Author or
publisher _____ Page _____ Call number _____

**8.** *Readers' Guide to Periodical Literature (index shelves):*

- Select a magazine article that will provide further background or supportive information on your science project or experiment.
- Choose only *one* article that is in a magazine or journal in our own THS media center. Use the gold *"THS Media Center Periodicals Holdings"* to check for the periodical title and date needed.
- Fill out a "Periodical Request Form" and *attach this form* to your worksheets.

Subject heading _____ Subheading _____

Article title _____

Author _____ Journal title _____

Pages _____ Date _____

· · · · · · · · · · · · · · · · · · · · · · · · · · · · · · · · · · · · · ·

**Careers**

**9.** Magazine Index on Computer (*Wait* until second day of class):

- Find a magazine article on career possibilities for your branch of science. For example type in "agronomy and (career or job)."
- If no article is listed, use a related term such as "agriculture" or "farming."
- If an article is still not found, use a more general term such as "biology" and find a similar career that would be appropriate.
- Choose only *one* article that is in a magazine or journal in our own THS media center. Use the gold "THS Media Center Periodicals Holdings" to check for the periodical title and date needed.
- *Attach a printout* for the magazine citation that you have chosen.
- Add this magazine to the "Periodical Request Form" that you used for the previous question, #8.

# MEDIA CENTER ORIENTATION: ELEVENTH GRADE—AMERICAN HISTORY

*Lesson* The Gilded Age

*Objectives*

1. To discover facts concerning the Gilded Age of American history.
2. To be introduced to the resources in the media center.
3. To develop research strategy skills.
4. To understand the importance of documentation of information.

*First Day—Classroom—Date:* _____

1. Introduce resources to be used, including the automated card catalog and magazine index on the computer network.
2. Students begin working independently.

*Third Day—Media Center—Date:* _____

1. Students continue to work independently on their assignment sheets.

*Due Date—Date:* _____

1. The teacher will collect and grade the assignments for a grade in his/her class. The suggested due date is one week from the first class day held in the media center.
2. Students will be expected to return to the media center on an individual basis to complete the assignment.

## Important People of the Gilded Age

| | |
|---|---|
| 1. Adams, Henry | Literature |
| 2. Addams, Jane | Reform leader |
| 3. Barnum, Phineas Taylor | Entertainment |
| 4. Bell, Alexander Graham | Invention |
| 5. Bennett, James Gordon, Jr. | Journalism, Business & Invention |
| 6. Carnegie, Andrew | Business & Philanthropist |
| 7. Clemens, Samuel Langhorne | Literature |
| 8. Cleveland, Stephen Grover | President |
| 9. Cody, William F. (Buffalo Bill) | Thought & Culture |
| 10. Crane, Stephen | Literature & Journalism |
| 11. Dewey, John | Reform leader, Thought & Culture |
| 12. DuBois, William Edward Burghardt | Reform leader |
| 13. Edison, Thomas Alva | Invention |
| 14. Field, Cyrus West | Business & Invention |

| | | |
|---|---|---|
| 15. | Harrison, Benjamin | President |
| 16. | Hearst, William Randolph | Journalism, Business, & Political |
| 17. | Hoar, George | Reform leader & Political |
| 18. | Holmes, Oliver Wendell, Jr. | Thought & Culture |
| 19. | Howells, William Dean | Literature |
| 20. | Hunt, Richard Morris | Architecture |
| 21. | James, William | Thought & Culture |
| 22. | McKinley, William, Jr. | President |
| 23. | Moody, Dwight Lyman | Reform leader |
| 24. | Olmsted, Frederick Law | Art & Architecture |
| 25. | Pulitzer, Joseph | Journalism & Business |
| 26. | Pullman, George Mortimer | Invention |
| 27. | Reed, Thomas Brackett | Political |
| 28. | Sullivan, Louis Henri | Architecture |
| 29. | Tweed, William Marcy | Political |
| 30. | Washington, Booker Taliaferro | Reform leader |
| 31. | Whitman, Walt | Literature |

# MEDIA CENTER ORIENTATION: ELEVENTH GRADE—AMERICAN HISTORY

Student _____ Topic _____

Teacher _____ Period _____ Due Date _____

Lesson Components (Staple together. Blanks are for teacher use.)

_____ 3 page worksheet

_____ 1 computer encyclopedia printout (#1)

_____ 1 card catalog bibliography (#5)

_____ 1 periodical request form (#7)

_____ 1 periodical bibliography (#8)

*Note:* Every topic will not be in every reference source. You may need to use *related terms.* If information cannot be found in a particular source, show your teacher or one of the media personnel where you have looked and we will indicate this on your assignment sheet.

· · · · · · · · · · · · · · · · · · · · · · · · · · · · · · · · · · · · · · · · · ·

**Biographical Sketch**

**1.** *Information Finder* or *Software Toolworks Illustrated Encyclopedia* (computer versions of two encyclopedias): (Browse titles, type in your person's last name, "Alt E" to mark your text, "Alt P" to print your marked text *up to the first five frames,* and *attach printout.*

**2.** Biographical dictionaries: Use one of the following dictionaries to find basic biographical information on your person and list your source.

**a.** American Biographies (R 920.073 WEB)
**b.** American Reformers (R 973 AME)
**c.** Webster's Biographical Dictionary (R 920.02 WEB)
**d.** Webster's New Biographical Dictionary (R 920.02 WEB)
**e.** Who Was Who in America (R 920 MAR)

Birth/death dates _____ Birthplace _____

Parents _____ Education _____

Career or position _____

_____

Major influence or contribution _____

_____

_____

_____

_____

Title of source _____ Page _____

· · · · · · · · · · · · · · · · · · · · · · · · · · · · · · · · · · · · · · · ·

### Description of Era

**3.** Magill's History of North America (R 970 MAG): Using the "Principal Personages Index" in volume 12 (copies of index on pink paper), read an article about your person and answer the following:

Title of article _____

Type of event _____

Time _____ Locale _____

Volume _____ Pages _____ Principal personages:

a. _____   b. _____

c. _____   d. _____

e. _____   f. _____

g. _____   h. _____

i. _____   j. _____

Summary of event _____

_____

_____

_____

_____

_____

_____

_____

**4.** Special encyclopedias (Do not use a general encyclopedia.): Using one of the following special encyclopedias, describe three characteristics of the Gilded Age and give an example of each.

   **a.** *The American Destiny* (R 973 AME)
   **b.** *American Heritage Illustrated History of the United States* (R 973 AME)
   **c.** *Annals of America* (R 973 ANN)

#1 _____

_____

_____

_____

#2 _____

_____

_____

_____

#3 _____

_____

_____

_____

Title of source _____ Volume _____ Page _____

  5. Card Catalog on Computer

  • Type in your topic and/or a combination of related terms (person's name
    and/or area of significance, plus Gilded Age).
  • Arrange books in call number order by pressing "F 9" to sort results.
  • Delete the fiction.
  • Delete multiple copies of the same title.
  • Select up to 15 titles that can be used for future reference. If there are more
    than 15 titles, read the notes on each catalog card, and *delete* those which
    do not seem to be helpful.
  • Print the remaining bibliography by pressing "F 10" and *attach printout.*

  6. Bibliography from Card Catalog: Using the bibliography that you printed for
  #5, locate a book from your list. Show one of the media personnel where the book
  should be located on the shelf and ask him/her to sign this sheet.

  _____

  . . . . . . . . . . . . . . . . . . . . . . . . . . . . . . . . . . . . . . . . . . .

**Current Information**

  7. Readers' Guide to Periodical Literature (Index Shelves).

  • Select a magazine article on your topic (person's name and/or area of
    significance).
  • Choose only one article that is in a magazine or journal in our own. THS
    media center. Use the gold "THS Media Center Periodicals Holdings" to check
    for the periodical title and date needed.
  • Fill out a "Periodical Request Form" and *attach this form* to your worksheets.

Subject heading _____ Subheading _____

Article title _____

Author _____ Journal title _____

Pages _____ Date _____

**8.** Magazine index on computer:

- Type in your topic (name and/or area of significance).
- Choose up to five articles that are in magazines or journals in our own THS media center. Use the gold "THS Media Center Periodicals Holdings" to check for the periodical titles and dates needed.
- *Attach a printout* for the magazine citations that you have chosen.

# MEDIA CENTER ORIENTATION:
# NINTH GRADE—GEOGRAPHY CLASSES

This lesson on countries was cooperatively planned by the THS geography teachers and media specialists.

## *Objectives*

1. To discover facts on a specific country.
2. To be introduced to the resources in the media center.
3. To develop research strategy skills.
4. To understand the importance of documentation of information.

## *First Day—Classroom—Date:* _____

1. View and discuss the fifteen-minute videotape, "How to Use the Reader's Guide."
2. Introduce assignment sheets, especially new terminology. (Transparencies of pages are available.)
3. Inform students of seating chart arrangement.
4. Assign each student to one of the countries listed below.
5. Review pages 18–19 of the *THS Student Handbook,* which explains the media center's policies and services.

## *Second Day—Media Center—Date:* _____

1. Introduce resources to be used, including the automated card catalog and magazine index.
2. Students begin working independently.

## *Third Day—Media Center—Date:* _____

1. The teacher will collect and grade the assignments for a grade in his/her class. The suggested due date is two weeks from the first day of class held in the media center.
2. Students will be expected to return to the media center on an individual basis to complete the assignment.

## List of Countries

| | | |
|---|---|---|
| 1. Afghanistan | 13. France | 25. Liberia |
| 2. Argentina | 14. Germany | 26. Mexico |
| 3. Australia | 15. Great Britain | 27. Nigeria |
| 4. Austria | 16. Greece | 28. Norway |
| 5. Belgium | 17. Iceland | 29. Pakistan |
| 6. Bolivia | 18. India | 30. Peru |
| 7. Botswana | 19. Iran | 31. Philippines |

8. Brazil
9. Canada
10. China
11. Egypt
12. Finland

20. Israel
21. Italy
22. Japan
23. Kenya
24. Korea, North

32. Spain
33. Sudan
34. Sweden
35. Thailand

# MEDIA CENTER ORIENTATION: NINTH GRADE–GEOGRAPHY

Student _____ Country _____

Teacher _____ Period _____ Due Date _____

Lesson Components (Staple together. Blanks are for teacher use.)

_____ 4 page worksheet

_____ 1 computer encyclopedia printout (#1)

_____ 1 card catalog bibliography (#7)

_____ 1 periodical bibliography (#10)

_____ 1 periodical request form (#11)

**1.** *Software Toolworks Illustrated Enciclolpedia* (computer version of encyclopedia)

• Choose Browse titles, type in your country's name, "Alkt P" to print, choose "page," then "begin printing."

**2a.** General Encyclopedias (Located on bottom shelves in Reference)

• *Academic American Encyclopedia, Compton's Encyclopedia Americana, Merit Student Encyclopedia, The New Book of Knowledge,* or *The World Book Encyclopedia.*

**a.** Using the *index* volume, find a *subheading* that is listed under your country.

Title of encyclopedia _____

Index–Volume # _____ Page _____ Subheading _____

Where does the index tell you to go? Text–Volume _____ Page _____

**b.** Using the *text volume* of the same encyclopedia, find the general article on your country. *Skim* the article, list one important *person* in your country's *history,* and briefly explain his/her significance.

Text–Volume # _____ Page _____ Person _____

_____

_____

_____

_____

**c.** Does this encyclopedia have a separate article on the person? _____

If yes, list where the article was found. (Use the index volume.)

Index–Volume # _____ Page _____ Text–Volume _____ Page _____

3. *World Almanac and Book of Facts* (R 317.3 WOR) (Wait until second day.)

- Using the index in the front of the book, find your country. Look at the pages listed until you find the "Nations of the World" section.

    Page(s) _____ Year/edition _____

    **a.** Official name: _____

    **b.** Population (Date: _____) _____ Density: _____ per square mile

    **c.** Ethnic groups: _____

    **d.** Languages: _____

    **e.** Religions (%): _____

    **f.** Geography—Area in square miles: _____

    **g.** Geographic location: _____

    **h.** Capital: _____

    **i.** Government type: _____

    **j.** Economy—Labor force (%): Agriculture _____, Industry and

    commerce _____, services _____, and other _____

    **k.** Finance—Currency (date _____): Name of currency _____

    U.S. equivalency _____

    **l.** Per capita income (date _____): _____

    **m.** Health—Life expectancy (years): Male _____ and female _____,

    Births _____ per 1,000, deaths _____ per 1,000, and

    infant mortality rate _____ per 1,000

    **n.** Education—Literacy rate (date _____) (%): _____

4. *Geography on File* (R 912 GEO)

- Using the "Statistical Resources" section of this book, describe your country's *terrain.*

    _____

    _____

    _____

    _____

    Section # _____ Section title _____ Page _____

5. *Maps on File* (R 912 MAP)

- Using the index, locate a *map* of your country's continent that shows surrounding countries. Show this map to your teacher or the media staff so your worksheet can be *initialed.* Teacher/Media Staff _____

Section # (page) _____ Section title _____

**6.** *Day by Day: The Seventies* (R 909.82 LEO)

• Using the *index* in Volume II, find an entry for your country on the dateline and write it here.

_____

_____

_____

_____

**7.** Card Catalog on Computer

• Type in your country.
• *Arrange* books in call number order by pressing "F 9" to sort results.
• *Delete* the fiction.
• *Delete* multiple copies of the same title.
• *Select up to 5 titles* that concern your country. If there are more than 5 titles, read the notes on each catalog card, and *delete* those that would *not* be a general description of the land or history.

**8.** *Abridged Readers' Guide to Periodical Literature* (Index shelves)

• Select *one* magazine article on your country that is in a magazine or journal which is in our own THS Media Center.
• Use the gold "THS Media Center Periodical Holdings" to check for the periodical title and date needed.

Subject heading _____ Subheading _____

Article title _____

Author _____ Journal title _____

Pages _____ Date _____

**9.** Index Shelves (outside office/conference rooms).

• Indexes for several social studies magazines are shelved here. Using the National Geographic Index, find an article on your country.

Article Title: _____

Author _____ Date _____ Page _____

Is this magazine in the THS collection? Yes _____ or No _____

**10.** Magazine Index on the Computer (Wait until second day.)

• Find magazine or journal articles concerning your country. Choose "Search," then type in your country. Use "F 9" to mark the *first title* which is included in our own Media Center. To determine which magazines are included, check the gold "THS Periodical Holdings" list. Push "F 4" to print. Then choose "Long (Citation and abstract)" and "Marked items." Attach printout to assignment.

**11.** Using the magazine articles that you found for #8–10, fill out the "Periodical Request Form." Check the *gold list* of THS holdings and list *only* the magazines in our collection and check the correct *format* for each. *Attach this form* to your worksheets. (Wait until second day.)

(For future assignments, the computer printout is for you to *keep* with your notes while doing research. The "Periodical Request Form" is needed for borrowing magazines from the backfile room. Overnight checkout must be done at the circulation desk with your THS identification card.)

**12.** *The Marshall Cavendish New Encyclopedia of the World and Its People* (R 910.3 MAR)—Describe your country's climate and how it affects the peoples' life-styles (weather, food, products, housing, clothing).

_____

_____

_____

_____

_____

_____

_____

_____

Volume _____ Pages _____

**13.** *The Illustrated Encyclopedia of Mankind* (R 306.03 ILL)

- Using the *index,* list four of the *ethnic groups* found under your country.
- Look up one of the ethnic groups and describe one unique characteristic of that ethnic group. Briefly explain why they are significant.
- If specific ethnic groups are not listed, show your teacher or media staff where you have looked. Then use the general article on your country.

a. _____    b. _____

c. _____    d. _____

*Index* (volume page _____ *Text* volume _____ Pages _____

Ethnic group described: _____

_____

_____

_____

_____

_____

_____

# MEDIA CENTER ORIENTATION:
# TWELFTH GRADE–GOVERNMENT CLASSES

This lesson on researching current issues was cooperatively planned by the THS government teachers and media specialists.

## Objectives

1. To discover facts concerning a current issue in order to provide preliminary information for the annual bill writing assignment.
2. To be introduced to the resources in the media center.
3. To develop research strategy skills.
4. To understand the importance of documentation of information.

*First Day: Classroom–Date:* _____

1. View and discuss the fifteen-minute videotape, "How to Use the Reader's Guide."
2. Introduce assignment sheets, especially new terminology. (Transparencies of pages are available.)
3. Inform students of seating chart arrangement.
4. Assign each student to a different general topic related to the proposed bill that he or she wishes to write.
5. Review pages 18–19 of the *THS Student Handbook,* which explains the media center's policies and services.

*Second Day: Media Center–Date:* _____

1. Students continue to work independently on their assignment sheets.

*Due Date: Date:* _____

1. The teacher will collect and grade the assignments for a grade in his or her class. The suggested due date is two weeks from the first class day held in the media center.
2. Students will be expected to return to the media center on an individual basis to complete the assignment.

# MEDIA CENTER ORIENTATION: TWELFTH GRADE–GOVERNMENT

Student _____    General topic _____

Teacher _____    Period _____    Due date _____

Lesson Components (Staple together. Blanks are for teacher use.)

_____ 5 page worksheet

_____ 1 computer encyclopedia printout (#2)

_____ 1 card catalog bibliography (#7)

_____ 1 periodical request form (#8)

_____ 1 periodical bibliography (#9)

*Note:* Every topic will not be in every reference source. You may need to use *related* terms. If information cannot be found in a particular source, show your teacher or one of the media personnel where you have looked, and we will indicate this on your assignment sheet.

. . . . . . . . . . . . . . . . . . . . . . . . . . . . . . . . . . . . . . . . . . . .

Proposed bill: _____

_____

_____

. . . . . . . . . . . . . . . . . . . . . . . . . . . . . . . . . . . . . . . . . . . .

## Definition

1. Keywords and Important People

• Using your previous knowledge and the definitions that you get for #2–3, list keywords and important people that can be used for researching more information on your topic. Add more terms as they are found.

Keywords and important people:

a. _____    b. _____

c. _____    d. _____

e. _____    f. _____

g. _____    h. _____

2. *Information Finder* or *Software Toolworks Illustrated Encyclopedia (computer versions of two encyclopedias)*

- Browse titles, type in topic, "Alt E" to mark your text, "Alt P" to print your marked text *up to the first five frames,* and *attach printout.*

**3.** Using *one* of the following books and the printout for #1, read the definitions for your topic. After reading, *list important people* and *keywords* that can be used for researching more information on your topic and *write a complete definition* in your own words. As more names and terms are noticed in later books, *add* these to this list.

    **a.** *Black's Law Dictionary* (R 340 BLA) page _____

    **b.** if not found in *Black's,* use any unabridged dictionary.

Definition _____

_____

_____

_____

_____

_____

. . . . . . . . . . . . . . . . . . . . . . . . . . . . . . . . . . . . . . . . . . . . .

**Historical Background**

**4.** *Chronology:* Use one of the following books and write a description of an important event that is related to your topic:

    **a.** *The Almanac of American History* (R 073.02 ALM)

    **b.** *Day by Day: The Forties, . . . The Fifties, . . . The Sixties, . . . The Seventies* (R 909.82 LEO)

_____

_____

_____

_____

_____

_____

_____

Title of source: _____ Page: _____

Subject heading: _____ Date of event: _____

**5.** *Reference books:* 300s and 900s. (Do not use a general encyclopedia.)

- Using the *index volume,* which is usually the last section of a book or the last volume in a set of books, find an article that will provide *background or supportive information* for your topic.

• Write a summary of this article and list the source.

Subject heading or title: _____

_____

_____

_____

_____

_____

_____

_____

_____

_____

_____

Title of source _____

Author or publisher _____ Page _____ Call number _____

6. Historical Documents (R 917.3 HIS)

• In this set of books with primary sources of information, locate a document related to your topic and describe it below.

Title of document: _____

Author or responsible group: _____

Date of document _____

Edition year of historic documents _____
Type of document: treaty, speech,
report, course case, etc. _____ Pages _____

_____

Summary _____

_____

_____

_____

_____

_____

_____

_____

7. Card Catalog on Computer

• Type in your topic and/or a combination of related terms.
• Arrange books in call number order by pressing "F 9" to sort results.

- *Delete* the fiction.
- *Delete* multiple choices of the same title.
- *Select up to 15 titles* that can be used for future reference. If there are more than 15 titles, read the notes on each catalog card, and *delete* those that do not seem to be helpful.
- Print the remaining bibliography by pressing "F 10" and *attach printout.*

. . . . . . . . . . . . . . . . . . . . . . . . . . . . . . . . . . . . . . . . . . . . . .

**Current Information**

8. Readers' Guide to Periodical Literature (Index Shelves).

- Select a magazine article that will provide further background or supportive information on your topic.
- Choose only *one* article that is in a magazine or journal in our own THS media center. Use the gold *THS Media Center Periodicals Holdings* to check for the periodical title and date needed.
- Fill out a Periodical Request Form and *attach this form* to your worksheets.

    Subject heading _____ Subheading _____

    Article title _____

    Author _____ Journal title _____

    Pages _____ Date _____

9. Magazine Index on Computer.

- Type in your topic and/or a combination of related terms.
- Choose up to ten articles that are in magazines or journals in our own THS media center. Use the gold *THS Media Center Periodicals Holdings* to check for the periodical titles and dates needed.
- *Attach a printout* for the magazine citations that you have chosen.

10. Bibliography from Card Catalog (green paper on desk)

- Using a bibliography on the Supreme Court and Constitution (several copies have already been printed to save time at the computer), find a Supreme Court case that deals with your topic and answer the questions below.

    Name of case _____

    Date _____

    Summary of the issues and verdict: _____

    _____

    _____

    _____

    _____

    _____

_____

_____

_____

Title of source _____

Author or publisher _____ Page _____ Call number _____

**11.** Congressional Record (Next to Bookroom)

- Using the index volumes marked with yellow spines, find a recent entry concerning your topic.

Subject heading _____
Type of entry: letters,
remarks . . . , testimonies, etc. _____

Reference number _____ Page in index _____

Date of text volume _____

Summary: _____

_____

_____

_____

_____

_____

**12.** Washington Information Directory, 1987–1988 (R 975.3 CON)

- List three organizations, government or nongovernment group, agencies, support groups, lobbyists, etc., where more information can be obtained concerning your topic.

**a.** Group _____

Contact person _____ Page _____

Address _____

Phone _____ Type of group _____

**b.** Group _____
Contact person _____ Page _____

Address _____

Phone _____ Type of group _____

**c.** Group _____

Contact person _____ Page _____

Address _____

Phone _____ Type of group _____

*29* *Curriculum Unit* Visions of the Future

*Subject Areas* History

*Recommended Grade Level* High school

*Summary* The student will explore the perspective that the concepts of technology, change, conflict, systems, human dignity, and interdependence give us on current issues that may affect our global future.

*Objectives* The student will:

- Classify visions of the future in terms of their basic outlook/bias.
- Apply a process of issue analysis to explore current issues that may have important implications for the future.
- Apply tools of the futurist (e.g., trend analysis and extrapolation scenario writing, futures wheel, future problem solving) to generate a variety of alternative possibilities for the future.
- Analyze and evaluate a variety of visions of the future.
- Apply a model of questioning to lead discussion of reading selections.

*School and Contact Persons*

Spartanburg High School
500 Dupre Drive
Spartanburg, SC 29302
(803) 594-4410

Joseph P. Carke, Principal
Suzanne McDaniel

**Preassessment**

Please place a check after each book below that you have already read.

Asimov. *I, Robot.*
Bellamy. *Looking Backward.*
Clarke. *Childhood's End: 2001.*
Crichton. *The Terminal Man.*
Frank. *Alas, Babylon.*
Heinlein. *Starship Trooper.*
Herbert. *Dune.*
Huxley. *Brave New World.*
Miller. *A Canticle for Leibowitz.*
Orwell. *1984.*
Skinner. *Walden Two.*
Verne. *The Mysterious Island; 20,000 Leagues Under the Sea.*
Zamyatin. *We.*

Please indicate on the lines provided your level of expertise (e.g., no experience, some knowledge, lots of experience) in using each of the strategies listed.

Future problem solving _____

Scenario writing _____

Trend extrapolation _____

Futures wheel _____

Cross impact analysis _____

Delphi technique _____

Mind mapping _____

Creative problem solving _____

Please check the discipline(s) that you prefer or in which you think you have the greatest interest and strength.

| | |
|---|---|
| Mathematics | Language/literature |
| Biology | Chemistry |
| Physics | History |
| Political science | Psychology |
| Sociology | Geography |
| Economics | |

Please list below the periodicals to which you have access.

After each of the concepts listed below, write a few statements to indicate your present understanding of the nature of that idea.

Technology:

Conflict:

Systems:

Human dignity:

Change:

Interdependence:

What do you see as the current issues most likely to have an impact on our future?

Please describe what you think the world will be like in the year 2050.

*What Is Futures Studies?* Futures studies is an attempt to examine systematically the factors that can influence the future . . . then project possible futures based on the interaction of those factors. This involves the exploration of alternative futures in hopes of imaging and inventing new ideas, options, and goals to pursue actively.

. . . futures studies is an interdisciplinary, conceptually based, process-oriented approach to exploring and investigating alternative futures from a personal and global perspective. It is a topical/thematic area of study that brings higher order thinking skills, creativity, and sensitivity to bear on real-life issues and trends (Charles E. and Helen Whaley, *Future Images: Futures Studies for Grades 4 to 12*).

**The ODYSSEY seminar *Visions of the Future* focuses on global futures. The *Community Internship Program* focuses on personal futures.**

**In** *Visions of the Future* you will be exploring the perspective that the concepts of technology, change, conflict, systems, human dignity, and interdependence give you on current issues that may impact our global futures and on a variety of visions of the future that have been advanced by writers and futurists over the years.

**Course objectives on which we will focus for the first six weeks:**
The student will

1. Classify visions of the future in terms of their basic outlook/bias.
2. Apply a process of issue analysis to explore current issues that may have important implications for the future.
3. Apply tools of the futurist (e.g., trend analysis and extrapolation, scenario writing, futures wheel, future problem solving) to generate a variety of alternative possibilities for the future.
4. Analyze and evaluate a variety of visions of the future.
5. Apply a model of questioning to lead discussion of reading selections.

**Visions of the Future: Preliminary Syllabus**

*First Six Weeks*  Who are the futurists and what is "future studies"? What tools do futurists use?

Scheel, *Introduction to the Future*
Naisbitt, *Megatrends*

*Second Six Weeks*  What kinds of futures are possible, probable, preferable, undesirable?

Selected science fiction and utopianm/dystopian literature
Issue analysis

*Third Six Weeks*  Developing a synthesis

Toffler, *The Third Wave*

*Note*  This preliminary outline will be expanded through seminar group planning.

*Requirements*

Reading as assigned, along with discussion leadership
Journal: Four sections (What-if, Reaction/Response, Issue Analysis, Interviews/
Data Collection)
Presentation on individual novel
Group presentation on trends in a certain area
Scenarios
Issue analyses
Future problem solving
Parent presentation (group synthesis)
Personal synthesis

*Journal Assignments*

*Interview Assignment #1:* Interview four people—two male, two female, different ages. Note age and sex of each on the interview. Use as the interview question: "What do you think the world will be like in the year 2050?"

*Data Collection #1:* Find the date of the specific advancement/innovation/ technological development(s) assigned to you in Thursday's class.

*Issue Analysis #1:* What is the nature of the current crisis in the Middle East? How do you think it will come out? Why?

Please bring your journal with you each day you have a journal assignment due. Your entries will be the basis for your discussion that day.

**Visions of the Future**

*Due Monday*

Interview Assignment #1
Data Collection Assignment #1

*Due Wednesday*

*Introduction to the Future,* pp. 5–9
Reaction/Response Assignment #1: React/respond to anything in the assigned pages of *Introduction to the Future* that strikes you. First, summarize the idea, point, or whatever, that caught your attention. Then react or respond. Some possible openers:

I don't understand . . .
This idea is significant because . . .
This idea interested me because . . .
This idea can easily be applied to . . .
This information could be better presented by . . .
I can relate this idea to . . .
I already knew . . .

*Due Friday*

*Introduction to the Future,* pp. 9–11
*Interview Assignment #2:* Interview your parents about their jobs. How has the nature of their business/industry/workplace changed over the time they have been in it? To what factors do they attribute those changes? (Consider a home executive's workplace the home.)

**Analyzing and Studying Issues**

The following four-step method outlines a process for studying and analyzing an issue. This is the process we will use in *Visions of the Future* as we look at current issues and their possible impact on future events.

**1.** Identify and define the issue by using a conceptual approach. (Look at the information about the issue in terms of the six major concept themes of the course: conflict, change, technology, systems, interdependence, and human dignity.)

**2.** Gather the viewpoints of others on the issue. Identify the stakeholders and understand the reasons for their concerns or involvement.

**3.** Consider the impact and implications (with respect to such things as the environment, technology, society, global equity, etc.) of various possible outcomes of the issue.

**4.** Develop a personal viewpoint with supporting rationale.

### Issue Analysis Presentation—Evaluation Criteria

*Criterion*　　　　　　　　　　　　　　　*Rating*

I. The presentation shows evidence that the issue analysis process was followed:

- Information is presented in relation to the six course themes.
- The information falls into abstract categories as well as concrete categories (i.e., it goes beyond "types" and "characteristics").
- Stakeholders and their views are accurately delineated.
- A variety of outcomes is presented.
- Impacts and implications of the outcomes are projected to at least the middle term future or beyond.
- A group response/resolution of the issue is presented and supported within the context of information and ideas developed through steps 1–3.
- The bibliography shows use of good quality and appropriate references.

II. The presentation itself meets the following criteria:

- It is complete within the time limit.
- It is clearly presented.
- It is illustrated with appropriate and well-designed visuals.
- There is participation by each group member.
- It is organized and coherent (each piece builds on the one before, each part of the presentation is essential to the whole).
- It is audible.
- It is interesting.

# HOW WELL DID YOUR SYSTEM WORK?

Name _____ Group _____ Role _____

Use the questions below to evaluate how the parts of your group worked to perform the function assigned to it. Use a G = good, F = fair, and P = poor.

### Discussion Leader

Did the discussion leader make sure everyone participated in the discussion?

_____

Did the discussion leader make sure no one dominated the discussion?

_____

Did the discussion leader keep the discussion moving and purposeful?

_____

Did the discussion leader make sure the final response was a consensus of the group? _____

### Materials Coordinator

Did the materials coordinator wait until the group had a clear plan before going to get materials? _____

Did the materials coordinator procure the proper materials? _____
Did the materials coordinator participate in the discussion? _____

### Reporter

Did the reporter clearly convey the primary idea of the group? _____
Did the reporter clearly explain the groups idea? _____
Did the reporter represent the group's ideas rather than simply his or her own? _____

Did the reporter make reference to the visual in the presentation? _____
Did the reporter participate in the discussion? _____

Overall, how well did the group function as a unit? _____

What do you think your group could do to improve its functioning next time? (Elaborate)

# GROUP PRESENTATION—ISSUE ANALYSIS

Name _____

### Assessment of Group Process

This time your group contained half the class rather than three to four members. Did the larger size of the group have any impact on

- how well each member was able to stay on task?
- how much each member participated actively?

What role(s) did you play in your group?

How important was the role you played to the ultimate success of the group?

Did each of the group members make significant contributions to the group effort or did a few group members shoulder the responsibility?

If your group were to work together again, what changes do you think the group should make to ensure that the work proceeds effectively and efficiently and everyone makes significant contributions?

### Visions of the Future: Assignments, Week

*Due Wednesday*

Read the "Universal Declaration of Human Rights" and the "Declaration of the Rights of the Child" in preparation for discussion of the concept of human dignity.

Continue to research the Middle East crisis, sorting your findings according to the six themes of this course and step #1 of the Issue Analysis process. This will be part of Issue Analysis Assignment #2, due Wednesday.

*Due Friday*   What-If Assignment #1: Respond to *one* of the following:

What if there were no bees?
What if there were no zero?
What if there were no principal at SHS?

### Assignments, Week

*Due Monday*
Read *Introduction to the Future*, pp. 21–27.

*Due Wednesday*

Issue Analysis #2: Use the issue analysis process to assess the current Middle East crisis. Be sure your journal is clearly labeled so that the steps you followed in the process are clear. Include a bibliography to indicate what sources you consulted in preparing your analysis.

*Due Thursday*

Read the information on two systems for classifying views of the future and the sample views of the future provided for study.

Reaction/Response Assignment #3: Classify each of the views of the future provided by using both of the classification systems. Where does each fit? Why? (Use specific evidence to support your thinking.)

**Journals will be handed in for evaluation today.**

*Due Friday*

Read *Introduction to the Future*, pp. 26–38.

**Visions of the Future: How to Improve Your Journal—A Checklist**

*Organization*

Is your journal separated into the four sections assigned?
Is each entry labeled with the assignment name and number and due date?
Do you have tabs or dividers that make it easy to find the sections?

*What-Ifs*

Does your entry show some knowledge of the systems of which the item is a part and the impact of the interdependence of this item with other items?

Does your entry get down to specifics?
Have you carried impact/implications to the second, third, and further levels?
If the form of the "what-if" has been specified, have you used that form?

*Reaction/Response*

Have you been clear and specific about what you are responding to?
Have you gone beyond generalization to support your thinking with details, examples, etc.?

Have you included your own thinking and elaborated on your reasoning process? (In other words, have you gone beyond what was said in the reading or in class or something you've heard or read?)

*Interview/Data Collection*

Have you clearly labeled the kind and source of the data?
In an interview, have you used follow-up questions to get elaboration?
Have you organized the data in any way to make it easier to interpret or use?

*Issue Analysis*

Are the four steps of the issue analysis process clear in what you have written?
Have you focused on specifics in steps 1 and 2?
Have you brainstormed possible outcomes and then traced possible impact/implications of a variety of outcomes in step 3?

Have you pulled everything together in a personal interpretation in step 4?
Can you see the use of the raw material you developed in steps 1–3?

Have you provided a list of sources if that was required?

**Throughout the journal, are you showing your thinking processes, how you are thinking through the questions posed or the tasks assigned?**

# VISIONS OF THE FUTURE: JOURNAL EVALUATION

Name _____ Date _____

Criteria _____ Assessment _____

## Organizations

Sections
Entry labels
Tabs, dividers

## Assignments Completed

## What-Ifs

Knowledge of systems/interdependence
Specifics
Implications carried to second, third, and further levels
Use of specified form

## Reaction/Response

Clear, specific subject
Generalizations supported
Own thinking
Elaborated reasoning process

## Interview/Data Collection

Kind and source labeled
Follow-up questions used for elaboration
Organization of data

## Issue Analysis

Process steps are clear
Steps 1 and 2 include specifics
Brainstormed possible outcomes
Impact/implications traced
Personal interpretation based on steps 1–3
List of sources

**Demonstration of thinking processes**

**Visions of the Future: Assignments, Week of**

*Due Wednesday* Review the handouts on "Orientations to the Future" and "Schools of Thought in Future Studies" and the three reading selections (Bell, Kahn, and Schumacher) so that you will be prepared to discuss the approach of each of the three writers in terms of their "orientation" and "school of thought."

*Due Friday* Read "What May Happen in the Next Hundred Years" by John Elfreth Watkins, Jr. and "The World of 1990" by Isaac Asimov. Be prepared to discuss these in terms of the "orientation" and "school of thought" as well as in terms of the ideas themselves.

**Assignments, Week of**

*Due Monday* Bring in articles, data collected for your group's issue so the group can spend this class session working on the issue analysis process in preparation for the group presentation due later. Date to be set in class on Tuesday.

*Due Tuesday* Read the introduction to *Megatrends* and be prepared to discuss it in terms of "orientation" and "schools of thought."

*Due Wednesday* Read Chapter 1 of *Megatrends*.

*Due Thursday* Read Chapter 2 of *Megatrends*.

*Journal Assignments: Over these two weeks do these entries* Do two (2) of these what-ifs in futures wheel form:

The rain forests disappeared.
Pollution contaminated all ground water.
Each schoolchild was required to have a computer.
One of your choice suggested by the reading or class discussion during the week.

Do two (2) reaction/response entries, reacting/responding to something discussed in class or something in the reading.

**Visions of the Future: Assignments,**

*Due Friday* Read the article by Neil Postman, "The Day Our Children Disappear: Predictions of a Media Ecologist." Be prepared to discuss Postman's views with our guest teacher, Dr. Thomas R. McDaniel, Professor of Education and Dean of the College of Arts and Sciences, Converse College.

*Due Monday* Any additional information about the issue your group is analyzing. You will spend this class session completing the issue analysis process and planning your presentation for the other group.

*Due Wednesday* Your group presentations: Each group will have 22 minutes. Presentations will be evaluated based on the criteria handed out on October 1.

*Due Thursday*   Reaction/Response #6: React/respond to the class session with Dr. McDaniel. Your journal entries will be the basis of class discussion.

Journals will be handed in for a grade at the end of class. Be sure that you have checked the suggestions for improving your journals as you prepare yours for evaluation.

### Visions of the Future: Assignments,

*Due Tuesday*   Read Chapters 7 and 8 from Rifkin's *Time Wars*. Be prepared to discuss these questions: What does Rifkin see as the impact of schedules and computers? What are the characteristics of what he calls the "efficient society"? How does he feel about this society? (Cite specific evidence.) How does his approach/attitude compare with that of Naisbitt? with that of Postman?

*Due Friday*   Read Chapters 3 and 4 in *Megatrends*. For each chapter do a Data Collection entry in your journal (#2 and #3), using a mind map or some other graphic organizer to delineate the structure and main points of each chapter.

*Due the Week of* _____   Complete the reading of *Megatrends*. Work with a partner to present the particular chapter assigned to the pair of you. The chapters and dates of presentation will be assigned in class.

  Chapter 5 –
  Chapter 6 –
  Chapter 7 –
  Chapter 8 –
  Chapter 9 –
  Chapter 10 –

Write Data Collection entry #4 for your assigned chapter in *Megatrends:* a graphic organizer for the chapter.

### Visions of the Future: What Makes a Good Presentation?

1. The presenter is clearly prepared: fluent, comfortable with the subject (can answer questions), organized, and thorough (covers the material completely).
2. The presenter uses good quality visuals that attract attention: colorful, clear, readable, legible, not too small.
3. The presenter uses examples familiar to the audience, especially ones related to the local community.
4. The presenter draws things from her or his own thoughts to go beyond the basic material.
5. The presenter uses ways to tie the listeners into the presentation and makes sure the audience is attending: for example, posing questions to the audience, allowing for audience participation, moving around the room.
6. The presenter directs attention to all members of the audience, making eye contact.
7. The presenter's posture and facial expressions (smiles) convey self-confidence.
8. The presenter speaks clearly and loudly enough for all to hear.

**Visions of the Future: Chapter Presentations**

1. What does it say?
   - Main points?
   - Key terms?
   - Significant examples?

2. What does it mean?
   - In terms of the six themes we are looking at?
   - In relation to the other trends Naisbitt has discussed so far?
   - In terms of our local community?

3. How can we use it?
   - To plan for our personal futures?
   - To understand current events and issues?
   - To determine directions we want to work for or against?
   - To redesign or restructure the world or parts of it for the far future?

# VISIONS OF THE FUTURE: CHAPTER PRESENTATIONS

Names _____ Chapter _____

1. What does it say?
   • Main points?
   • Key terms?
   • Significant examples?

2. What does it mean?
   • In terms of the six themes we are looking at?
   • In relation to the other trends Naisbitt has discussed so far?
   • In terms of our local community?

3. How can we use it?
   • To plan for our personal futures?
   • To understand current events and issues?
   • To determine directions we want to work for or against?
   • To redesign or restructure the world or parts of it for the far future?

**Visions of the Future: Schedule,**

| | |
|---|---|
| Tuesday: | Essays/projects on *Megatrends* due |
| | *Walden Two* introduced, assignment sheet handed out |
| | Introduction to scenario writing |
| Wednesday: | Scenario writing (Bring your journal) |
| Thursday: | Scenario writing (Bring your journal) |
| Friday: | Work session on Issue Analysis presentations |
| Wednesday: | Issue Analysis presentations |
| Thursday: | FPS—Dropouts |
| Friday: | FPS—Dropouts |
| Monday: | FPS—Dropouts |
| Tuesday: | FPS—Dropouts   (Mail date for FPS and scenarios) |
| Wednesday: | Discussion of *Introduction to the Future*, pp. 11–18 |
| | Discussion of *Walden Two* |
| | Individual novel assigned |
| Thursday: | Discussion of *Walden Two* |
| Friday: | Written exercise on *Walden Two* |
| | Journals due |

*Assignments*

Finish work on Issue Analysis presentation. See due dates above.
Read *Introduction to the Future*, pp. 11–18. In the Reaction/Response section of
your journal, compare and contrast the role of the writer of fiction with the
writer of nonfiction in expanding our understanding of the future. See due
date in schedule above.

Read *Walden Two*. In the Data Collection section of your journal, keep a record of the characteristics of the society that Skinner describes in the novel. In the Reaction/Response section of your journal, make two entries. In each of these entries, react or respond to some aspect of *Walden Two* that you feel is noteworthy and that you would like to discuss in class. See due dates above.

### Visions of the Future: Essay Assignment

As the culmination of our study of Naisbitt's *Megatrends*, each of you needs to reflect on the meaning of the book as a whole. This essay assignment is designed to provide a vehicle through which you can do that. Select one of the questions below which interests you. (Or see the alternative at the end.) Use the question as the focus for your reflection on the book as a whole. **Rough drafts are due Friday, Final drafts are due Tuesday.**

1. An implication of Naisbitt's analysis in *Megatrends* is that a new concept of leadership must emerge for the decades ahead. Based on *Megatrends* and your own analysis, what qualities, skills, and attitudes do you think must characterize the leader of tomorrow? Support your answer with specific evidence and examples, and make sure you use a clear line of reasoning.
2. "In the midst of change people constantly try to maintain a balance in their lives." Assess the validity of this statement, using *Megatrends* as a point of reference.
3. It can be argued that an understanding of the nature of systems and patterns of interdependence is essential for anyone who wishes to study the future. Develop an argument to support this view, using *Megatrends* as a point of reference.
4. "Wherever there is change there will be conflict." Assess the validity of this statement, using *Megatrends* as a point of reference.
5. Select any one of the six themes of this course. Develop an essay in which you synthesize what you have learned from *Megatrends* about the nature of that idea (change, conflict, technology, human dignity, systems, or interdependence) that you did not know before. (*Note:* You may want to use some of the key words from Kaplan's "content continuum" to help you develop generalizations around which you will organize your essay. Be sure to use key words from the abstract end of the continuum.)
6. "Change occurs when there is a confluence of both changing values and economic necessity, not before." Naisbitt argues that we have reached the "end of denial." Discuss what forces have brought about the change in values and what economic necessities have brought us to the realization of the necessity of change.
7. The image of the future world presented by Naisbitt is one that suggests a move to greater individualism, greater direct involvement, and greater ranges of choice. By looking at the ten trends he discusses, assess that image.

*Alternative* If you wish to use a medium of expression other than the essay, please develop a proposal for your teacher to consider. Your proposal should describe the medium you intend to use and the question you intend to address as a way of synthesizing what you've learned through reading and discussing *Megatrends*.

*Glossary*

*Analysis:* A separation of a whole into constituent parts, a study of the nature and essential elements of something.

*Assess:* To estimate the value or significance of, to judge critically the merits of.
*Assess the validity of:* See *Assess.*
*Develop an argument:* To present and elaborate upon a line of reasoning in order to persuade the reader to a particular point of view.

*Discuss:* To treat fully, providing background information and explaining how parts relate to each other.

*Generalization:* A broad inference based on data, a statement of a basic principle or idea that can be applied and that holds true in many different situations. (Note: The quotations in questions 2, 4, and 6 above are examples of generalizations.)

*Synthesize:* To bring things together into a complex whole, to combine pieces or elements to create a new understanding.

## VISIONS OF THE FUTURE: WALDEN TWO

Please respond in essay form to *both* of the following.

**1.** In discussing *Walden Two* in class, we used the theme of *systems* to examine the novel. Of the other five themes of this course, which do you feel is most important for analyzing and interpreting the book? Why? (Be very specific in your answer, showing precisely how the theme you've selected is significant and explaining why it is more important than others you might have chosen.)

**2.** If you had the opportunity to use any of the ideas Skinner advances in *Walden Two* to improve society as we know it today, what aspect of our society would you choose to improve? Why would you choose that aspect? What idea from *Walden Two* would you draw upon to change that aspect of society? Explain how that would work (be specific) and why you think that would be an improvement.

## VISIONS OF THE FUTURE: FINAL ASSIGNMENTS

Read *The Third Wave* by Alvin Toffler. Complete the following journal assignments related to the book. (You will need to do some reading over the holidays!!)

In the Data Collection section, as you read, write a one-paragraph summary of each chapter. This will help you in our discussions after Christmas break.

When you have finished the book, in the Reaction/Response section, compare and contrast Toffler's approach to/view of the future with that of Naisbitt. Be sure to use specifics from both books to support your points about similarities and differences.

**Be finished with the book and ready for discussion on Tuesday, _____.**

Individually or with a partner, develop a description of your version of the ideal world of the future. You may be creative in the format in which you write this; e.g., you may want to write it in short story form or comic book form, to name a few ideas. In your planning, determine what systems you want to/need to address in your ideal society and why those are important to an understanding of what your ideal world would be like. Make sure you have thought about the interdependence of systems in your society and the ways in which changes you make in one system may have implications for the organization of other systems in your society. Also in your planning consider how your society will deal with change, conflict, human dignity, and technology. (Does this sound like you're to use this assignment to pull together the ideas that this course has generated in you?!) **Due date: Monday, _____.**

*Revision of Assignment for Exam Period*   Read the Environment/Ecology chapter (Chapter 5) in *Introduction to the Future* and the Ozone Depletion research packet in preparation for the Ozone Depletion FPS session that will take place during our exam period.

# VISIONS OF THE FUTURE: PARTICIPATION ASSESSMENT

Name _____ Date _____

Criteria _____ Assessment _____

**Comes to class prepared for the day's discussion/presentation**

**Participates in discussion by:**

- Contributing ideas
- Answering questions when called on
- listening carefully and courteously to others
- Focusing on discussion without distraction
- Asking for clarification
- Elaborating ideas
- Building on the ideas of others
- Questioning
- Supporting or challenging ideas through use of specific data or logical analysis, whichever is most appropriate

**Works effectively in a cooperative group by:**

- Staying on task
- Carrying out an assigned role
- Making contributions of ideas and information
- Supporting and encouraging other group members.

## VISIONS OF THE FUTURE: INDIVIDUAL PROJECT ON A NOVEL

Select one of the following novels which you have not read previously.

Asimov. *I, Robot.*
Bellamy. *Looking Backward.*
Butler. *Erewhon.*
Burgess. *A Clockwork Orange.*
Clarke. *2001.*
Crichton. *The Terminal Man.*
Frank. *Alas, Babylon.*
Herbert. *Dune.*
Huxley. *Brave New World.*
Miller. *A Canticle for Leibowitz.*
Orwell. *1984.*
Shute. *On the Beach.*
Verne. *The Mysterious Island. 20,000 Leagues Under the Sea.*
Wells. *The Time Machine.*
Zamyatin. *We.*

*Note:* If you have another suggestion for a book you'd like to read instead of one of those listed above, please consult with your teacher before you make a suggestion.

As you read, develop an entry in the Data Collection section in your journal in which you make note of the characteristics of the future world which the author describes. Make particular note of systems described or implied by the novel.

When you have finished reading, make an entry in the Data Collection section in which you classify this novel using either the Whaley system or the Haas system (be sure you specify which you're using and give evidence to support your classification). Also, classify the novel in relation to the terms *science fiction*, *dystopian literature*, or *utopian literature*, and support your classification.

Write one entry in the Reaction/Response section of your journal in which you react or respond to the novel as a whole or to any part of it.

Design a visual that will fit on one side of a poster to convey the author's vision of the future to someone who has not read the book. Use as few words as possible.

**30**  *Curriculum Unit*  Pursuing the Dream: Puritans and Immigration

*Recommended Grade Level*  High school

*Subject Area*  American history, American literature

*Summary*  This American Studies course is, an eleventh-grade, team-taught, interdisciplinary course, which combines American social history with American literature. Its curriculum design is thematic rather than chronological. In this course students explore three major questions: What is the American dream? Who has pursued the dream and why? How has the dream been challenged in American society?

*Objectives*

- To understand the relationship between American history and literature.
- To learn about our nation's past through primary and secondary sources.
- To present social and cultural history of America through thematic rather than chronological goals.
- To develop social awareness among students in units on African Americans, women, Native Americans, and various ethnic groups (immigration).

*School and Contact Person*

Upper Darby High School
Lansdowne Avenue
Upper Darby, PA 19082
(215) 622-7000

Gil Minacci, Principal
Elizabeth McDonald
Martha Menz
Margaret Preis

*Procedure*  The history and English sections in this course each take their own perspective. In history, students study how each large groups of Americans have shaped their concept of the American dream and pursued it, either eventually reaching it or having it elude them. Examples of such groups include the pioneers moving westward or women striving for equality. These dreams might be termed collective dreams, for they are common goals shared by many, and the effect of their success or failure is recorded in history.

In English, students read classics of American literature to determine the effect of the dream on the individual. Fiction provides students with an intimate look at the individual dream, focusing on how people define the dream for themselves. Whereas the collective dreams form the substance of history, individual dreams compromise the themes of many literary works; thus, the student is able to take a personal view of the American experience. The women's movement, for example, takes on a poignant quality when seen through the eyes of Charlotte Perkins Gilman's long-suffering wife in *The Yellow Wallpaper*.

The juxtaposition of these two perspectives gives students a rich and varied appreciation of the American cultural heritage, celebrating its glory without shunning its complexity.

**Course Content**

    **I.** Introduction: What Is the American Dream?

   **II.** Pursuing the Dream: Seeking New Frontiers
      **a.** Puritans
      **b.** Immigration
      **c.** Pioneers Go West

  **III.** Pursuing the Dream: Seeking Success
      **a.** Industrialization
      **b.** The Twenties

  **IV.** Preserving and Extending the Dream
      **a.** The Thirties: FDR and the Depression
      **b.** World War II and the Fifties: Cold War and Conformity
      **c.** The Sixties: Affluence and Dissent
      **d.** The Seventies and Eighties: The Me Decade and Watergate

The course sequence for this unit is quite detailed. Goals have been established for each of the learning objectives. The content to be understood, the activities, and the evaluation methods to be used are described. Any resources or materials that are required are also listed. Two examples are illustrated here: one from Pursuing the Dream: Seeking New Frontiers, Puritans, and one from Pursuing the Dream: Seeking New Frontiers, Immigration.

*Textbooks*

*Legacy of Freedom*, 1986, Laidlaw
*Accent, USA*, 1972, Scott Foresman
*United States In Literature*, 1989, Pegasus Edition, Scott Foresman
*USA Series*, 1974, McDougal, Littell and Company (Government, Foreign Policy, Economy, Social Change, American Character).

*The American Dream*, 1986, Scott Foresman
*A Nation of Immigrants*, Torch, by John F. Kennedy.

*Novels and Plays*

| | |
|---|---|
| *The Assistant* | *Catcher in the Rye* |
| *Breadgivers* | *My Antonia* |
| *Giants in the Earth* | *Hawaii* |
| *The Crucible* | *The Jungle* |
| *Sister Carrie* | *The Great Gatsby* |
| *The Glass Menagerie* | *Death of a Salesman* |
| *The Yellow Wallpaper* | *Johnny Got His Gun* |
| *The Sun Also Rises* | |

# BASIC CONCEPT: AMERICAN STUDIES
# PURSUING NEW FRONTIERS: PURITAN SETTLE A NEW LAND

*Grade: 11*

| Quality Goal | Learning Objective | Content | Learning Activities/Evaluation | Resources and Materials |
|---|---|---|---|---|
| 4-(i,ii) 4-(iii) 6-(i,ii) 1-(i) 12-(i) 12-(ii) | Students will understand the basic tenets of Puritanism and how they related to life in New England politically (theocracy), socially (rigid conformity) and economically (work ethic). | Puritans came to America in 1630 seeking the dream of religious freedom in a new land. The Puritans endeavored to build a society in which the achievement of salvation coincided with the achievement of material success. Their ethic of hard work and Godliness has left an indelible mark on American life. To achieve spiritual success, the Puritan had to have a calling, a conversion experience, and worldly success. | The student will learn about Puritan life-styles through lecture by the teacher (see Alice Morse Earle's) *Life in Colonial New England* for information. Topics are: Puritan theology and Calvin. Puritan split from Church of England, settlement of Massachusetts Bay, governing the colony, Sunday in the colonies, courtship and marriage, homes and home furnishings, food, baptism and childhood, music and art, the Puritan village, and education. | Students will view videotape on Hawaii. *Hawaii* by James Michener (optional) *The Crucible* by Arthur Miller "Young Goodman Brown" and "Minister's Black Veil" by Nathaniel Hawthorne "We Aren't Superstitious" by Stephen Vincent Benêt in *Accent USA* |
| 4-(i) 6-(ii) | Students will understand the roots of Puritanism in the Protestant Reformation and 17th-century Calvinism. | | | |
| 1-(i) 6-(i,ii) 1-(i,ii) | Students will examine the puritan life-styles, values, and the results when rigid orthdoxy gets out of hand (witch hysteria and trials). | As a cultural group the Puritans valued education, hard work, thrift, attendance of church services several times a week, marriage, democracy through the town meeting, simplicity in home and personal decoration, moderation in life, and spreading the word of God to the heathen. Their life-style reflected these values, and the characters in Hawaii, Chapter 3, also reflect these values. | MOE: UNIT TEST QUIZ Read the article "The Sermon" and its importance in Puritan life and do questions. | *Life in Colonial New England* by Alice Morse Earle |
| 1-(iv) 5-(ii) 5-(iv) | Students will see Puritan ideals, thought, and values in the works of Hawthorne, Miller, and James Michener. | | MOE: CLASS DISCUSSION Read article "The Puritans and Education," read printed notes on topic, or take notes from transparency. | *Films and videotapes:* 1. "Home from Home" 2. "Witches of Salem" 3. *Hawaii* 4. "Young Goodman Brown" 5. The Puritan Experience |
| 4-(i) 6-(i,ii) | Students will compare the witch trials of 1692 with the McCarthy era of the 1950s. | Although the Puritans came to America seeking religious toleration, they did not often extend this benefit to others, like the Quakers. Such intolerance led to the witch hunt trials in Salem and other New England towns. | | |
| 6-(i,ii) 4-(i) | Students will compare life in the Middle Colonies with life in Virginia. | The play *The Crucible* by Arthur Miller shows the mob hysteria of the Salem witch hunt and trials. It is a good example of the problems of a theocratic government and authoritarian rule. It questions the results of being honest and principled. | | |

# BASIC CONCEPT: AMERICAN STUDIES
# PURSUING THE DREAM: NEW FRONTIERS
# IMMIGRATION

*Grade: 11*

| Quality Goal | Learning Objective | Content | Learning Activities/Evaluation | Resources and Materials |
|---|---|---|---|---|
| 1-(i,ii) 4-(i) 6-(i,ii) | Students will understand the concept of a nation of immigrants, a nation of nations. | America is a nation of nations, a melting pot of nationalities. | Read *A Nation of Immigrants* and do study guide questions for each chapter. | *Breadgivers* by Anzia Yezierska |
| 1-(i) 4-(i) 6-(i) | Students will identify the motives for immigration, patterns of settlement, contributions of immigrants, resistance to immigration, and hardships in adapting to a New World. | America as a nation of immigrants is unique in the world. Even our native peoples migrated to America from Russia, it is believed.

America is a blending or melting pot of nationalities, with each nationality retaining some of its individuality such as customs and physical features. | MOE QUIZ Make a chart of who came, when, why, where they settled, using Chapter 4 in *A Nation of Immigrants*.

MOE: UNIT TEST Make a map showing patterns of settlement using outline desk map of United States. | *The Assistant* by Bernard Malamud

From *The Bitter Land*

*A Nation of Immigrants* by John F. Kennedy

"The Case of John Nichols" by John S. Nicholas |
| 1-(i,v) 4-(i) 12-(i) 12-(ii) 12-(iv) 12-(v) | Students will investigate the conflict between the Old World and the New World in the following areas: values, customs, role of women, social mobility, experiences. | Immigration has strengthened the American dream of equality, freedom, and boundless opportunity.

As immigrants sought new physical frontiers, they also sought new political and economic frontiers. Their strivings brought new meaning to the words *social mobility*, as seen in *The Assistant* by Bernard Malamud. | Read *Breadgivers*. In connection with the novel, do the following:

Listen to teacher lecture on life of Anzia Yezierska and take notes. Compare Anzia to Sara on unit test in essay form. | "The Free Man"

"In Jewish Harlem" by Sam Levenson

"The Crossing" in *The Uprooted* by Oscar Handlin

"The First Seven Years" by Bernard Malamud |
| 4-(i,ii) 1-(ii) 11-(i) 11-(ii) 11-(iii) | Students will describe how native Americans have stemmed the tide of immigration from 1880 to the present through legislation and unofficial restriction. | Immigrants came for a variety of reasons from a variety of countries. Religious persecution, economic hardships, and political oppression are the most common motives. | Take quiz on characters in chart form. Compare Bessie, Mashah, Fania, Sara with respect to: name meaning, loves, why Reb rejected loves, their fate. | *The Immigrant* by Neil Sedaka

Films: *Island Called Ellis*

*The Huddled Masses* |
| 1-(i) 4-(i,ii) 4-(iii) 6-(i,ii) 6-(iii) 6-(iv) | Students will analyze the question of admitting "new" immigrants from Central America and Southeast Asia and examine current immigration policy. | Before 1880 most immigrants were from northwestern Europe. After 1880 a great influx from southeastern Europe came.

The immigrant's experience of merely getting here and adjusting to American life, customs, language, ideals is one of hardship. | Discuss the following themes in the novel and take class notes (MOE: UNIT TEST) role of women, Image of New | *Hester Street*

*Immigrant Experience: Long, Long Journey* |

*31* **Curriculum Unit** The Southern Way

**Subject Areas** English, history, music

**Recommended Grade Levels** High school

**Summary** Students explore Alabama and Southern heritage as a whole.

**Objectives** The student will:

- Demonstrate an expanded knowledge of what Alabama and the SOuth have to offer an individual.
- Gain an understanding of the historical development of Alabama, including its people, manners, and customs.
- Develop an appreciation of the literature of the South.
- Transfer knowledge learned in history to the understanding of southern writing and literature.

**School and Contact Person**

Vestavia Hills High School
2235 Lime Rock Road
Vestavia Hills, AL 35216
(205) 823-4044

Michael Gross, Principal
Melissa Caffey

**Procedures** In a thematic study of Alabama and the great South, you will be studying, observing, and developing an awareness of the past as well as the current South. A cross-section of Southern literature, history, architecture, celebrities, cooking, customs, crafts, and folklore will be studied in the true Southern spirit.

*Each* student is required to prepare a five- to ten-minute presentation on the following:

**Southern Writers** Make an oral presentation to the class on a Southern piece of literature. The selection may be a short story, poems, essay, or chapter from a novel. In your discussion, include what makes your selection truly Southern. Concentrate on characterization, theme, setting, plot, dialect, language, word choice, and tone.

**Group Activity** (no more than four people per group): For your group activity, choose one of the following:

1. *"Down Home Cookin'"*: What makes Southern cooking different from other cooking? What is considered a truly Southern meal? A vittle samplin' and recipe sharin' is required.

2. *Southern Architecture:* Tara was only the beginning. . . . Through discussion, pictorial study, or models, present an in-depth study of Southern architecture. Include architecture varying from the "ole log cabin" to the grand antebellum mansion. Models will be accepted.

3. *"Stars" Fell on Alabama:* Many "stars" are famous Alabamians or Southerners. Prepare a mock interview, Barbara Walters style, on a famous Alabamian. Videotapin' and a script is required.

4. *Foot-Stompin', Knee-Bangin', Banjo-Playin' Music:* A cross-section of great Southern music is to be presented to the class. Characteristics of the music as well as the music itself are needed in order to get into the swing of things. Spirituals, bluegrass, jazz, and more recent music from Southern groups are needed for a true display of music Southern style.

5. *For Folks That Take a Likin' to Arts and Crafts:* Quilting, whittling, and basket weaving are only a few of the many great Southern crafts. Present to the class various "traditional" great crafts or possibly let the class participate in a "mini-craft" session.

6. *Alabama Folklore:* Recollections from the past as presented in Carl Carmer's book, *Stars Fell on Alabama,* will bring back times from long ago. Spirituals, all-day singings, foot washings, and square dancing are only a few of the traditional beliefs, practices, and legends that have been verbally retold generation after generation. Through storytelling, present to the class an array of great Southern tales. A possible idea may be interviewing someone from the old South and sharing the story with the class.

7. *For Those Who Like to Write:* Create an original Southern short story, poem, or song. Be sure to keep in the Southern tone. Your piece will be read or sung to the class. Remember to consider dialect, tone, and other elements that will make your writing a true Southern work.

**Lesson One**

Exploring What We Know about *Alabama* and the *South.*

*Preparation*   Place Alabama-related reading material around the room. Set up a card table in the back of the room that has a red-checkered tablecloth. On the table place books such as *The Autobiography of Miss Jane Pittman, The History of Alabama* and short story collections by such authors as William Faulkner, Truman Capote, Flannery O'Connor, and Mark Twain. Place lyrics of famous Southern songs, pictures of famous Southerners, and copies of *Southern Living* and *Southern Accents* on the table as well.

*Activity*   Let students browse around the room and look at the various books, pamphlets, etc. After about twenty minutes, have students brainstorm and write down as many facts as they can about the information they have just viewed, as well as facts they already know about the South and Alabama. Share the information with the class.

**Lesson Two**

Is That What They Really Think?

*Preparation*   Make copies of Lewis Grizzard's "Is That What They Really Think?" Make copies of the Lewis Grizzard handout "Between the South and Chicago, the Choice Is Simple," "Getting Even Is the Best Revenge (or Something)."

*Activity*   Have the class list what comes to their mind when they think of the South. Read handout, "Is That What They Really Think?"

Discuss stereotypes. Have the class write down positive images of the South. Pass out brochures from the Chamber of Commerce. List all the interesting things that Alabama has to offer. With a partner, have students prepare a ten-minute interview. Students will designate one person to be the "Alabamaian" and the other student to be the "non-Alabamaian." The non-Alabamaian is considering moving to Alabama and will write questions about things that concern his or her family. The non-Alabamian should try to ask questions that require detailed information. The Alabamian will write questions about the newcomer's interest and family. The Alabamaian should gather information and attempt to prove that Alabama would be a good home for the non-Alabamian.

**Lesson Three**

*Preparation*   Make copies of Grizzard's "Southerners Need Not Fret over Accents." Get copy of Capote's "A Silver Jug."

*Activity*   Discuss dialogue. Discuss dialect. Read "A Silver Jug." Pass around a container with candy in it. Let students guess the amount of candy in the jug. Discuss the use of dialect in the story and what makes "A Silver Jug" a true Southern story. At the end of class, let the student who guessed the closest to the correct amount have the candy jar.

**Lesson Four**

*Preparation*   Get copies of Capote's "A Christmas Memory."

*Assignment*   Have the class write a one-page story about one of their Christmas memories. Read "A Christmas Memory" and answer questions concerning characterization and setting. Discuss why this story is a true Southern story. Share the students' stories with the class.

**Lesson Five**

*Preparation*   Get a copy of "A Rose for Emily."

*Assignment*   Read "A Rose for Emily." Place an overhead projector the following:

1. Write a short poem that sums up "Rose for Emily."
2. Draw a picture that illustrates the story.
3. Write three adjectives that express how this story makes you feel.

Have the class divide into groups of four to complete the three steps above. Allow only ten minutes to complete the steps.

**Lesson Six**

*Preparation*   Have one of the Alabama history teachers or someone from the community come and talk with the class about slavery and the Civil War. Have students prepare specific questions that they would like the speaker to answer.

*Assignment*   View "The Autobiography of Miss Jane Pitman." Discuss how this book represents Southern history from the perspective of a black woman born into slavery on a Louisiana plantation. Miss Jane tells her story, summarizing "The American history of her race."

*32* *Curriculum Unit* This Land Is Your Land: A Festival of Ecological Activities

*Subject Areas* Chemistry, biology, earth science, language arts, social studies

*Recommended Grade Levels* High school

*Summary* The preservation of the environment is a crucial issue in today's society. Students will be made aware in this unit of the ecological problems and how they effect human life. They will also learn how the earth's precious resources can be saved.

*Objectives*

1. Awareness of the earth's/current environmental problems and illustration of man's impact on our world will be promoted.
2. Problems that affect human life today and in the future will be identified.
3. Solutions to the earth's environmental problems will be addressed.

*School and Contact Persons*

Tavravella High School
10600 Riverside Drive
Coral Springs, FL 33076
(305) 344-2315

M. E. Huber, Principal
Duke Donatucci
Kathy Guilbert
J. P. Keener

*Procedures* This unit is divided into 11 separate lessons plus one culminating actively at the end of the four-week unit plan. The culminating unit is described first so the reader may understand how the lessons fit together.

### . . . From California . . .

*Eco-fest* An ecological culminating activity.
     The eco-fest displays many of the findings made by the participating classes over a period of four weeks. This will be a multipurpose assembly for the entire school, conducted as a fair held in the school gym. The design will motivate uninterested students to participate and will enable interested, motivated students to develop a better understanding of confusing issues. The scope of this activity will be of interest to the entire school staff as well.
     Following is a list of many eco-fest activities:

- Environmental awareness will be demonstrated by a slide show emphasizing the problems of our environment in a variety of geographical locations.

- Landfill use will be demonstrated with critical statistics, problems, solutions, and goals. Research will be displayed, and questions will be addressed.
- Recycling will be addressed from an analytical viewpoint, displaying critical data, future ideas, and solutions to pressing problems.
- A collaborative musical event, entitled "This Land Is Your Land," will be presented to the collective assembly group.
- Environmentally safe foods will be served in environmentally sound dishware, with emphasis on recycling, landfill surplus, litter, and waste management.

### Lesson 1: . . . to the New York Island . . .

*Rate of Decay for Common Throw-away Items*   Students will select a variety of common types of garbage, organic and inorganic, to be placed in an area of soil outside of the school. Each item will first be massed and then critically examined with a microscope and hand lens. A picture and detailed observation report will be kept. At the end of the four-week period, the garbage will be brought back inside for a second massing to determine the amount of decay. Analysis via microscope will be redone with close attention to the nature of decay and to any bacterial growth. Data tables and graphs will be constructed to show short-term decay.

For evaluation, an oral discussion will be held to discuss the various findings. Students will be asked to self-evaluate their studies and to determine what might be changed to guarantee better results. A list will be composed assessing the decomposition qualities of various items. Students will submit a formal lab report, which will include a written conclusion of ideas. The results will be displayed at the eco-fest for peer evaluation.

Materials needed for this lesson are: common garbage, balances, microscopes, slides, cover slips, and hand lenses.

### Lesson 2: . . . From the Redwood Forest . . .

*"A Day in Life of the Earth"*   Students will be asked to envision themselves as a living, breathing earth. The students will be required to assimilate feelings that the earth might have under present conditions and to write about them creatively in poetic rhythm. Some of the best works will be displayed at the eco-fest culminating activity.

For evaluation, students will submit a correct version for grading. Students will read their poem to the class and allow for self and peer evaluation.

### Lesson 3: . . . to the Gulf Stream Waters . . .

*Ecological Disasters*   Students will be asked to develop a list of ecological tragedies and then choose one to research (e.g., Love Canal, Three Mile Island). Through the use of reference materials, the students will be asked to prepare a cause-and-effect summary of their event, and then to propose a list of "what if" solutions, and alternatives to the problem. Their research will be displayed at the eco-fest activity.

For evaluation, students will submit their written findings and bibliography to the teacher. The students will discuss their individual findings with the class as a group and present their research to the school at the culminating assembly.

## Lesson 4: . . . This Land Was Made for You and Me!

*Recycling*  Students will be given a garbage bag and plastic gloves to collect daily trash. The next day, students will separate their trash into paper, plastic, glass, aluminum, metals, and other materials. This collection process will continue for one week. During this time, students will group and research methods for recycling and prepare a factual poster demonstrating their research. At the end of the week the garbage will be individually weighed, and a bar graph will be constructed and displayed with the poster and other findings at the eco-fest culminating activity.

For evaluation, students will discuss their findings with the students at the assembly. Self and peer evaluation will be encouraged.

## Lesson 5: . . . to the New York Island

*Preparing the Eco-fest*  Students will write and send letters to prominent people in the community to determine if they are interested in participating in the "This Land Is Your Land" eco-fest. Students will also formulate questions that will be used to interview potential presenters. To complete this assignment, students will brainstorm who should be invited and what should be written in the letter. Questions will be formulated that will be used to interview the guests.

For evaluation, students will exchange their letters and interview questions for peer and self-evaluation. The teacher will then review the letters and questions. The students will select which letters and questions could be used.

## Lesson 6: . . . From the Redwood Forest . . .

*Ecology T-shirts*  The class will brainstorm ideas for "ecology T-shirts." The ideas will center around the theme "This Land Is Your Land." After all the ideas have been presented, a final design will be selected by the members of the class. The students will then decorate their own individual shirts, using the design selected by the class. Materials such as paint, lettering, glue, and glitter should be available. The students will wear the shirts on the day of the eco-fest and be prepared to explain their origin to students at the assembly.

For evaluation, students will self- and peer evaluate the T-shirt design.

## Lesson 7: . . . to the Gulf Stream Waters . . .

*Futures Wheel*  Students will be divided into groups of four or five to create a Futures Wheel. This wheel will demonstrate a problem and/or a solution to an ecological situation or crisis. The final Futures Wheel will be presented by the group to the other members of the class and then to students at the assembly.

Both peers and the teacher will evaluate the Futures Wheel and the presentations.

### Lesson 8: . . . This Land Was Made for You and Me!

*Theme Song*  The class will brainstorm ideas for a theme song for the eco-fest. Ideas will be shared by the entire class. After a class consensus is reached, a theme song will be written and will be presented by class members at the eco-fest.

The teacher will have final approval of the theme song.

### Lesson 9: . . . to the New York Island . . .

*Polling*  Students will set up four large writing pads in the classroom. All students will brainstorm questions they can ask people in the community about ecological problems. Then they will formulate the questions under main topics. Students will group themselves into teams of about five students each and select four questions for their team. In one week's time, the students on the team should ask these questions of adults in the community. The students will discuss the results and share their responses and opinion with classmates. Final results will be written and shared at the eco-fest.

The evaluation for this unit will consist of peer and teacher evaluation of the polling results.

### Lesson 10: . . . from the Redwood Forest . . .

*National Parks*  The students will write letters to superintendents of various national parks requesting material (photos, maps, records, graphs, etc.) depicting landscapes before and after extended periods of time. The students will compose a slide show based on their findings, and narrate the show at the eco-fest assembly using information gathered from the various sources.

The students will self-evaluate their input and then discuss their slide shows in a group, allowing for criticism, improvement, and peer evaluation.

### Lesson 11: . . . to the Gulf Stream Waters . . .

*The Menu of Foods*  Students will research recycling and garbage to determine which items are best suited for the environment. On the basis of their findings, students will develop a menu of foods prepared using safe supplies and will serve their creations on environmentally safe products at the eco-fest. Students will discuss their findings at the eco-fest with students and faculty.

For evaluation, students will work in groups to encourage self- and peer evaluations. A final menu will be submitted to the teacher for official evaluation.

## *33* *Curriculum Unit* Rocketry

*Subject Areas* Technology, science, math

*Recommended Grade Levels* High school

*Summary* Using a model rocket, students will learn the technology of rocketry and the application of mathematical formulas to solve problems related to flight of the rocket.

*Objectives*

- To learn how to build a model rocket
- To understand how a rocket flies
- To be able to calculate data about a rocket's flight
- To be able to apply mathematical formulas

*School and Contact Person*

Kennebunk High School
89 Fletcher St.
Kennebunk, ME 04043
(207) 985-1110

David McConnell, Principal
Amos McCallum, Department Chairperson
David Mitchell, author of unit

*Procedure* Students were given instructions on how to build a rocket that would successfully launch and release a parachute at the highest point and then safely return to the ground. The challenge was to build a rocket that would go the highest and the fastest. Along with specific instructions each student received vocabulary words pertaining to their rocket launch. These words would help them assemble their rockets, calculate the height and speed of each successful launch, and understand the physical aspects of rocketry.

Mathematically, students were instructed in how trigonometry is used to calculate the altitude of each successful rocket launch. We first used an inclinometer to calculate the angle of elevation that the rocket obtained from the ground level to its maximum apogee. We knew how far away from the launch pad we were, so we could then use this angle to calculate the altitude.

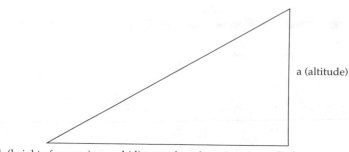

h (height of person)     d (distance from launch pad)     Pad

Altitude = (tan $\theta$ × d) + h

Students learned that when you have a right triangle, trigonometry can be used to find desired lengths. With respect to the angle of elevation that we found, we want to calculate the opposite side of the triangle, and we know the adjacent side. This information tells us to use the tangent function.

$$\text{Tan } \theta = \frac{\text{Opposite}}{\text{Adjacent}} = \frac{a}{d}$$

Using a calculator, we find the tangent of the angle of elevation and multiply it by the distance from the launch pad. This calculation gives us the length of the opposite side of the triangle. To calculate the altitude of the rocket's flight, we must add in the height of the person. This gives us the total length of the path traveled by the rocket from launch to apogee. This is known as the rocket's *altitude.*

While one student was calculating the angle of elevation with the inclinometer, another student was timing the length of time the rocket took to get to its maximum height. This time divided into the distance traveled (altitude) will calculate the average speed of the rocket.

$$\text{Rate (average speed)} = \frac{\text{Distance}}{\text{Time}}$$

By multiplying the average speed by 3,600 seconds, we change the seconds to hours. Now we divide this answer by 8,200 feet to put the answer in final form as miles per hour.

Finally, we decided to take another step and calculate the speed of the rocket at ignition. This required a formula used in calculus that takes into consideration the pull of gravity against the rocket while in flight.

$$S(t) = at^2 = V_0 t = S_0$$

$S(t)$ = maximum height of the rocket (altitude)
$a$     = pull of gravity ($-32$ ft/sec)
$t$     = time of the flight
$V_0$   = initial velocity or speed at ignition
$S_0$   = initial height of the rocket while on the launch

Because the rocket starts on the ground, the initial height is zero and is not a factor in the formula. The pull of gravity is $-32$ feet per second squared and is placed into the formula to give us:

$$S(t) = -16t^2 = V_0 t$$

We now solve for the initial velocity ($V_0$)

$$\frac{S(t) = 16t^2}{t} = V_0$$

By putting in all our known information—that is, the altitude and the time—we can solve for the initial velocity, in units per second. Because students can relate better to miles per hour, we change the average speed and initial velocity.

$$V_0(ft/sec) \times \frac{3,600 \text{ seconds}}{5,280 \text{ feet}} = V_0(m/h)$$

By multiplying the initial velocity by 3,600 seconds, we change the seconds to hours. We now divide this answer by 5,280 feet to finalize the answer to miles per hour.

For example:

Height of person = 6 feet
Angle of elevation (0) = 57°
d = distance to launch pad = 420 feet

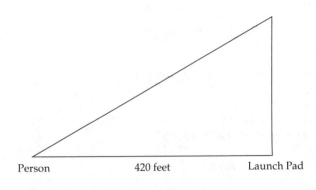

Person                    420 feet                    Launch Pad

Altitude = (Tan 0 × d) + h
        = (Tan 57 deg. × 420 ft.) + 7 ft.
        = (1.5399 × 420 ft.) + 6 ft.
        = 646.8 ft. + 6 ft.
        = 652.8 ft.

Maximum height or altitude is 652.8 feet
Time of flight = 5.3 seconds

$$\text{Rate (average speed)} = \frac{\text{Distance}}{\text{Time}} = \frac{652.8 \text{ ft.}}{5.3 \text{ sec.}} = 123.2 \text{ ft./sec.}$$

$$123.2 \text{ ft./sec.} \times \frac{3,600 \text{ sec.}}{5,280 \text{ ft.}} = 84 \text{ mi./hr.} = \text{average speed}$$

$$V_0 = \frac{S(t) + 16t^2}{t} \quad \frac{652.8 \text{ ft.} + 16\text{ft./sec.}^2 (5.3 \text{ sec.})^2}{5.3 \text{ sec.}} = 208 \text{ ft./sec.}$$

$$208 \text{ ft./sec.} \times \frac{3,600 \text{ sec.}}{5,280 \text{ ft.}} = 141.8 \text{ mi./hr.}$$

This figure, 141.8 miles per hour, is the initial velocity or velocity at take-off.

### Rocket Launch Program

```
10    PRINT "THIS PROGRAM WILL CAL
      CULATE THE HEIGHT OF THE ROC
      KET,AVERAGE SPEED, AND INITI
      AL VELOCITY."
20    PRINT
30    PRINT "WHAT WAS THE ANGLE OF
      ELEVATION OF YOUR ROCKET?"
40    PRINT
50    PRINT "WHAT IS THE TANGENT V
      ALUE FOR THIS ANGLE"
60    INPUT T
70    PRINT "HOW FAR AWAY FROM THE
      ROCKET WAS THE ANGLE OF ELE
      VATION DETERMINED FROM?"
80    INPUT D
90    PRINT "HOW TALL IS THE PERSO
      N THAT DETERMINED YOUR ANGLE
      OF ELEVATION?"
100   INPUT X
110   PRINT "HOW LONG WAS YOUR RO
      CKET IN FLIGHT?"
120   INPUT Y
130   LET H = (T * D) + X
140   PRINT "THE HEIGHT OF THE RO
      CKET IS: "H"FT
150   LET S = (H / Y) * 3600 / 52
      80
151   LET S = INT (100 * S + .5)
      / 100
160   PRINT "THE AVERAGE SPEED OF
      YOUR ROCKET IS: "S"M/HR"
161   LET V = (H + (Y ^ 2 * 16)) *
      3600 / (Y * 5280)
162   LET V = INT (100 * V + .5)
      / 100
163   PRINT "THE INITIAL VELOCITY
      OF YOUR ROCKET IS: "V"M/HR"
170   PRINT "WOULD YOU LIKE TO DO
      ANOTHER PROBLEM(1 = YES, 0 = NO)
      "
180   INPUT A
190   IF A = 1 THEN GOTO 10
200   END
```

**34** *Curriculum Unit*  The Spirit of Romanticism

*Subject Areas*  English, world history, art, music

*Recommended Grade Level*  High school

*Summary*  This project is aimed at enabling students to see the interrelatedness of history, literature, art, and music of the Romantic Age, particularly that of the period surrounding the French Revolution.

*Objectives*

- Students will understand the historic causes and effects of the French Revolution.
   a. They will recognize the roles played by the figures of Robespierre and Napoleon.
   b. They will study the effects of the Revolution in America as well as on the Continent.
- Students will become familiar with the literature of the age, appreciating in particular the character of the new romantic hero.
- Students will see the evolution of the symphony from the Neoclassical Age to the Romantic.
- Students will appreciate art as the product of the age that produces it.

*School and Contact Persons*

Tavavella High School
10600 Riverside Drive
Coral Springs, FL 33071
(305) 344-2315

M. E. Huber, Principal
Margery Marcus
Penelope Fritzer
Fran Tankovich
J. P. Keener

*Procedure*  The curriculum unit is established according to a timetable of approximately four weeks from February to March. This unit can be used at any time of the school year according to the teacher's needs.

*Week One*  Introduction of the unit in world history and in English classes. The following two novels are distributed to all the students. In world history class the students are expected to read *A Tale of Two Cities*. In English class the students will read *The Count of Monte Cristo.* The French Revolution as well as the reign of Napoleon is studied in both world history and English classes. The students will need to know about Napoleon as background to reading *The Count of Monte Cristo.*

*Week Two*   In English class the students are taught the music of the Neoclassical and the Romantic Age. The best way to achieve this is for one of the school's music teachers to come into the English class. In some cases a substitute teacher or coverage for one or two periods may be needed to schedule this. The concentration should be on Mozart for the Neoclassical period and Beethoven and Tchaikovsky for the Romantic period.

*Week Three*   One of the school's art teachers visits the English classes to show a slide presentation entitled "Appreciating Art." The emphasis is on the elements of art and how to view a painting. In addition, students view a slide presentation on "Painting from the French Revolution to 1900" and an audio/filmstrip set entitled "Eighteenth Century Art and Music."

*Week Four*   Students take a field trip to a local art museum. Students must take a notebook with them to record the name of a painting, the artist, and their feelings after viewing it. Students are encouraged to discuss quietly in groups of two or three particular paintings at the museum. In English class the students complete a writing assignment incorporating an experience with their own life with feelings they have after viewing a painting at the museum. Students must write a book report on both novels read.

### Materials

One audio/filmstrip set entitled "Eighteenth Century Art and Music." Educational Audio Visual Inc.

One set of slides entitled "Painting from the French Revolution to 1900." Educational Audio Visual Inc.

**35** *Curriculum Unit*  Amusement Park Science (the course is called Trisics)

*Recommended Grade Level*  High school

*Subject Areas*  Mathematics (trigonometry) and physics

*Summary*  This course requires that students go on rides at a local amusement park to collect data related to physics concepts.

*Objective*

- To demonstrate physical phenomena and laws of nature from bodily experience.
- To create scientific/mathematical models for similar occurrences in nature.

*School and Contact Person*

Heritage High School
1401 West Geddes
Littleton, CO 80120
(303) 795-1353

James Ferguson, Principal
Ronald Hogan
Judy Westerberg

*Procedure*

**Trisics . . . The Mathematical Universe**

(offered jointly between the science and math departments)

*Credit*  5 hours science laboratory credit (equivalent to physics), 4 hours mathematics credit (equivalent to trigonometry)

*Course Outline*

*Unit I*  Thinking

- The Process of Science
- The Art of Measurement
- Thinking with Mathematical Relations
- Principles of Conservation

*Unit II*   Plotting

- Functions
- Slopes and Changes

*Unit III*   Directions

- Trigonometric Functions and Definitions
- Vectors and Scalars
- Resolution and Addition

*Unit IV*   Motion I

- Kinematics–Rectilinear
- Changes and Proportions–Graphs

*Unit V*   Forces

- Resolution of Vectors
- Friction
- The Inclined Plane
- Gravity
- Trigonometric Identities

*Unit VI*   Waves

- Graphing of Energy–Potential and Kinetic as Trigonometric Functions
- Simple Harmonic Motion
- Waves: A Transfer of Energy
- The Wave Equation
- Waves on Water
- Trig Functions: Graphing

*Unit VII*   Motion II

- The Resolution of Projected Velocities
- Circular Motion: Torques and Balance
- Sinusoids

*Unit VIII*   Universe

- Stellar Distances
- Plotting of Orbits
- Relativity and Limits
- Special Topics

*Unit IX*   Energy

- Work and Power
- Energy of Motion and Position
- Momentum
- Solutions to Trigonometric Equations

This is an experiment in Mathematics, Physics, and the Senses. Please—do not attempt to have any fun, or enjoy yourself in any way.

Take appropriate notes, estimates, and ride sketches as necessary. Think about the ride as you wait in line—discuss it with your colleagues. Rides may be taken in any order—but cover them all. Many times, if necessary!

### The Wave Swinger

What motions do you observe other than rotation?

What forces act to make the motion fun?

Can you think of any analogous or similar motions?

### Scooters

How does this ride work?

Is the steering responsive?

How might a law of action/reaction be demonstrated on this ride?

### Roundup

How *fast* are you going? What data do you need?

Does your body go horizontal? If not . . . how close do you come to being horizontal?

*Sky Ride*

How fast are you going?

How high do you get?

How is the chair balanced—empty or full?

*Tilt-a-Whirl*

Identify primary and secondary axes of rotation.

What other rides or physical phenomena have two axes of rotation?

How do you adjust your position to rotate faster?

What if you're alone?

*Sea Dragon*

During the ride—do you ever look straight down?

Over how large an angle—measured from the top, does the boat extent?

How long is the boat? . . . give your answer in feet.

When do you feel the strongest push at your back? the most pressure against your seat?

When did you feel you were going the fastest?

What time is required for one *period?*

Sketch a graph to show how your distance from the ground changes with time?

How does this ride stop?

### Ferris Wheel

How fast are you going?

Where do you feel yourself moving the fastest? The slowest?

In what order are the cars loaded, and why?

### Troika/Spider

What different motions are there? Identify axes and radii of motions.

Sketch the path of a rider.

*Holland Express*

What differences in "seat pressure" do you detect (backward, forward, etc.) as the ride continues?

What is the effect of the uneven surface? All things being equal, what if the ride were flat?

*Rainbow*

Compare the ride at these clock positions:
12:00

3:00

6:00

9:00

How many revolutions per minute for this ride?

After you ride observe, from the front, a person sitting in your former seat. Is the path of travel a circle?

*Roller Coasters*

Plot the path followed . . . labeling "critical" points and sections.

Describe the "energy" of the ride.

*Ride Follow-up*   Which ride was:

Fastest?

Most exciting?

Most "secure"?

Complete this table for at least four rides:

| *Ride* | *Pulse before* | *Pulse after* | *Comments* |
| --- | --- | --- | --- |
| | | | |
| | | | |
| | | | |
| | | | |

Which ride(s) gave the greatest illusion of speed and danger?

## TRISICS AMUSEMENT PARK TERMS

        Energy:

        Rotation:

        Swing:

        Inertia:

        Rolling:

        Probability:

        Revolution:

        Axis:   Primary

                Secondary:

        Force:

        Reaction:

        Speed:

        Steer:

        Degrees:

        Angles:

        Distance:

        Arc length:

        Period:

        Radius:

        Clockwise:

        Estimate:

        Frame of Reference:

### 36   *Curriculum Unit*   Journeys

*Recommended Grade Level*   High school

*Subject Areas*   Social studies, English, music, art

*Summary*   The course is built around different themes, socialization, ancestry, life and death, and secular belief systems. Each year the teachers pick and choose "areas" and follow the interest of the students. The course is flexible and adaptable to current events.

*Objectives*

- To decompartmentalize and demonstrate to students the integration of various disciplines.

*School and Contact Person*

South Brunswick High School
P.O. Box 183, Major Road
Monmouth Junction, NJ 08852
(908) 329-4044

Richard Kaye, Principal
Lou Pini
Joyce Greenberg Lott

*Procedure*   The following schemes for each of the four major themes are included here.

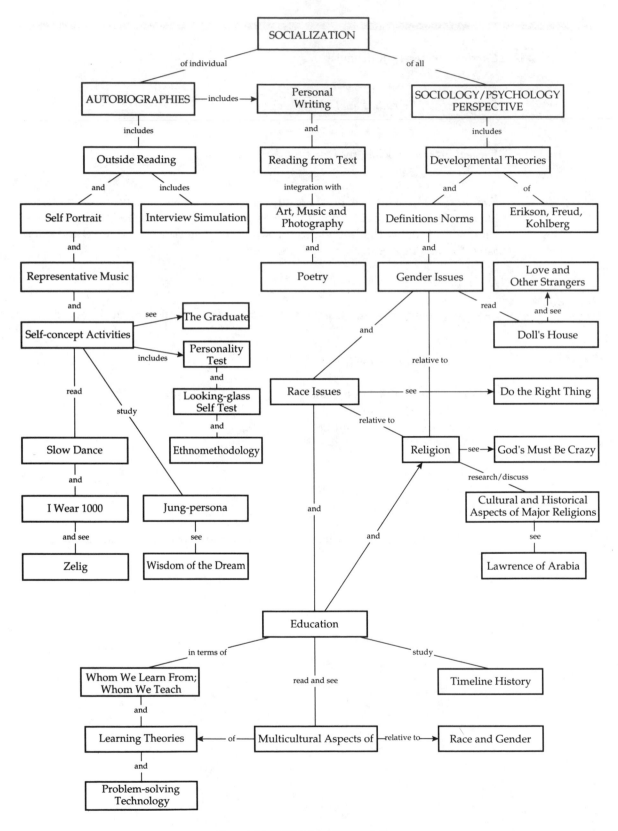

SOCIALIZATION

of individual | of all

AUTOBIOGRAPHIES —includes→ Personal Writing | SOCIOLOGY/PSYCHOLOGY PERSPECTIVE

includes | and | includes

Outside Reading | Reading from Text | Developmental Theories

and | includes | integration with | and | of

Self Portrait | Interview Simulation | Art, Music and Photography | Definitions Norms | Erikson, Freud, Kohlberg

and | and | and

Representative Music | Poetry | Gender Issues | Love and Other Strangers

and | read | and see

Self-concept Activities —see→ The Graduate | Doll's House

includes → Personality Test | relative to

and | read | Race Issues —see→ Do the Right Thing

Looking-glass Self Test | relative to

study | and | Religion —see→ God's Must Be Crazy

Slow Dance | Ethnomethodology | research/discuss

and | Cultural and Historical Aspects of Major Religions

I Wear 1000 | Jung-persona | see

and see | see | Lawrence of Arabia

Zelig | Wisdom of the Dream

and

Education

in terms of | read and see | study

Whom We Learn From; Whom We Teach | Timeline History

and | relative to

Learning Theories ←of— Multicultural Aspects of —relative to→ Race and Gender

and

Problem-solving Technology

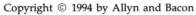

Copyright © 1994 by Allyn and Bacon

230

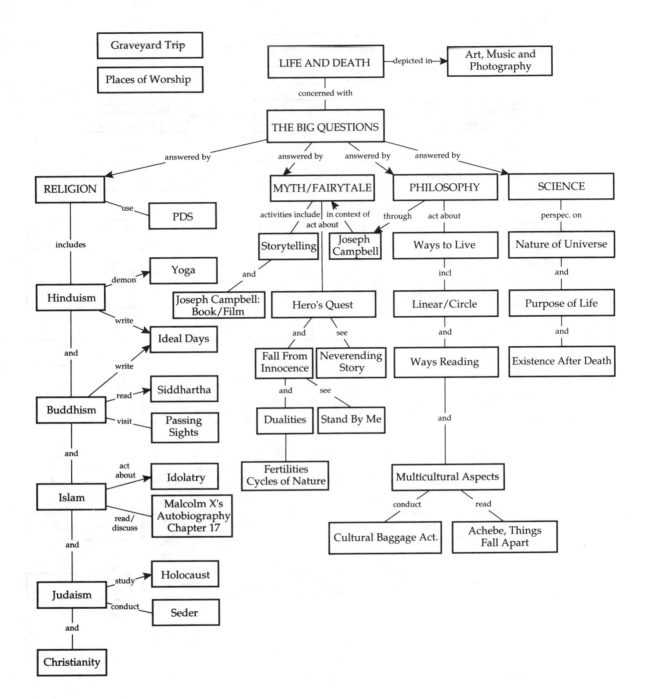

Graveyard Trip

Places of Worship

LIFE AND DEATH —depicted in→ Art, Music and Photography

concerned with

THE BIG QUESTIONS

answered by — RELIGION
answered by — MYTH/FAIRYTALE
answered by — PHILOSOPHY
answered by — SCIENCE

RELIGION — use → PDS

includes

Hinduism — demon → Yoga
Hinduism — write → Ideal Days

and

Buddhism — write → Ideal Days
Buddhism — read → Siddhartha
Buddhism — visit → Passing Sights

and

Islam — act about → Idolatry
Islam — read/discuss → Malcolm X's Autobiography Chapter 17

and

Judaism — study → Holocaust
Judaism — conduct → Seder

and

Christianity

MYTH/FAIRYTALE — activities include → Storytelling; in context of / act about → Joseph Campbell

Storytelling — and → Joseph Campbell: Book/Film
Hero's Quest

Hero's Quest — and → Fall From Innocence; see → Neverending Story

Fall From Innocence — and → Dualities
Neverending Story — see → Stand By Me

Dualities — Fertilities Cycles of Nature

PHILOSOPHY — through / act about → Ways to Live

Ways to Live — incl → Linear/Circle
Linear/Circle — and → Ways Reading
Ways Reading — and → Multicultural Aspects

Multicultural Aspects — conduct → Cultural Baggage Act.
Multicultural Aspects — read → Achebe, Things Fall Apart

SCIENCE — perspec. on → Nature of Universe
Nature of Universe — and → Purpose of Life
Purpose of Life — and → Existence After Death

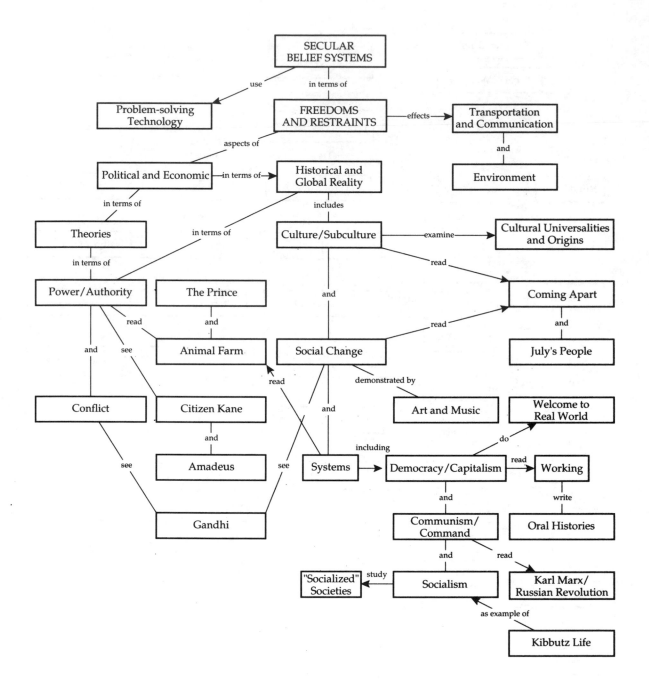

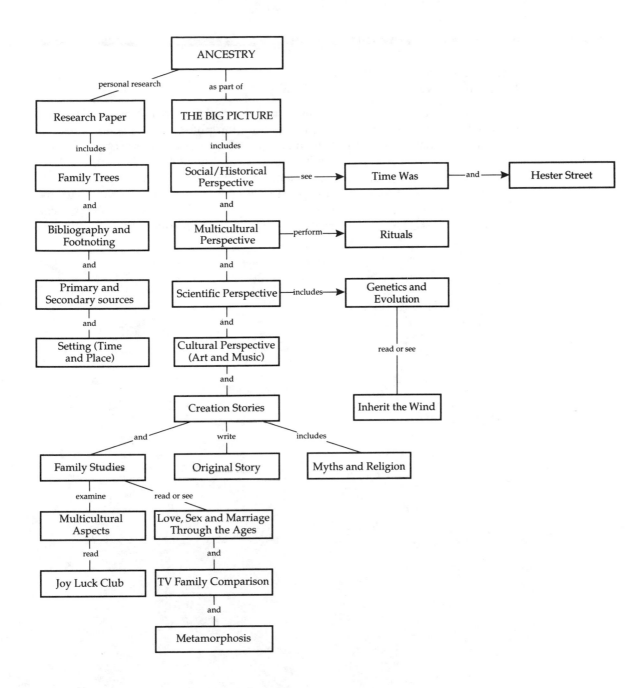

ANCESTRY

personal research — Research Paper

as part of — THE BIG PICTURE

Research Paper
includes — Family Trees
and — Bibliography and Footnoting
and — Primary and Secondary sources
and — Setting (Time and Place)

THE BIG PICTURE
includes — Social/Historical Perspective
and — Multicultural Perspective
and — Scientific Perspective
and — Cultural Perspective (Art and Music)
and — Creation Stories

Social/Historical Perspective — see — Time Was — and — Hester Street

Multicultural Perspective — perform — Rituals

Scientific Perspective — includes — Genetics and Evolution — read or see — Inherit the Wind

Creation Stories
and — Family Studies
write — Original Story
includes — Myths and Religion

Family Studies
examine — Multicultural Aspects — read — Joy Luck Club
read or see — Love, Sex and Marriage Through the Ages
and — TV Family Comparison
and — Metamorphosis

## 37 The Creation and Organization of the Pacific Northwest States

This comprehensive unit of 31 pages covers the exploration and organization of the Pacific Northwest. In studying the exploration phase, students analyze and evaluate the moral and ethical dilemmas faced by the early explorers. In the organization phase the students gain an understanding of why Washington State and the surrounding states were formed, how the present form of government operates, and how students can become involved in government to be active participants in the future. Students become involved in a mock trial involving facts from a real court case. Special emphasis is devoted in this unit to fostering higher order thinking skills.

*Contact*

Anacortes High School
20th and "J" Avenue
Anacortes, WA 98221
(206) 293-2166

John Irion, Principal
Kevin Miller
Mark Knight

## *38* Philosophers' Party

This "party" is part of a much broader humanities unit that is taught with three teachers in a two-hour block of scheduled time. It incorporates six major areas of study: Satire, Tragedy, Sociology, Civics, Current World Problems, and Philosophy. The focus for seminar discussion are seven themes: the Nature of Man, Power and Authority, the Search for Truth, Metaphysics, Love and Human Relationships, Ethics, and Utopia. For example, the interdisciplinary approach applied to the Power and Authority unit might require students to participate in several activities; a critical analysis of *Antigone*; a seminar discussion of Machiavelli's *Prince*; a role-playing debate between philosophers based on readings from the Great Books; a formal synthesis paper investigating the nature of the drive for power within humans; a guest speech from a well-known political figure; a visit from Dostoevsky's *Grand Inquisitor* (teacher role-play); and a satirical skit portraying historical world leaders dealing with current world problems.

### *Contact*

Mission Viejo High School
25025 Christana Drive
Mission Viejo, CA 92691
(714) 837-7722

Robert Metz, Principal
Jerry Chris
Robert Minier
Judy Hewett

## 39 Study Trips

Study trips are conducted throughout the school year at this Department of Defense school. The trips are cross-curriculum related and are planned by the school's interdisciplinary teams. The trips take advantage of the approximation to the various cultures from Germany and the four other countries that are ninety minutes' drive. Many of the trips are timed to the current events at the time. The host nation is active in coordinating student exchange programs and school visitations as well.

### Contact

Department of Defense Dependents Schools, Germany Region
Hahn American High School
APO AE 09122

Richard S. Tom, Principal

## 40 Great Books Honors Program

This course is offered to all four grade levels and follows the Great Books program. The curriculum at each level stresses historical, moral, theological, and sociological perspectives. The freshman study English and world cultures; the sophomores, English and theology; the juniors, English and U.S. history; and the seniors, English, theology, and philosophy.

### Contact

Xavier College Preparatory
4710 North 5th Street
Phoenix, AZ 85012
(602) 277-3772

Sister Joan Fitzgerald, Principal
Janet Burke, coordinator

## *41* Food Science

This course is an integration of the concepts and theories studied in traditional science chemistry classes with the analytical and production processes found in home economics classes. The students learn about the scientific methods in studying foods, about the relationship between water, acids, and bases, the importance of carbohydrates and fats, proteins, vitamins, and minerals to health. The students apply food science techniques to solutions, colloidal dispersions, emulsions, and dairy products. A unit on careers in food science will also be completed.

*Contact*

Apple Valley High School
14450 Hayes Road
Apple Valley, MN 55124
(612) 431-8244

James Boesen, Principal
Sharon Mitchell
Christopher Lee

## 42   Scholars' Academy

Every May the freshmen and sophomores in this school participate in an annual fair, "Partnerships on Our Planet." The fair is a culminating, multifaceted, interdisciplinary project. The freshman students, as part of a requirement in the Scholars' biology classes, prepare an in-depth study of the life functions of a variety of marine and land organisms. The sophomore students enrolled in Scholars chemistry classes prepare extensive literary research reports on environmental problems that impinge on living things. Each participant is responsible for understanding and interpreting scientific, historical, and socially important data relative to the quality of the environment; using and combining skills in reading, research, organization, writing, art, home economics, mathematics, and measurement; selecting a recipe that utilizes the organism as a source of food for humans; purchasing the food source; preparing the food source; and serving the food at a "tasting fair." Artistic ability and creativity come into play when students prepare posters to accompany the reports.

In addition, many cultural trips are part of the Scholars program. The students saw eight live productions of plays and stories they read in their respective English classes (e.g., *The Miser, To Kill a Mockingbird, Hamlet*). A visit to the Metropolitan Museum of Art in Manhattan allowed the students to study paintings, sculptures, and artifacts that correlate with the history curriculum. Other trips to the Stock Exchange, Ellis Island, the Asia Society, the science laboratories at the International Flavor and Fragance Company and at John Jay College of Criminal Justice, the Bronx Zoo, and the National Aquarium in Baltimore, Maryland, also enriched the curriculum.

*Contact*

   Susan E. Wagner High School
   1200 Manor Road
   Staten Island, NY 10314
   (718) 698-4200

   Ralph Musco, Principal
   Naomi Kirsch, coordinator of Scholars Academy

# Section Four
## Conclusion

*The effort of restructuring U.S. secondary schools is gaining momentum. In the area of curriculum, one of the more promising and more frequently advocated restructuring efforts is the implementation of interdisciplinary curriculum designs. This book's purpose is to introduce you to what interdisciplinary curriculum is all about.*

*An understanding of integrated curriculum begins with a knowledge of its nine basic purposes, which range from "teaching students to transfer knowledge" to "having fun." Interdisciplinary curriculum is viewed in this book as providing opportunities for students to think, to learn to work cooperatively, and to become proficient in certain performance outcomes. Advocates of this interdisciplinary restructuring of curriculum include government-sponsored agencies, professional educational organizations, national curriculum associations, and leading educational and professional research groups.*

*The process of designing integrated curriculum begins with the development of common course objectives, common themes, and common time, particularly in school scheduling procedures. Five diverse sequencing patterns can be used to help organize the redesign of curriculum into an interdisciplinary format. You should view the process of integration along a continuum from simple to complex. The opportunity to design curriculum using higher order thinking strategies is discussed in this book. The use of varied models of assessment or more authentic assessment needs to be advanced when you begin to think about how to measure what a student learns from an interdisciplinary curriculum approach.*

*The real heroes are the teachers like you who will be the redesign experts of our schools. Curriculum, particularly at the secondary level, needs to be viewed from a team perspective across traditional discipline lines. The process by which how successful teams of teachers work together is discussed at length in this book.*

*Efforts to redesign the curriculum of U.S. schools are coming from many different directions. Some advocate a national curriculum and/or national standards. Others call for individual state curriculum requirements. Still others take more traditional philosophical and/or cultural approaches to teaching and learning. Interdisciplinary curriculum can flourish within all these different orientations to redesign.*

*The 42 examples of middle/junior high and high school interdisciplinary curriculum provided in this book offer you a rich source of ideas from which to develop your own interdisciplinary curriculum. These curricula range from simple correlated designs to sophisticated thematic integrated examples. You may want to adopt some of the examples outright, or you may use them as a springboard in developing your own interdisciplinary designs.*

*Restructuring curriculum toward an interdisciplinary design is not a simple task in today's schools. Simple correlated designs are common in classrooms, but true thematic interdisciplinary curricula are hard to find, for many reasons. Most states still require examinations at different grade levels in specific content areas. Many states even require so-called program evaluations, which test students in specific curriculum areas but provide a test score for the school, not for individual students. The evaluations measure how well the school "covers" the curriculum rather than how individual students perform. In addition, parent and community groups often have misinformation about interdisciplinary curriculum. Interdisciplinary curriculum activities are viewed as nice projects, but when the report card comes home the parent wants to know the grade the child received in each specific subject. Part of this problem arises from expectations; most school districts publish report cards with individual subject categories like spelling, history, and English.*

*Even among teachers and administrators, the redesign of curriculum will necessitate new expectations. As we mentioned in the text, schools are organized for teachers to teach apart from each other. If the building structure does not impede collaboration, then "the schedule" inhibits creativity. Visionaries at the local level will need to place curriculum in the center of a school's design and build the structure and the schedule around it rather than the reverse. One teacher's comment—"How can I teach interdisciplinary studies when my students need to know grammar for the SATs?"—expresses the frustration that comes from the demands placed on teachers today. The fact so many teachers and administrators have been able to develop interdisciplinary curriculum, even with correlated designs, speaks of their courage in breaking the mold.*

*The use of interdisciplinary curriculum will grow in U.S. schools with time. Nurturing this restructuring will require the efforts of many different interest groups. Colleges and universities will need to train teachers in the design of interdisciplinary curriculum. Professional curriculum associations need to build bridges to each other and foster more collaboration. National and state curriculum redesign teams need to view integration as a curriculum necessity rather than a luxury. State education departments need to take another look at certification requirements and need to dismantle many of the specific curriculum departments that can hamper the development of integrated curriculum. Finally, following the truism that what gets measured is what gets done, the whole process of assessment needs to be restructured. If interdisciplinary studies are to grow in this country, then the testing industry must redesign the ways it measures student learning. A test that assesses how much of the curriculum was covered forces teachers to teach to cover the curriculum. If, however, students are tested for higher order thinking skills such as comprehension, analysis, or evaluation across the various disciplines, teachers will redesign curriculum toward an interdisciplinary approach.*

*The future of interdisciplinary curriculum is strong in the United States. As you can see in the 42 examples presented in this book, there is outstanding curriculum thinking going on in this country today. There are other schools, many others, that have developed excellent interdisciplinary curriculum. All these schools present the U.S. commitment to provide a high-quality educational experience for our students well into the next century.*

# Appendix A

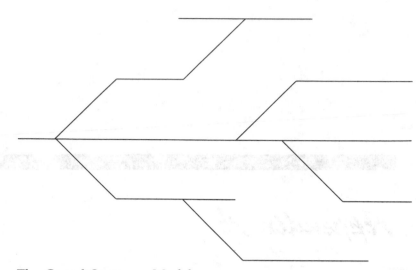

The Causal Sequence Model

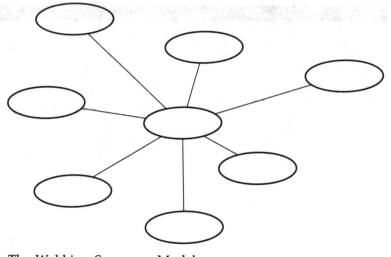

The Webbing Sequence Model

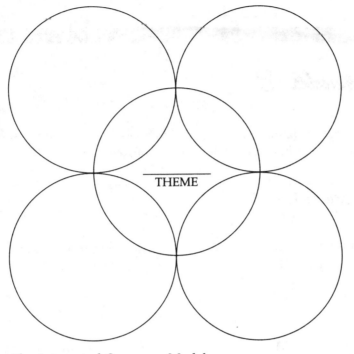

THEME

The Integrated Sequence Model

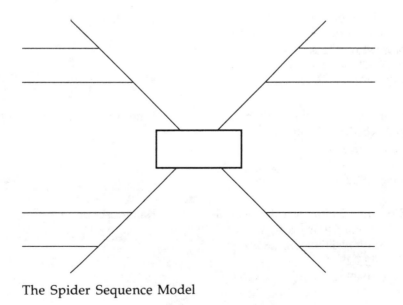

The Spider Sequence Model

## Appendix B

Here is a list of Nationally Recognized Schools, showing the year of recognition, the name of the integrated curriculum unit, and the unit number in this text.

## Middle Schools and Junior High Schools

| *School* | *Unit* |
|---|---|
| Alcott Middle School<br>1490 Woodtick Road<br>Wolcott, CT 06717<br>(203) 879-2517<br>1990–1991 | Back to the Past: An Immigration Experience, #8 |
| Anne M. Dorner Middle School<br>Van Cortlandt Avenue<br>Ossining, NY 10562<br>(914) 762-5740<br>1988–1989 | Storytelling through Dance, #23 |
| Arcola Intermediate School<br>Eagleville Road<br>Norristown, PA 19403<br>(215) 631-9404<br>1990–1991 | The Planets, #21 |
| Blair Junior/Senior High School<br>440 North 10th Street<br>Blair, NE 68008<br>(402) 426-4941<br>1988–1989 | Suite for the Endangered, #13 |
| Bloomfield Hills Middle School<br>4200 West Quarton Road<br>Bloomfield Hills, MI 48302<br>(313)626-2517<br>1988–1989 | Kaleidoscope, #2 |
| Brewster Middle School<br>Building 40 MCB<br>Camp Lejeune, NC 28542-5005<br>(919) 451-2561<br>1988–1989 | The Spirit of America, #11 |

Caloosa Middle School                     Middle East, #19
610 South Del Prado Boulevard
Cape Coral, FL 33990
(813) 574-3232
1990–1991

Canyon Vista Middle School                We Didn't Start the Fire, #17
8455 Spicewood Springs Road
Austin, TX 78759-1049
(512) 331-1666
1990–1991

Conway Middle School                      Walk across Orlando, #14
4600 Anderson Road
Orlando, FL 32812                          Ancient Greece, #10
(407) 275-9263
1988–1989

Cross Keys Middle School                  Historic "Dig," #1
14205 Cougar Drive
Florissant, MO 63033
(314) 831-2700
1988–1989

East Hills Middle School                  Dickens' England, #15
2800 Kensington Road
Bloomfield Hills, MI 48304
(313) 332-9286
1990–1991

Edgewood Middle School                    Cultural Fair, #12
929 Edgewood Road
Highland Park, IL 60035
(312) 432-3865
1988–1989

Fugett Middle School                      History through Literature, #5
500 Ellis Lane
West Chester, PA 19380
(215) 436-7242
1990–1991

Greater Atlanta Christian School          Kentucky–Tennessee Experience, #16
P.O. Box 4277
Norcross, GA 30091
(404) 923-9230
1988–1989

Helen Cannon Junior High School           Annual Science Olympiad, #18
5850 Euclid Avenue
Las Vegas, NV 89120
(720) 799-5610
1988–1989

St. Louis Park Junior HIgh School        Slake's Limbo, #3
2025 Texas Avenue South
St. Louis Park, MN 55426
(612) 541-1884
1988–1989

The Bishop's School                      Humanities Program, #7
7607 La Jolla Boulevard
La Jolla, CA 92037
(619) 459-4021
1990–1991

Timberlane Regional Middle School        Reader's Digest, #20
44 Greenough Road
Plaistow, NH 03865
(603) 382-7131
1988–1989

Washington Middle School                 A Minority Study: The
1st and Vine                             African-American Experience, #9
Maryville, MO 64468
(816) 562-3244
1990–1991

Wassom Middle School                     Vacation USA, #4
Forest and Gorgas Avenue
Fort Campell, KY 42233-5000
(502) 439-1832                           Manufacturing Technology, #22
1988–1989

Wydown Middle School                     Study Wydown Style, #6
6500 Wydown Boulevard
Clayton, MO 63105
(314) 726-5222
1990–1991

## High Schools

Apple Valley High School                 Food Science, #41
14450 Hayes Road
Apple Valley, MN 55124
(612) 431-8244
1988–1989

Anacortes High School                    The Creation and Organization of
20th and "J" Avenue                      the Pacific Northwest States, #37
Anacortes, WA 98221
(206) 293-2166                           Like the Stars That Never Set: A
1988–1989                                Study of Native American Cultures
                                         of the Pacific Northwest, #24

Convent of the Sacred Heart
1 East 91st Street                       History in the Making, #26
New York, NY 10128
(212) 722-4745
1990–1991

Department of Defense
Dependents School
Germany Region
Hahn American High School
APO AE 09122-0005
1990–1991

Study Trips, #39

Heritage High School
1401 West Geddes
Littleton, CO 80120
(303) 795-1353
1990–1991

Amusement Park Science, #35

Psychology in Literature, #25

Kennebunk High School
89 Fletcher Street
Kennebunk, ME 04043
(207) 985-1110
1990–1991

Rocketry, #33

Mission Viejo High School
25025 Chrisanta Drive
Mission Viejo, CA 92691
(714) 837-7722
1988–1989

Philosopher's Party, #38

Niles Township High Schools
7701 Lincoln Avenue
Skokie, IL 60077
(708) 673-6822
1990–1991

Algebra/Chemistry, #27

South Brunswick High School
P.O. Box 183 Major Road
Monmouth Junction, NJ 08852
(908) 329-4044
1990–1991

Journeys, #36

Susan E. Wagner High School
1200 Manor Road
Staten Island, NY 10314
(718) 698-4200
1988–1989

Scholar's Academy, #42

Spartanburg High School
500 Dupre Drive
Spartanburg, SC 29302
(803) 594-4410
1988–1989

Visions of the Future, #29

Tavavella High School
10600 Riverside Drive
Coral Springs, FL 33071
(305) 344-2315
1988–1989

The Spirit of Romanticism, #34

This Land Is Your Land: A Festival
of Ecological Activities, #32

Thomson High School                         Research Skills, #28
P.O. Box 1077
Thomson, GA 30824
(404) 595-9393
1990–1991

Upper Darby High School                     Pursuing the Dream: Puritans and
Lausdowne Avenue                            Immigration, #30
Upper Darby, PA 19082
(215) 622-7000
1988–1989

Vestavia Hills High School                  The Southern Way, #31
2235 Lime Rock Road
Vestavia Hills, AL 35216
(205) 823-4044
1990–1991

Xavier College Preparatory                  Great Books Honors Program, #40
4710 North 5th St.
Phoenix, AR 85012
(602) 277-3772
1990–1991

# *Appendix C*

## BLUE RIBBON SCHOOLS PROGRAM

Since 1982 the U.S. Department of Education has recognized outstanding schools throughout the nation. As part of the Blue Ribbon Schools program, over 2,000 schools from every state have been recognized as outstanding. These schools are diverse—they come from inner cities as well as rural and suburban areas; private, parochial, and public schools are represented. But these schools share a number of common characteristics. The chief one is that they have successfully mobilized their respective resources, staff, and community to meet the educational and social needs of the students entrusted to their care. These schools are special, reflecting all that is outstanding in U.S. education today.

The process of becoming a nationally recognized school begins at the school building level. The staff of the building must decide to look at itself and decide what is working well, what is working O.K., and what needs improvement. An elaborate application form asks a number of questions about the status of education in the school building. During the 1988–1989 and 1990–1991 period from which the secondary schools in this book were chosen, the following criteria were judged:

- Leadership
- Teaching environment
- Curriculum and instruction
- Student environment
- Parent and community support
- Indicators of success
- Organizational vitality
- A special emphasis area:
  - Geography and strengthening curriculum requirements (1988–1989)
  - Content-rich arts and history (1990–1991)

In alternate years, either the elementary or the secondary division of the schools is recognized. The chief school officer of each state can nominate a certain number of schools for recognition. Recommendations are also received from the Council for American Private Education. Once the applications are received in Washington, they are read by a peer review panel, which recommends the most promising schools for site visits. Another two-member peer review team visits the schools, verifies the information submitted by the school, and reports on the school climate and instruction. After a review of the site reports, the original panel makes its recommendations to the U.S. secretary of education, who announces the names of the schools selected. The recognized schools are honored at a national ceremony in Washington, D.C.

# Index